The Men and Women We Want

Gender and Race in American History

Alison Parker, The College at Brockport, State University of New York

Carol Faulkner, Syracuse University

ISSN 2152-6400

The Men and Women We Want
Jeanne D. Petit

The Men and Women We Want

Gender, Race, and the Progressive Era Literacy Test Debate

JEANNE D. PETIT

UNIVERSITY OF ROCHESTER PRESS

Copyright © 2010 Jeanne D. Petit

First published 2010

University of Rochester Press
668 Mt. Hope Avenue, Rochester, NY 14620, USA
www.urpress.com
and Boydell & Brewer Limited
PO Box 9, Woodbridge, Suffolk IP12 3DF, UK
www.boydellandbrewer.com

ISBN-13: 978-1-58046-348-5
ISSN: 2152-6400

Library of Congress Cataloging-in-Publication Data

Petit, Jeanne D.
   The men and women we want : gender, race, and the progressive era literacy test debate / Jeanne D. Petit.
       p. cm. — (Gender and race in American history, ISSN 2152-6400 ; v. 1)
   Includes bibliographical references and index.
   ISBN 978-1-58046-348-5 (hardcover : alk. paper)
   1. Literacy—Social aspects—United States—History—20th century. 2. Literacy—Ability testing—United States—History—20th century. 3. Immigrants—Education—United States—History—20th century. 4. United States—Emigration and immigration—Social aspects. 5. United States—Emigration and immigration—History—20th century. 6. Progressivism (United States politics) I. Title.
   LC151.P48 2010
   325.7309'41—dc22

                                                                                    2010009781

A catalogue record for this title is available from the British Library.

This publication is printed on acid-free paper.
Printed in the United States of America.

For my parents, in great appreciation and
love for all you have done for me

Contents

Illustrations

Acknowledgments

I am grateful for the remarkable support I have received as I have worked on this project. Over the years, I have incurred debts to many individuals and institutions. Generous assistance from the University of Notre Dame Zahm Grant, the American Historical Association Littleton Griswold Grant, and numerous Hope College Summer Grants has supported the archival research necessary for this project. I am deeply grateful to the archivists and librarians at the Department of Special Collections of Richard M. Daley Library at the University of Illinois at Chicago, the Regenstein Special Collections at the University of Chicago, the Houghton Library of Harvard University, and the Massachusetts Historical Society for allowing me access to their collections and for their guidance and knowledge.

My experience working with the University of Rochester Press has been uniformly positive, and I would like to thank Alison Parker, Carol Faulkner, and Suzanne Guiod for their encouragement and advice. The anonymous readers of the manuscript provided me with clear and cogent criticisms that improved this book immeasurably. Many other scholars have generously given their time to read and comment on my work over the years. On this score, I would particularly like to thank Matthew Jacobson, Victoria Brown, Elisabeth Israels Perry, Trisha Franzen, Barbara Steinson, Ellen Eslinger, and Laurie Matheson. Part of this work was published as an article in the *Journal of the Gilded Age and Progressive Era*, and the feedback provided by Maureen Flanagan and the anonymous readers helped me move this book in productive directions.

This project began at the University of Notre Dame. The intellectual community I enjoyed there has shaped me in more ways that I can say. Gail Bederman was an ideal advisor, generous with her time and effort both during and after graduate school. I especially appreciate her willingness to push me in new directions in both my writing and research. The advice and support of Walter Nugent and Suellen Hoy have been particularly important. I am also grateful to Scott Appleby, Kathleen Biddick, Jay Dolan, Philip Gleason, John McGreevy, and Doris Bergen for their learning, comments, and guidance. Anita Specht, Bill Svelmoe, and Angela Gugliotta were there for me from the first and helped see me through every step of the way. Rachel Koopmans has been and continues to be an essential sounding board. I also appreciate the feedback and encouragement provided by so many others, especially Carolyn Edwards Adler, Laura Brady, Kathy Cummings, Lezlie Knox, Daniel

Hobbins, David and Emily Mengel, Nicole Guenther Discenza, Christine Caldwell Ames, Scott Flipse, Jane Hannon, Sofie Lachappel, Estelle McNair, Dottie Pratt, and Amy England.

I am fortunate to work at Hope College; the support of my colleagues here has been essential in my completion of this project. Many Hope faculty members have taken the time to help me at different stages, and I would like to thank in particular my current and former colleagues of the Hope History Department: Marc Baer, Albert Bell, Fred Johnson, William Cohen, Larry Penrose, Neal Sobania, James Kennedy, Gloria Tseng, Tamba M'Bayo, Jonathan Hagood, and Kathleen O'Connor. Janis Gibbs deserves special thanks for her crackerjack editing skills and her leadership of the department. Many other colleagues have also shared their time and expertise: I am grateful to Elizabeth Trembley, John Cox, William Reynolds, Heather Sellers, Anne Heath, and Julie Kipp. Natalie Dykstra and John Hanson deserve special thanks and mention: they spent countless Saturday mornings over eggs and toast reviewing my work and helping me find my voice.

Finally, I want to thank my family. My sister and brother-in-law, Claire and Lance LaForge, gave me a place to stay on research trips. They also gave me my nephew, Mckinley, who has added a great deal of delight to my world. My sister Sara has generously shared her editing skills. They, along with my brother David Petit, have been encouraging through this whole process, and I appreciate that they have mostly repressed the impulse to ask, "Is it done yet?" My parents, Martin and Christine Petit, have always encouraged my curiosity by listening to me and letting me ask questions. It is to them that I dedicate this book.

Introduction

Prescott Hall feared for the future of the nation. He observed nearly twenty million immigrants arriving in the nation's ports between 1880 and 1910, more than twice the number that had arrived in the previous hundred years. Unlike the familiar immigrants from England, Scandinavia, Germany, or even Ireland, the vast majority of these "new" immigrants came from southern Italy, Russia, the Austro-Hungarian Empire, and other poverty-stricken and remote countries in southern and eastern Europe.[1] These new immigrants met the technical requirement of "free white persons" set out in the Naturalization Act of 1790, but their racial unfitness, for Prescott Hall, was evident.[2] These people toiled for low wages, lived in wretched conditions, and had children, lots and lots of children, so many children that they threatened to swamp the offspring of the strong, noble Anglo-Saxon race, the race to which Hall believed he belonged. Hall, a Boston Brahmin and Harvard graduate, founded the Immigration Restriction League (IRL) in order to advocate for the restriction of these undesirables. When, in 1909, the Senate Immigration Commission, also known as the Dillingham Commission, asked the IRL to submit a statement, Hall leapt at the chance to push for severe restrictions on immigration.

Hall's solution to the threat of immigration may seem, to modern eyes, curious. Since the 1890s, he and other members of the IRL had proposed that Congress pass legislation requiring adult immigrants to prove they could read and write at least fifty words of English or some other language before entering the United States. In recommending this solution in his statement, Hall said almost nothing about the importance of literacy or an educated citizenry. Instead, he made a racial case in support of the literacy test. Most immigrants to the United States, he warned, "are from races . . . which have not progressed but have been backward, downtrodden and relatively useless for centuries."[3] He then pointed to statistics about the lower literacy rates among immigrants from southeastern European nations and insisted that a literacy test would be the best means to keep those immigrants out. Hall dismissed arguments that poverty and oppression in southeastern Europe led to higher rates of illiteracy or that the educational opportunities in the United States would uplift immigrants. For Hall, inborn, immutable racial qualities prevailed over any attempts by reformers to improve individuals or groups. "Education," he insisted, "can develop what is in an immigrant, but can not supply what is not there," and "there is no reason to suppose that a change in location will result in a change of inborn tendencies."[4]

For Hall, though, the threat of immigration was not just about race, but also about sex and gender. In the longest section in his statement, titled "Restriction Needed from a Eugenic Standpoint," he declared that the main goal of immigration restriction should be "the selection of the alien men and women who are coming here to be the fathers and mothers of future citizens." If these fathers and mothers were not racially desirable, the result would be, in Hall's words, "'that watering of the nation's lifeblood' which results from their breeding after admission."[5] For Hall, then, ensuring the nation's racial strength, its "lifeblood," meant making sure the right men had sex with the right women in order to reproduce desirable future citizens. Having the government institute a simple literacy test, Hall maintained, would safeguard the population of the United States by making sure immigrant men and women were "the best specimens to breed from."[6] Without it, he warned, the nation would fill up with servile immigrant men and fecund immigrant women whose sons would inherit their smaller physique, lower intelligence, and questionable moral sense. When these races came to predominate, Anglo-Saxon men would lose their place of authority, and instead of a strong, steady hand guiding the ship of state, the nation would come under the power of races that had shown no capacity to rule themselves. Eventually, the bountiful American countryside would begin to look like the ghettos of Eastern Europe, and the freedom and opportunity that Anglo-Saxons had fought for in the past would be frittered away by those who could not possibly appreciate it.

When the Dillingham Commission released its report in 1911, it recommended that Congress pass literacy test legislation to restrict immigration. Yet this proposed solution to the problem of immigration did not go uncontested. Opponents of the literacy test countered that such a test was unjust, impractical, and would hurt rather than help the nation. Yet, like Hall, opponents of the literacy test framed the debate not in terms of education, but in terms of race, manhood, womanhood, and sexuality.

These opponents included Louis Hammerling and the members of the American Association of Foreign Language Newspapers (AAFLN). Hammerling had originally organized AAFLN to sell advertising and advocate for the Republican Party in immigrant newspapers, but by 1912, the year after the Dillingham Commission released its report, he had become a leading critic of immigration restriction. As an immigrant from Austria-Hungary, Hammerling took the criticisms against southeastern European immigrants personally, and he used the pages of the AALFN's journal, the *American Leader*, to warn that government meddling in the free flow of broad-shouldered, willing working men could lead to economic collapse. Hammerling and others in the AAFLN maintained that overeducated, neurasthenic Anglo-Saxon men could no longer handle the exertion necessary to build bridges, man factories, or perform the other tasks necessary to make the United States an industrial power. Nor were Anglo-Saxon men "rearing their sons for such tasks." Then, taking a swipe at Anglo-Saxon virility, Hammerling claimed, "all their sons combined would not number enough to tackle a good-sized job."[7] The men of southeastern European races, on the other hand, provided the nation with muscular bodies and hearty sons who could do the nation's work. They were, in the words of another editorialist for the *Leader*, "supplying fresh vigorous blood to the beating heart of the nation."[8] The AAFLN opposed the literacy test, then, by turning the eugenic logic of the IRL on its head by asserting that southeastern European immigrant men and women—but especially men—would introduce a revitalizing racial element to the American bloodstream.

In a different twist, progressive reformer Grace Abbott eschewed Hall's and Hammerling's notion that blood or virility determined the quality of an immigrant. Instead, she proposed a solution that focused on the creation for immigrant families of safe, nurturing havens in dangerous, exploitative urban environments. She was the director of the Immigrants' Protective League, a group that was founded by a cooperative effort between the Women's Trade Union League and Jane Addams' Hull House and that sought to improve the plight of immigrants in Chicago. Abbott also contributed a report to the Dillingham Commission and used the opportunity to redefine the problem of immigration. Instead of focusing on issues of race, she told stories of immigrant men struggling with crooked employment agencies and of young immigrant women being preyed upon by white slavers. Then she complained, "The Federal Government, in emphasizing and constantly developing the restrictive features of [immigration] legislation, has allowed the equally important function of protection to fall into comparative insignificance and disuse."[9] If the government really cared about the future population, she argued, it should stop worrying about literacy tests and instead follow the lead of the women in the IPL by protecting immigrant husbands and fathers from the economic exploitation of industrialization and safeguarding immigrant mothers and daughters from sexual exploitation. For, as Abbott declared, immigrants needed social supports if they were going to "become the sort of men and women we want."[10]

This book explores the racialized, gendered, and sexualized dynamics of the Progressive Era literacy test debate by analyzing the ways the members of the IRL, AAFLN, and IPL fought for or against this restriction legislation. Even though these groups do not represent the full spectrum of the debate over the literacy test, focusing on their public writings, private musings, and social context reveals specific ways Americans linked race, gender, and sexual ideologies to define the stakes of the literacy test debates. During the long fight, they mobilized interconnected arguments about racial superiority and inferiority, fatherhood and motherhood, and virility and fertility as they made their cases. In debating whether the government should use literacy as a tool to exclude immigrants, all three of these groups took competing stands on the ability of southern and eastern European immigrant men and women to work, vote, marry, and procreate in the United States. Moreover, as members of the IRL, AAFLN, and IPL debated about the kind of men and women the nation wanted, they made larger claims about which native-born men and women were true citizens who had the authority to shape the nation's laws and institutions. For them, the debate became about expanding political, economic, and social possibilities for immigrant and native-born men and women or shutting those possibilities down.

The IRL and other racial restrictionists achieved success in promoting the threat posed by immigration by playing on powerful Progressive Era fears about race and gender. Over the years, they developed arguments about a dystopic eugenic future, one where hordes of puny immigrants, aided by sentimental women reformers, would push aside Anglo-Saxon men from their traditional place of power and authority. The central question about the literacy test was, according to IRL leader Prescott Hall, "who will be the fathers and mothers of our future citizens?" Would future American men be like the stalwart, physically strong men of America's past? Would future women still be attractive? Would Anglo-Saxon men be able to maintain their dominance over Anglo-Saxon women, as well as all other women? If the answer to these questions was negative, the men of the IRL warned, the fate of the United States as a nation looked dim. The national government needed to have the guts to take the actions necessary to protect the nation's racial heritage from those who would outbreed or, worse, interbreed with the Anglo-Saxon race. The literacy test, insisted the IRL, would be a step in setting up these protections.

The more optimistic race and gender scenarios, spun out by groups like the AAFLN and the IPL as they opposed the literacy test, were also powerful. The AAFLN also used eugenic logic, but they insisted that immigrant men—because they were strong, uncomplaining, and safely white—would invigorate the American gene pool and revitalize white American manhood. Southeastern European immigrant men, they argued, were the new pioneers, cultivating their muscles and manhood as they conquered the modern industrial frontier. The women of the IPL touted their direct experience working with immigrants and offered themselves up as models for how the United States should handle immigration. Following the principles of progressive women reformers, they insisted, would lead to the growth of a strong, interdependent nation, one where the best qualities of all races would be enhanced and men and women would work together to build strong families and communities. These more optimistic outlooks, however, could not compete with the fear promoted by the restrictionists, especially in the World War I era. In the end, the ways immigration opponents like the IRL conceptualized gender and race in relation to government power allowed them to make immigration restriction into an imperative for a majority of native-born white Americans.

The arguments of the men of the IRL would eventually become the basis for the most restrictive immigration legislation in the nation's history—the 1924 Johnson-Reed Act, which severely limited immigrant numbers and established harsh quotas for southeastern European immigrants. Before that, though, Americans worked through questions of whether and how to exclude immigrants in the literacy test debate.

The History of the Progressive Era Literacy Test

The Progressive Era literacy test debate was long, dynamic, and consequential. It began during the depression of the 1890s, continued through times of prosperity and political reform in the early twentieth century, and concluded on the eve of the U.S. entry into World War I, when the literacy test became law. This debate developed in unpredictable ways, with support and opposition cutting across party and regional lines, and positions shifting over time. Other forms of immigration restriction were proposed during this time, including the exclusion of immigrants who participated in radical politics, who exhibited mental illness or physical incapacity, who migrated back and forth from the United States to their homelands, or who were "likely to become a public charge" because of their poverty.[11] These methods of restriction, however, either passed into law fairly quickly or fell to the wayside. The literacy test, by contrast, generated more passionate support and opposition than these other methods of restriction. Proposals for a literacy test kept coming back to the forefront of political debates about immigration and came to dominate the ways Progressive Era Americans talked about restriction. By the time the literacy test law passed in 1917, the debate had transformed the way Americans understood immigration, and created the logic that would shape immigration policy throughout the twentieth century.

Immigration restriction first became an issue in the United States in the years before the Civil War, as an influx of immigrants arrived from Ireland and Germany. Laws restricting immigration, however, did not emerge until later in the nineteenth century. Before the 1890s, Congress had turned to a variety of methods to restrict immigrants whom they deemed to be threats, whether moral or economic. Between 1875 and 1891, Congress had passed laws that excluded contract laborers, criminals, paupers, prostitutes, and those who trafficked in prostitution.[12] Congress also excluded immigrants from an entire nation in the 1882 Chinese Exclusion Act, which barred all Chinese laborers, and later merchants, from entering the United States on the grounds, in part at least, that Chinese immigrants were racially "incapable of attaining the state of civilization of the Caucasian."[13] Moreover, since Chinese immigrants were not categorized as white, they did not meet the requirement for United States citizenship established by the

Naturalization Act of 1790, which made it easier to argue that they could never be part of the nation.[14] By the late 1880s, many Americans began to express fears about the changes they perceived in newly arriving immigrants. The origin of the majority of immigrants had shifted from nations in northwestern Europe to those in southern and eastern Europe, and the overall number of immigrants nearly doubled. Immigrants from all European nations were classified as white, so something comparable to the Chinese Exclusion Act would not work to restrict immigration from southern and eastern Europe.[15]

In the early 1890s, a chief critic of those southern and eastern European immigrants, Massachusetts Senator Henry Cabot Lodge, came across a new solution—the literacy test. He submitted a bill to the 54th Congress of 1895–97, a proposal to exclude "all persons over 14 years of age who cannot read and write the language of their native country or some other language."[16] The debate over this bill took place in the midst of the most severe economic depression up to that time, and most of the debate centered on the question of whether or not southern and eastern European immigrants hurt the American labor force. In the end, although the bill passed, Grover Cleveland vetoed it, calling the literacy test a "radical departure" from the nation's heritage of open borders.[17]

In the first decade of the twentieth century, however, the literacy test debate emerged in the transformed political context of the Progressive Era.[18] Congress passed immigration reforms in 1903 and 1907, which included provisions that excluded anarchists, beggars, and physical and mental "defectives"; increased the head tax; made knowledge of English a prerequisite for naturalization; and legalized the "Gentleman's Agreement," which severely limited immigration from Japan.[19] Congressmen tried to attach literacy test provisions to these acts, but opponents, who had become more organized, managed to scuttle them. President Theodore Roosevelt maneuvered to put off the issue of the literacy test by asking Congress instead to undertake a multiyear scientific study of immigration to the United States and come up with recommendations for government action.[20] Named after its chairman, Republican Senator William Dillingham of Maine, the Dillingham Commission spent the next four years studying the impact of immigration on all levels of society and deciding whether a literacy test was the best legislative approach to what Progressive Era Americans termed the "immigrant problem."

In 1911 the Dillingham Commission released its report and made a series of recommendations, including improving steerage conditions and implementing legislation to prevent exploitation, but its main recommendation, and the one that gained the most public attention, was a call to restrict immigration, with a literacy test being "the most feasible" method.[21] While some of the commissioners saw this provision as a way to curb the racial threat of immigration, the final report emphasized that restriction was needed to protect the nation's economic and social standards from low-wage immigrants. Yet as historian Robert Zeidel points out, the perceived economic problems caused by southeastern European immigrants were not backed up by the actual data in the report, which showed that the social and economic conditions of immigrants actually improved over time.[22] Nevertheless, restrictionists in Congress had their ammunition, and literacy test bills were introduced in the 63rd Congress of 1911–13, the 64th Congress of 1913–15, and the 65th Congress of 1915–17; all passed both houses of Congress.[23]

While support for the literacy test grew in Congress, however, all the Presidents who were presented with the bills refused to sign them. Republican William Howard Taft vetoed it in 1913, one of his last acts as President, because he believed it would cause too much disruption in the migration of much-needed laborers.[24] Democrat Woodrow Wilson, who had been elected in 1912, also vetoed the bill twice, contending that literacy tests were "not tests of quality or of character or of personal fitness but tests of opportunity."[25] Woodrow Wilson's last veto came in January of 1917, two months before he would ask Congress to declare war on Germany. By that point, immigration had dwindled to a fraction of what it had been before World War I began in Europe. Growing suspicion of immigrants and congressional support for a literacy test law, however, overrode that practical fact.[26] There were enough votes in the House and Senate to override Wilson's veto, and on February 9, 1917, the literacy test became law.

The twenty-year debate over literacy test legislation intertwined with many of the contradictions and tensions of the Progressive Era. For one, the literacy test debate became linked with ongoing conflict between capital and labor in the late nineteenth and early twentieth centuries. The first literacy test bill was debated during a severe economic depression marked by high unemployment, deteriorating working conditions, failed businesses, and rising labor violence.[27] But the debate also continued during the first decades of the twentieth century, which saw periods of tremendous economic growth. The demand for labor became acute, and to fill these jobs, over ten million immigrants arrived between 1900 and 1910, the vast majority from southern and eastern Europe.[28] During these economic swings, unions usually supported the literacy test as a means to keep out low-wage labor, while organizations like the Chamber of Commerce and other representatives of business usually aligned against it as they believed it would lead to labor shortages.[29] They used the classic Liberal argument that the government should not interfere with economic activities—such as the migration of laborers—as a way to justify its opposition to immigration restriction.

By the early twentieth century, however, this argument had begun to hold much less sway, and the debate over the literacy test reflected this change. As historian

Steven J. Diner argues, "The central issue of politics became not whether government could restore individual autonomy and preserve democracy in an age of industrial concentration, but how."[30] Progressives instituted many legislative attempts to protect and improve the population. For instance, supporters of protective labor legislation for women and children—laws that regulated the hours they could work or the weight they could be expected to lift—justified it as a means of ensuring that potential mothers and their children would remain healthy and productive members of the nation.[31] Progressive ideologies about government, though, could cut both ways in the literacy test debate. While supporters of the literacy test tapped into the belief that the government needed to use its power to control and shape the population, opponents drew more on the optimism of progressivism and insisted that positive government actions, rather than restrictive measures, could transform almost any immigrant into a good citizen.

The literacy test debate also reveals contradictions in progressive views on education—particularly how education, or the lack thereof, could be a means to expand or limit access to political power. The idea of making immigrants prove they could read or write could fit well in the era's focus on self-improvement through education. It was during this time that states adopted compulsory school laws and extensive educational reforms, promoting the idea that the government needed to take an active part in ensuring an educated citizenry.[32] Many reformers pushed for education as a way to advance disadvantaged groups politically or socially.[33] By the early twentieth century, W. E. B. Dubois had begun promoting his idea of creating a "talented tenth," a group of highly educated African Americans who would advocate for rights and work to uplift less educated African Americans.[34] Progressive women reformers who worked with immigrants, such as Jane Addams, saw educating immigrant children as key to raising the position of immigrant groups in the community and making them into good citizens.[35]

At the same time, immigration restriction legislation like the literacy test was not so much about the optimistic idea of improving individuals to become better citizens but instead about the more pessimistic idea of excluding individuals and groups from access to citizenship. The choice of the literacy test as a means to restrict undesirable immigrants echoed the methods used by whites in the South to exclude African Americans from suffrage. By the 1890s, white Southern Democrats, who had recently retaken control of their states after the failure of Reconstruction, started rewriting their state constitutions to require all who wanted to vote to pass a literacy test—to be able to read a section of the United States Constitution—before being granted the right. While these provisions sometimes targeted poor whites who might have voted for a Republican ticket, the enforcers of the law mostly used them to prevent African Americans from voting, while allowing illiterate white men to do so.[36]

Race, Gender, and the Literacy Test Debate

It is this idea—the literacy test as a race test—that became the central point of contention during the literacy test debate. The debate emerged at a time when scientists and social scientists, politicians and commentators were attempting to pin down the meaning of race. Most took for granted the idea that lighter skinned people of European ancestry were racially distinct from darker skinned people indigenous to Africa, Asia, and the Americas. In the mid to late nineteenth century, as nationalist struggles in Europe became more heated and migration patterns shifted from northwestern to southeastern Europe, Americans and Europeans sought to make racial distinctions among different European groups. Those who sought to do this, however, had a difficult time articulating a logical demarcation of different European races. Some based racial differences on nationality, others on broader geographic regions, and yet others on language groups.[37] Most viewed Jewish people as a distinct racial group, often defined as the Hebrew race, no matter what nationality or language they spoke.[38]

During these years, Americans did not struggle just to define racial differences but also to advocate for their perspective about racial hierarchy. Some, such as reformer Jane Addams, took a cosmopolitan view, believing that each immigrant race could fully adapt and contribute as an equal in American society.[39] Some in anthropology, notably Franz Boas, began to question the whole notion of racial difference and instead postulated that environment and culture had more to do with differences among groups of people than inherent racial traits.[40] By the early twentieth century, the eugenics movement, which sought to promote procreation among the fit and discourage it among the unfit, came to predominate racial thinking in academic and popular discourse. This movement was linked with a wider acceptance of the belief in fixed racial differences between northwestern and southeastern Europeans and the importance of the propagation of superior races.[41]

When historians have examined Progressive Era immigration restriction debates, they have mainly focused on how they reflected and shaped American racial identities and hierarchies. The literacy test debate in particular revealed what historian Gary Gerstle defines as a central tension in American national identity—that between civic nationalism, which promoted a vision of national belonging based on the ability of individuals to participate in democratic institutions, and racial nationalism, a *Herrenvolk* vision that deemed particular races incapable of national belonging.[42] A literacy test had the potential to enhance civic nationalism and measure whether an immigrant had the potential to be an informed voter and citizen.[43] Most historians, however, have argued that the debates were a manifestation of what John Higham terms "racial nativism," a belief that only those of northwestern European descent, often called Anglo-Saxons or Nordics, truly belonged to the nation.[44]

Whiteness studies have complicated the racial category of "Anglo Saxon" and have shown how the massive migrations of southeastern European immigrants shifted the meaning of white racial identities as Americans constructed immigration policy. Matthew Frye Jacobson, for instance, argues that immigrants' white identity was contingent upon where they were in the legal process of migration. As the nineteenth century progressed, Jacobson writes, "peoples such as Celts, Italians, Hebrews and Slavs were becoming less and less white in debates over who should be allowed to disembark on American shores, and yet were becoming whiter and whiter in debates over who should be granted full rights of citizenship."[45] Thomas Guglielmo demonstrates this point further, showing that native-born Americans could denigrate Italian immigrants, and particularly southern Italians immigrants, as racially inferior when it came to questions of immigration restriction, but define them as white when it came to issues of naturalization, voting, housing, and other legal classifications.[46] In her study of the creation of the category of illegal aliens, Mae M. Ngai has shown that, even as the 1924 Johnson-Reed Act established a racial hierarchy for Europeans through its quota system, it also "solidified the legal boundaries of the white race" by excluding Asian immigration and severely controlling Mexican immigration.[47] Overall, the debates over literacy test legislation reflected larger debates about race and power in the United States. In the words of Desmond King, they "privileged an Anglo-Saxon conception of U.S. identity" and "helped solidify the second-class position of non-whites."[48]

Most historians of immigration restriction, however, have not systematically considered how the ways in which Americans set up, enforced, and resisted immigration policies like the literacy test depended on their understanding not only of race, but also of gender and sexuality.[49] As historians have shown, appeals to gender served as a powerful mediating force in Progressive Era political discourse. Such appeals could, in the words of Alice Kessler-Harris, "enhance the public appetite for some policies and silence resistance to others. They legitimized, rationalized, and justified policies that could and did serve many other ends, including maintaining [or challenging] a stratified and racialized social order."[50] Debates such as those over women's suffrage, maternal welfare policy, racial segregation, business regulation, protective labor legislation, imperialism, and, during the World War I era, pacifism and preparedness provoked larger debates about men and women in the workforce, polity, and family.[51]

As Americans struggled to understand the meaning of the massive southeastern European migrations, using gender imagery and allusions became a way for commentators to anchor their racial arguments and give them an emotional punch. Race and gender, in the words of Evelyn Nakano Glenn, "are positioned and therefore gain meaning in relation to each other."[52] In particular, demonstrating the sexual deviation or sexual conformity of groups who were racially suspect became a key way

Americans solidified or challenged racial hierarchies.[53] Participants in the literacy test debate used ideologies of manhood, womanhood, and sexuality to infuse their arguments about race with greater power and to push the debate toward the outcome they wanted. By portraying immigrant men as muscular, virile workers or dissipated, dependent paupers, by portraying immigrant women as nurturing, virtuous mothers or overly-fecund brood-mares, participants sought to either amplify or diminish the racial threat that southeastern European immigrants were believed to pose.

Moreover, in debating whether immigration restriction should be based on literacy, both proponents and opponents also had to contend with the issue of whether immigrant women should be subject to the test. In the process, they waded into the debate about the changing place of American women at the turn of the century. Nineteenth-century immigration laws had reinforced the idea of *femme covert*, the legal concept that women's legal position was under the protection of men, without the rights to own property, to sue in court, or even to make decisions about their children. Under the Naturalization Act of 1855, for instance, a foreign-born woman automatically became a citizen if her husband had American citizenship, even if the woman did not want it.[54] The first immigration exclusion law passed by Congress, the Page Act of 1875, targeted women, especially Chinese women, who were suspected of entering the country to engage in prostitution. Lawmakers justified this Act not by saying they were excluding these women because they would make poor workers and citizens but instead by arguing that they did not exhibit the sexual morality to be good wives and mothers and build good homes.[55] Even this law, however, emphasized the dependent status of women by placing blame on the men who trafficked in prostitution, and by depicting the women as victims in need of protection.[56] By the late nineteenth century, American women, especially white, middle-class women, had chipped away at the concept of *femme covert* and demanded more political and economic rights.[57] As participants in the literacy test debate took on questions about women's literacy, they made larger claims about whether women belonged in the nation as wives and mothers or as workers and citizens.[58]

Finally, the literacy test debate became a forum for defining the parameters of government power, and gender was at the center of this debate. As historian Arnoldo Testi argues, "The 'battle of the sexes'—the conflict between genders and over gender definitions—shaped the comprehensive development of the country's public life."[59] When participants in the literacy test debate disputed whether the literacy test was a justified use of government power or an abuse of it, they took part in this battle of the sexes. Like other policy proponents of the Progressive Era, they made a case about whether the progressive state should exert patriarchal control over its population, whether it should embrace a more laissez-faire policy, allowing for manly independence, or whether it should exhibit more maternal, protective qualities.[60] In staking a claim about which men and women deserved to enter the country and have access to the privileges of citizenship, participants made the literacy test debate about much more than whether an immigrant could read or write, or even about the racial composition of the nation. They also made a case about whether the newly empowered progressive state would be one in which the power and privileges of men would be upheld, or one that would include participation and visions of women.

The chapters of this book are organized chronologically and each focuses on key legislative moments during the literacy test debate. Chapter 1 explores the central role of the IRL in the creation of literacy test legislation in the 1890s and how its members struggled to introduce eugenic logic into the debate over immigration restriction. Chapter 2 shows how the IPL entered the debate and compares the ways the IPL and the IRL participated in the Senate Immigration Commission (a.k.a. Dillingham Commission). Both groups focused on immigrants as fathers and mothers, but the IRL argued that the government needed to keep out what they considered dangerous breeders while the IPL emphasized the role of the government in helping immigrants become good parents. Chapter 3 introduces the men of the AAFLN and compares their construction of immigrant and native-born manhood with the IRL's by examining both groups' participation in debates over the literacy test bills vetoed by Presidents Taft and Wilson in 1913 and 1915. Chapter 4 analyzes how Grace Abbott and the IPL offered an alternative vision of immigration during these years by de-emphasizing manhood and focusing on the contributions of women, both immigrant and native-born. Chapter 5 examines the final push for the literacy test in 1916 and 1917, on the eve of the U.S. entry into World War I. During these years, the gendered debate over pacifism and preparedness permeated the literacy test debate and affected the arguments of all three groups. My conclusion traces the fate of the three organizations and examines how their gendered views of immigrants affected the ways Congress established quotas in the 1924 Johnson-Reed Act.

Throughout the years of the debate, the arguments made by Hall, Hammerling, Abbott, and others about the literacy test ranged far beyond simple issues of reading and writing. The participants linked their arguments to the dominant issues of the age: the impact of industrialization; the shift from a rural to an urban society; the scope of government power; the growing influence of scientific thought; the meaning of American imperial might; the consequences of racial and ethnic diversity; and the increased demands of women, African Americans, and others who had been excluded from power. To address these myriad concerns, though, the members of the IRL, AAFLN and IPL returned to the same kinds of questions: did the literacy test ensure that the nation was getting the sort of men and women it wanted and needed? Would the test racially strengthen or weaken the nation? How would it effect the reproduction of future citizens? A question which was not directly asked, but was the subtext of their anxiety, was: what did the literacy test mean for the power and privileges of men and women already in the nation?

The literacy test debate had consequences. The ideological constructs set up during the debate led to policies that separated families, turned back people who were fleeing oppression, and hindered the nation's foreign policy. Moreover, these debates had consequences for the ways Progressive Era Americans understood race and gender. In the debates about which persons should be allowed to immigrate, Americans experimented with different meanings of racial desirability and ideal manhood and womanhood. Grace Abbott, Prescott Hall, Louis Hammerling, and the thousands of others who engaged in these debates were not just trying to create public policy. They were engaging in a battle to mold the men and women of the nation's future and to define the sort of men and women who counted as Americans.

–I–

Breeders, Workers, and Mothers

The Beginning of the Literacy Test Debate

The literacy test came into being through the political will of Senator Henry Cabot Lodge and the passion of Prescott Hall and Robert DeCourcy Ward, the young Harvard graduates who founded the Immigration Restriction League (IRL). In the 1880s, these men watched as immigration to the United States nearly doubled from the previous decade and, more worrisome for them, the sources of immigration shifted. The numbers of English, Scandinavians, and other northern Europeans whom they saw as racially compatible stagnated while the numbers of those whom they saw as less racially desirable—Italians, Russians, and other southeastern Europeans—tripled, or even quadrupled.[1] As the IRL's first pamphlet put it, "The quantity of our immigration is increasing . . . its quality is deteriorating," and "the results are very dangerous to the country."[2] By the early 1890s, the men of the IRL and Lodge hit upon a solution: since literacy rates in southeastern European nations were lower, making immigrants pass a literacy test before they could enter the nation would keep out undesirables.[3]

They worked together to write legislation, and in 1896 they saw their chance to get it passed.[4] In the spring of that year, Lodge, the Junior Republican Senator from Massachusetts, introduced a bill calling for Congress to exclude "all persons over 14 years of age who cannot read and write the language of their native country or some other language."[5] The bill decreed that when immigrants arrived at a port, they would choose the language with which they were most comfortable. The immigration officer would then present the immigrant with a box containing slips of paper with five lines of the United States Constitution written on it. The potential immigrant would draw a slip, read those lines to the inspector, and then copy them down to prove he or she could write. Besides children under fourteen, the only other immigrants exempt from the test would be "aged" parents or grandparents of an admissible or landed immigrant. Lodge hailed this literacy test as a practical method for restriction, as it could fit into the existing inspection system and provide inspectors with a uniform method with which to examine immigrants.

When Lodge defended the idea of a literacy test on the floor of the Senate in March of 1896, he spoke of his fear for the future of the nation. In that election

year, the fate of the United States did look grim. The American people had weath-
ered three years of depressions, with high unemployment, deteriorating working
conditions, failed businesses, and rising labor violence. Farmers were desperate, as
crop prices plummeted and farm foreclosures rose. The political order was shifting
as the Populist Party's radical calls for government-run railroads, an income tax, and
free coinage of silver had gained wider appeal. Members of Congress scrambled to
find solutions to the crisis, leading to vigorous debates over the hot political issues
of the late nineteenth century, like whether to raise the tariff or whether currency
should be valued on the gold standard.

Lodge sought to lift the "immigrant question" out of contemporary concerns
about unemployment, strikes, and overcrowded neighborhoods, and to place it
instead into a sweeping narrative of racial struggle and sexual competition. In his
speech introducing the bill before the Senate, he dismissed the nation's economic
problems and class divisions as insignificant and warned, "If any danger threatened
the United States it was not from a war of classes but a war of races."[6] On one side
of this potential race war would be his race, the race that descended from the original colonists from northern Europe, the one he saw as the genuine American race.
He painted a glorious past for this race, one in which it emerged from the forests of
ancient Germany, overthrew a weakened and decadent Roman Empire, carved out
the nations of northwestern Europe, particularly England, all the while building up
its manhood through feats of courage, self-denial, and intellect. Then "this vigorous body of men" came to North America and conquered savage races and hostile
environments. Overall, this race fashioned itself into one whose qualities mirrored
those of ideal late-nineteenth-century men: "An unconquerable energy, a very great
initiative, an absolute empire over self, a sentiment of independence . . . a puissant
activity, very keen religious sentiments, a very fixed morality, a very clear idea of
duty."[7] The present day descendents of those immigrants, Lodge argued, inherited
these mental, physical, and moral traits their ancestors acquired through "centuries
of toil and conflict."[8]

But Lodge warned that late-nineteenth-century immigrants were "of a totally
different race origin."[9] These foreigners from southeastern Europe had ancestors
who were the conquered, not the conquerors, and they inherited weaker bodies, passive dispositions, and less rigid moral sense. How, one might ask, could these lesser
races pose a threat to the superior, manly Anglo-Saxon race? Lodge declared that
there was only one way these races would lower the qualities that the Anglo-Saxon
and Germanic races had built up over centuries, "and that is by breeding them out."
He continued: "If a lower race mixes with a higher in sufficient numbers, history
teaches us that the lower race will prevail. The lower race will absorb the higher
not the higher the lower, when the two strains approach equality in numbers."[10] In
other words, while southeastern Europeans could not conquer Anglo-Saxons and

other Germanic races in combat or other forms of direct competition, they could do it in the more insidious manner of sexual competition.

Right from the first, then, defenders of the literacy test made the racial threat of immigration into a gender-based and sexual threat by using a eugenic framework.[11] While the term "eugenics" had been coined by British mathematician Francis Galton in 1883, it still had not entered the lexicon of most Americans in the 1890s. By the late nineteenth century, however, ideas about competition between races and the importance of heredity had begun to take root in popular discourse. In his speech, Lodge made allusions to the early-nineteenth-century naturalist Jean-Baptiste Lamarck and included long quotes from French psychologist Gustave LeBon. These men argued for the importance of heredity in different ways, but both posited that abilities, temperaments, and moral capacity were passed from parents to children, and that negative as well as positive characteristics could become part of the bloodstream.[12] If racially inferior immigrants came in greater numbers, Lodge warned, they could outbreed Anglo-Saxons, or, even worse, interbreed with them. This kind of sexual activity would lead to racial contamination and a nation full of weaker, more dependent men. Lodge insisted that Congress needed to pass a literacy test to restrict southeastern European immigration not only for the nation's future, but for the future of humanity himself. As he put it, "The lowering of the race means not only its own decline but that of human civilizations."[13]

This argument, which would also be developed by the men of the IRL, did not gain much traction in the 1890s, especially in the halls of Congress. Instead, when Congress debated the literacy test, the arguments with the most force were about how southeastern European immigrants affected the present-day working men of the 1890s, not the men of the nation's future. Supporters of the literacy test maintained that southeastern European immigrants undercut the ability of working-class men to fulfill their duty to their families because these immigrants were willing to work for low wages and to live in poor conditions. Opponents of the literacy test, in contrast, held that southeastern European immigrant men would enhance the working class and the nation at large through their strong backs and hard work, and a literacy test would be counterproductive to the nation's economic advancement. The unwillingness to accept the IRL's and Lodge's eugenic arguments about immigrant breeding would become particularly apparent when Lodge sought to extend the literacy test to the wives of immigrant men. In his view, women as well as men were responsible for breeding, and excluding immigrant wives was necessary in order to keep out undesirable race traits. Even many supporters of the literacy test, however, saw this measure as going too far. Most in Congress saw immigrant women outside the considerations of the literacy test because they did not compete in the male labor force. They classed immigrant women as wives and mothers, not workers, breeders, or future citizens.

From the beginning, then, the fight over the literacy test exposed competing views about the gendered implications of immigration restriction. The legislative debate became not only about the men and women the nation wanted to enter its borders, but also about the nature of American manhood and womanhood. By constructing immigrants in gendered ways—as breeders, workers, and mothers—participants in the literacy test debate sought to shape the ways native-born Americans understood immigration and whether it was a threat. More than that, though, they used the literacy test to thrash out the connections between race, labor, and American manhood and womanhood. The push for the literacy test in the 1890s gave the founders of the IRL a chance to cultivate arguments about the gendered threat of southeastern European immigrants that would resonate in the future.

The Immigration Restriction League and the Literacy Test

The young men who founded the Immigration Restriction League in 1894 believed they were the right sort of men—Harvard graduates, sons of long-standing New England families, embarking on successful, professional careers. Prescott Hall, the twenty-six-year-old son of a Boston merchant, had just become a lawyer when he helped found the IRL. He had a melancholy and obsessive temperament, and within a few years he let his law practice fall away and became almost monomaniacal about immigration restriction and the literacy test. Robert DeCourcy Ward found more balance in his life, maintaining a successful career in geology while never wavering in his devotion to immigration restriction.[14] These men graduated from Harvard in 1889, and they took to heart the lessons of their dynamic professors. From Charles Eliot Norton, Barrett Wendell, Nathaniel Shaler, and Francis Peabody, they learned that American democracy was made possible through the strength, intelligence, and grit of their Anglo-Saxon forefathers, who had the courage to stand up to both Indians and the King of England to demand their independence. These glorious founders set the stage for the greatness of the United States.[15] These history lessons contrasted with present-day reality, however, and the young founders of the IRL looked to the future with foreboding.

The views of the men of the IRL, along with those of Henry Cabot Lodge, were shaped by their particular regional context. As Bluford Adams argues, the social situation of Boston Brahmins in the late nineteenth century shaped them in distinctive ways. Their writings exhibited a "unique mixture of power and impotence, arrogance and despair, expansionism and defensiveness."[16] There were many reasons that young, privileged men of Boston Brahmin families would find the early 1890s to be a disconcerting time. Boston was a city coasting on former glory, as industrial powerhouses like New York and Chicago became the dominant cities of the Gilded Age. Although these upper-class Bostonians believed they had a "destiny as a chosen people," they were apprehensive about their decline as a force in American culture and politics as long-standing hierarchies were being upended.[17] "New Money" capitalists, with their gauche mansions and excessive spending, were becoming the center of economic and, increasingly, political power. The workers in these industrialists' factories had begun to behave like the radicals in Europe, demanding higher wages and union recognition. More and more often, labor agitation led to disconcerting violence, as seen in the 1886 Haymarket Riot in Chicago or the 1892 Homestead Strike. A severe depression that had begun in 1893 exacerbated the poor working and living conditions of these workers, leading to greater labor unrest and an increase of unemployed, wandering "tramps."[18] Concurrently, the so-called "New Women" challenged the notion that women should be relegated to the private realm and demanded more access to education and more fulfilling careers. They also claimed the right to participate in public political debates.[19]

There were other, more visible challenges for young Bostonians, namely the impact of immigration on *their* city. The ascendance to power of Irish Catholic immigrants and their sons disconcerted the Brahmin class. Starting in 1884, when Irish Catholic Hugh O'Brien was elected mayor of Boston, the Brahmin class found their right to rule challenged, and those who saw themselves as natural leaders had to recognize that their leadership was "undervalued, unappreciated and unwanted."[20] The most significant sign that something was amiss, however, came from the people these young men saw when walking in certain sections of Boston. They not only had to contend with rabble-rousing Irish, but more and more the men of the IRL saw the streets being taken over by immigrants from southern or eastern Europe— Italian, Slavic, and Jewish laborers whose appearance, language, and culture seemed entirely foreign. The 1885 Boston census had shown that over 63 percent of Bostonians were either foreign or of foreign parentage, and growing numbers of these foreigners were from southern or eastern Europe.[21] It was this change in the population that the founders of the Immigration Restriction League saw at the root of all the other threats to the nation. In the words of Robert DeCourcy Ward, no national problem could be solved "so long as our ports are open to the ignorant, the depraved and the vicious of all nations."[22]

The men of the IRL were not alone in their desire for immigration restriction. The call to close the borders to undesirables had flared up at different times in the nation's history, from the anti-Jacobin agitation in the late eighteenth century to the rise of the anti-Catholic, antiforeigner Know-Nothings of the pre–Civil War era.[23] In 1882, the United States established a principle of exclusion based on nationality with the Chinese Exclusion Act, and the Contract Labor Act of 1885 prohibited the importation of workers by industrialists.[24] In the 1890s, particularly after the start of the depression, the American Federation of Labor and other labor organizations began to call for immigration restriction as a way to protect workers. The Populist Party sought to appeal to the native-born urban working class by making immigration restriction part of their 1892 platform. The rabidly anti-Catholic American Protective Association grew tremendously, starting in the Midwest in the 1880s and then expanding into the Northeast. Their rallying cry was "America for the Americans," and they called on the nation to impose restrictions and increase the naturalization period to twenty years.[25]

While these groups could have been potential allies in the IRL's fight for restriction, Prescott Hall and his colleagues from Harvard sought to distance themselves from what they perceived as crude, partisan, or radical ways.[26] Instead, they cultivated a reputation as scholarly, scientific, and non partisan. As historian Roger Daniels points out, the IRL, similar to a modern-day right-wing think tank, was never a large organization.[27] In their 1894 constitution, the leadership of the IRL defined their primary goal to be to "arouse public opinion to the necessity of a further exclusion of elements undesirable for citizenship or injurious to our national character." They were careful to add that these "elements" did not include "laborers or other immigrants of such character and standards as fit them to become citizens."[28] They strove to present a face of reasoned authority and reached out to distinguished Bostonians to join the organization. A number of academics, businessmen, judges, and former politicians became vice presidents of the League.[29] The IRL also issued documents and circulars full of statistics, wrote letters to the editor and to congressmen, held public meetings, inserted articles into journals of opinion, and tried to persuade other influential men to join their organization.[30]

While most of the League's members were political conservatives as concerned issues of government interference in the economy, they did call on the federal government to use its power to protect the American population from undesirable immigration, preferably through a literacy test.[31] To argue for this test, they did not extol the virtues of literacy but instead sought to show that undesirable immigrants also had the highest rates of illiteracy. Their early pamphlets were full of statistics about the higher rates of illiteracy among southeastern European immigrants. For instance, an 1895 pamphlet titled "The Educational Test as a Means of Further Restricting Immigration" documented the increase in southern and eastern European immigrants, describing them as "foreign not only in race, language and customs, but in habits of thought, traditions and ways of living," and "the least capable of assimilation." To show that a literacy test would provide the best solution for limiting these immigrants, the pamphleteer then went on to give illiteracy statistics for the "undesirable" immigrant nationalities from 1894: Austro-Hungarians, 25 percent; Russians, 26 percent; Polish, 28 percent; Italians, 36 percent—figures much higher than the single-digit rates for England, Germany, and other northern European nations.[32]

The IRL's goal was to convince those in power that these immigrants were a racial threat, and to do so they echoed the language of those who had argued against Chinese immigrants in the previous decade, accusing southeastern European immigrant races of producing men incapable of being self-reliant workers, the heads of patriarchal families, or independent citizens. Worse than that, the IRL argued, these spiritless men would undermine the ability of native-born, working-class men to fulfill their duty to their families and their nation.[33] In other words, the IRL accentuated its critique of immigrant races by depicting them as incapable of maintaining high standards of white manhood.[34] As others had with the Chinese, the men of the IRL portrayed immigrant races as responsible for conditions "contrary to respectable domesticity and capable of undermining American morality and family life."[35] Their most widely distributed pamphlet of 1894, "Twenty Reasons Why Immigration Should Be Further Restricted Now," linked this economic and social threat to a political threat. The servility and dependence of southeastern European immigrant men showed that they were "elements unfitted to absorb democratic ideals of government or take part in the duties and responsibilities of citizenship."[36] The IRL expressed no doubt that Anglo-Saxon men set the standard for American citizenship, and emphasized that racially different immigrant men did not have the qualities to meet the challenges of participating in American democracy.

Since they were advocating for restriction during a severe economic depression, focusing on the plight of working men made tactical sense. Throughout the 1890s, though, the men of the League struggled to advance the debate beyond the question of how immigration affected working-class men to a question of how immigration affected all native-born white men in the nation. They began to make arguments about how inferior immigrant races would outbreed Anglo-Saxon men or, worse, interbreed with Anglo-Saxons, infecting their "blood" with unmanly traits. While not familiar with the technicalities of hereditary science at this point, IRL leaders did try to frame the problem of immigration as a eugenic one affecting the entire race through immigrants' passing on their weakness and dependency to future citizens. They struggled, however, to find a language to make this kind of argument. Their first pamphlet, "The Present Aspects of the Immigration Problem," came the closest of all the 1890s pamphlets to arguing that immigrant "blood" would hurt the Anglo-Saxon race. It complained that the bulk of immigration was no longer of a "related stock, such as the English, the Irish, the Germans or the Scandinavians," who were "some of the most intelligent and most desirable races of Europe." The pamphlet warned that the "new" immigrants' unmanly traits were intractable, and "unaffected by the higher civilization around them." It continued: "The safety of this country depends upon our assimilating and Americanizing all these heterogeneous elements, but the process of assimilation must become slower and more difficult as the foreign element increases."[37]

Richmond Mayo Smith, a political economist at Columbia University who became a vice president of the IRL, also toyed with this sort of eugenic argument in his scholarly writings. The leadership of the League promoted Mayo Smith as an important member of the organization because of his stellar social science credentials and his statistical work in support of immigration restriction.[38] In 1894, the same year the IRL was founded, he published in the *Political Science Quarterly* a series of articles on immigration entitled "The Assimilation of Nationalities," in which he advocated a literacy test and took aim at immigrant "breeding." Although he had an imprecise definition of race based more on sociological rather than biological differences, Mayo Smith felt certain that a mixture between native-born Anglo-Saxons and southeastern European immigrants did not produce a "high civilization," for "neither the Indian half-breed nor the mulatto has approached the white parent." Yet after he made this point, he retreated from it and argued that the American nation found coherence "not in unity of blood, but in unity of institutions."[39]

Prescott Hall, though, did see "unity of blood" as the most pressing issue. A series of letters to the editor of the *Boston Herald* shows how arguments about immigrant breeding were greatly favored by Hall, even as he came to recognize that they did not have much sway at the time. In his letters, Hall stated that immigration had become a "biological question." This was not always the case, he argued. The nation, he insisted, began with a strong racial heritage—those of "Anglo-Saxon descent, with the inborn spirit of freedom and a past history of conquest and success." Prior to 1880, immigrants had been "often inferior physically and mentally" to native-born Americans, but he declared that they were of "kindred blood." Around 1880 this demographic changed. Hall pointed out that the "new" immigrants were illiterate, politically downtrodden, and dirty. But most importantly, immigrants from southern and eastern Europe were "of different races from those already here, and they are physically inferior races." Hall's central concern was not that these immigrants would undercut native-born workers. Instead, he asked, "Shall we permit these inferior races to dilute the thrifty, capable Yankee blood of the sturdy qualities of the earlier immigrants?"[40] Hall stressed that the main racial threat of immigration was based not on immigrants' labor, but on their sexual activity. Immigrant procreation would water down the conquering blood of Anglo-Saxons and leave the nation vulnerable.

When faced with a challenge, however, Hall backed away from this argument. In a response to Hall, Alexander M. Craig wrote to the *Herald* and challenged the notion of innate biological and social difference differences between races. Craig admitted that many immigrants were ignorant and not very clean. "But surely," he declared, "these are not irremediable crimes." He delineated the criticisms of the Irish, German, and Scottish immigrants of the past, and concluded that "the more closely we come in contact with people of varied nationalities, the more irresistibly is the fact impressed upon us that underneath all racial differences the general traits of mankind are identical."[41] In his response to Craig's letter, Hall backed away from his original argument, saying "it is very far from my intention to draw race distinctions," and he went on to make an argument about immigration's undermining labor.[42] Hall came to realize that the argument about breeding did not resonate as much as the labor argument, and for most of the 1890s League publications de-emphasized it. But the men of the IRL would not forget this argument, and they would revive it with greater force after the turn of the century.

By turning to eugenic kinds of arguments, the men of the IRL were seeking to control a world that seemed to have lost its moorings.[43] They believed, as their Harvard professors taught, that they belonged to a superior race, and deserved a superior place in the nation. Their ancestors had borne out the Social Darwinist teachings of survival of the fittest, in the way they conquered Native Americans on the frontier and dominated enslaved African Americans. By the late nineteenth century, in fact, it was the common understanding of a number of social scientists that African Americans and Native Americans were on the verge of extinction as races.[44] At the same time, the Anglo-Saxon male grip on power in the nation seemed to be slipping. While Social Darwinism held that governments should follow a strict laissez-faire policy, what if circumstances in the industrializing United States were making it so the fittest race might not actually survive? While the men of the IRL disdained the idea of government interference to improve working or living conditions, legalize unions, or regulate the excesses of industry, they argued for the government to exert its power to protect the population from racially inferior immigrants. By 1896, the IRL had published seventeen pamphlets, written numerous letters, and seen to the publication of many articles, all of which promoted the literacy test as the best method for restricting immigration. Henry Cabot Lodge, their greatest ally in Congress, had introduced a literacy test bill, and it seemed poised for success.

The Literacy Test in Congress

Lodge's proposal would find widespread support in the 54th Congress of 1895–97, but most of its congressional supporters argued from a very different set of assumptions than Lodge and the men of the IRL. First, instead of ignoring the virtues of literacy, many of them promoted it as a desirable quality for a man to have if he were to become a voting citizen in a democratic society.[45] More than that, most in Congress made the literacy test about the economic problems of the present, not the eugenic problems of the future. This focus starts to become apparent when looking at the language of the literacy test bill in the House of

Representatives. It contained a key change from Lodge's bill: it required all *male* immigrants, not all persons, between the ages of sixteen and sixty to prove they were literate in either English or some other language.[46] Instead of focusing on protecting the breeding stock, restrictionists in the House debate framed the immigrant problem as one of men competing with men in the labor market, and the literacy test as a means to ensure that native-born men prevailed.

By the late nineteenth century, mechanization and the growth of corporate capitalism gave men much less control over their work, and downward wage pressure and periodic high unemployment damaged men's ability to earn a wage sufficient to support a family, and the 1890s depression aggravated this dynamic.[47] Members of the 54th Congress were eager to prove that they were doing something to confront the disruption caused by closed factories and high unemployment, and saw supporting the literacy test as a way to do this. They argued that southeastern European immigrant races would corrupt native-born, working-class manhood because, in their view, southeastern European immigrant men were unwilling or unable to stand up for themselves and demand a decent wage.[48] The threat to wage-earning capacity, in turn, threatened the ability of a working-class man to be the head of a patriarchal family.[49]

Congressmen also made it clear that they saw this problem as one that involved men exclusively. When Republican Richard Bartholdt of Missouri introduced the House bill he explained that it did not include women because of the "scarcity of female white servants."[50] In actuality, unmarried immigrant women had begun to shun domestic labor and entered the industrial workforce in increasing numbers, but Bartholdt and others disconnected women from the labor problem. Instead, they operated from the nineteenth-century, middle-class perspective that women's labor was relegated to the home.[51]

Yet, like Lodge, House supporters of the literacy test also made the test about protecting the prerogatives of *white* manhood, and, like Lodge, they posited that southeastern European immigrants were racially different from those from northwestern Europe. Restrictionists in the 54th Congress by and large agreed with Lodge about the racial difference of southeastern European immigrants. When he introduced the House's version of the literacy test bill, Bartholdt, himself a German immigrant, provided a table that showed that immigrants from countries like Italy, Poland, Hungary, and Russia had much higher illiteracy rates than those from Great Britain, the Netherlands, Germany, and Scandinavia (fig. 1.1).[52] He then said, "Call it race prejudice or any other name, but there is no denying the fact that the Anglo-Saxon feels an aversion against the Latin races."[53]

Instead of pointing to a glorious, manly, Anglo-Saxon past or intimating some horrific future race war, most restrictionists in the House accentuated the racial threat of southeastern European immigrant men by characterizing them as workers

Nationalities	Percentage of illiterates	Nationalities	Percentage of illiterates
Portugal	67.35	Spain	8.71
Italy	52.93	Ireland	7.27
Galicia and Bukowina	45.68	Finland	3.58
Poland	39.82	France (including Corsica)	3.50
Hungary	37.69	England	3.49
Russia (proper)	36.42	Netherlands	3.38
Other Austria	32.70	Scotland	2.83
Greece	25.18	Germany	2.49
Roumania	17.75	Norway	1.02
Belgium	15.22	Sweden	.74
Turkey in Europe	14.79	Switzerland	.60
Bohemia and Moravia	8.98	Denmark	.49

Figure 1.1. This listing of the numbers of illiterate immigrants by nationality was included in the Congressional Record by Representative Richard Bartholdt, who used it to illustrate the large numbers of southern and eastern European immigrants the literacy test would exclude. (*Congressional Record*, 54th Cong., 1st sess., 1896, vol. 28, pt. 6:5418.)

who could not live up to the standard of white, native-born male workers. A typical argument for the literacy test was made by Massachusetts Republican Samuel McCall, who explained that "the American workingman cannot support churches and decently clothe his children and send them to school and enjoy any of the comforts of civilization so long as he must come into this degrading competition."[54] In particular, restrictionists likened southeastern Europeans to Chinese laborers, who had been restricted in the previous decade. For example, Massachusetts Republican Elijah Morse declared that "a Chinaman can live on a little rice a day, and dress in paper; an Italian laborer, as I have seen with my own eyes, can make a satisfactory meal out of a half a loaf of dry bread, without meat, without butter, without education for his children, without the most common necessities of an American workman."[55] Thus Morse and others emphasized the racial inferiority of southeastern European immigrant races by accusing them of producing men who, like the Chinese immigrants, would undermine the ability of native-born, working-class men to fulfill their duty to their families and their nation.[56] In other words, thriftiness and personal economy—which was generally praised in American society—became a sign of racial inferiority.

The debate over the literacy test bill also revealed the attempts by some restrictionists to portray Jewish immigration as a distinctive racial problem. While the original House bill made literacy in "the English language or some other language," it emerged from the conference committee with the stipulation that immigrants "read and write the English language or the language of their native or resident country."[57] Lorenzo Danford, Republican representative from Ohio, admitted that the reason for this change was to exclude Russian Jews, many of whom could read Yiddish or Hebrew, but not Russian. He complained that Jews had "almost drained the magnificent charities of the city of London," and would do the same to the United States.[58] Representative Henry Johnson, Republican, of Indiana, also defended this change. While he claimed that he did not care whether an immigrant was a "Gentile or a Jew," he declared that the change in the bill would keep out those "utterly incapable of becoming good American citizens, but who would be a burden rather than an advantage if they were grafted upon it," immigrants who would not add "anything whatever to our energies and resources."[59] Both Danford and Johnson implied that eastern European Jewish immigrants did not possess manly independence—as evidenced by their need for charity and their lack of "energies"—and therefore threatened to diminish the nation. For most in Congress, however, this change in the bill went too far. Richard Bartholdt of Missouri declared that he could not support the change, finding it inhumane. He admitted that Russian Jews "have their great faults, just as we all have," but insisted that they were a "loving, peaceful race" who gave the world "some of its greatest actors, authors and composers."[60] In the end, opposition to the change was overwhelming, and it was removed from the final bill. While these kinds of anti-Semitic arguments did not gain much traction in Congress, they reemerged in the early twentieth century with even greater force.

The racial arguments made by restrictionists, and particularly by Henry Cabot Lodge, resonated the least with white Southern congressmen, even those from states which were considering or had already passed laws instituting literacy tests to restrict African American suffrage. Ironically, a few years before Lodge proposed his literacy test bill, he had stood out as a defender of African Americans in the South. He was a chief sponsor of the failed Federal Elections Bill of 1890, which would have required Southern states to grant full suffrage to African Americans.[61] By the 1890s, white Southern Democrats, who had recently retaken control of their states after the failure of Reconstruction, started rewriting their state constitutions to require all who wanted to vote to pass a literacy test—to be able to read a section of the United States Constitution—before being granted the right. While these provisions sometimes targeted poor whites who might have voted for a Republican ticket, the enforcers of the law mostly used it to prevent African Americans from voting while allowing illiterate white men to do so.[62] Therefore, even as Lodge promoted suffrage for African Americans, he adopted the tool of their exclusion from suffrage—the literacy test—to target races he believed should be excluded from United States citizenship.

But when it came to the literacy test debate in the 54th Congress, the most out-spoken opponents were Southern Democrats. Many of them were economic boost-ers who wanted to build the New South, and they viewed southeastern European immigrants as a cheap labor source, not as a racial threat.[63] Some Southern members of Congress even asserted that, during a time when socialism was gaining traction among the working classes, literate immigrants could be more dangerous than illiter-ates. Charles Buck, Democrat of Louisiana, made this point when he said that "the assaults upon civilization are committed not by the ignorant, but by those whose vicious tendencies and natures are made more powerful by the light of knowledge."[64] The other Democratic Senator from Louisiana, Donelson Caffery, echoed this senti-ment, arguing that a literacy test would exclude the "most laborious part of the popu-lation" while allowing in the youth, "corrupted, emasculated, diseased, through cheap journalism, bad tobacco, and the enforced physical idleness of the schools."[65]

Other Southern congressmen defended the racial credentials of southeastern European immigrants by arguing that even though they might be racially different from Anglo-Saxons, they were still white. Democratic Congressman John Hendrick of Kentucky asked if a restrictionist colleague "honestly believes that the immi-grants who are coming to our shores from foreign countries are worse than the uneducated Negroes of the South who were raised in slavery. We all know he will not say it. We all know he cannot say it truthfully."[66] Democratic Senator Charles Gibson of Maryland used this tactic to criticize Henry Cabot Lodge. Gibson won-dered why Lodge had in the past given passionate speeches against the sale of slave husbands away from their wives, yet could tolerate "the separation not of humble Negroes who are in the relation of husband and wife, but of those of the same race as the Senator from Massachusetts, humble and alien though they may be."[67] Here, Gibson was referring to a change made in the bill that made immigrant women a central part of the debate. When the conference committee met to resolve the differences in the House and Senate bills, Lodge managed to get them to add a provision that barred all illiterate women immigrants, even if they were married to literate men. This change set off a firestorm of criticism.

"This Worthy Woman, This Good Wife and Mother": Women and the Literacy Test

During the literacy test debate of the 1890s, the vast majority of congressmen saw the position of immigrant women, and women in general, through the lens of *femme covert*, a status in which women's legal and economic rights were under the control of her husband.[68] Even as American women, especially white, middle-class women, were chipping away at this concept and demanding more political and economic rights, members of the 54th Congress did not acknowledge that immigrant women, or any women, were participants in either the labor market or politics.[69] As Senator George Vest, Democrat, of Missouri, put it, "The great objection of illiterate immigration is that it corrupts our suffrage and endangers the basis of our Government, which is the virtue and intelligence of the people." He continued, saying that "there can be no danger either to our civilization or to our labor from allowing these girls to come into the United States whose labor is domestic in its nature."[70]

Henry Cabot Lodge, however, did see a danger that immigrant women could pose. He countered Vest's point, saying, "Of course it is perfectly true . . . that women do not affect the suffrage. I think they affect very largely the quality of citizenship in a somewhat broader way." In Lodge's eugenic framework, an immigrant woman's value to the nation came not in her ability to be a good mother, participate in domestic service, or live up to high moral standards. Instead, the "broader way" she could affect the quality of citizenship came from her role in the reproduction of her race. Lodge considered women from southeastern Europe to be just as racially undesirable as men when it came to breeding, and just as capable of passing objectionable qualities to their sons, the citizens of the future.[71] For Lodge it came down to the fact that he wanted a law that would "lower the number of immigrants coming to this country, and to do it by shutting out the most undesirable class," whether men or women.[72]

Lodge's argument that women were dangerous breeders who had the potential to lower the quality of citizenship did not find much backing in the 54th Congress. Instead, the arguments members made about women and the literacy test centered on the ways women fulfilled their duties to their families. Even some Republicans who previously supported the original bill would not do so after the language changed to keep out wives of literate men. This included the House bill's sponsor, Richard Bartholdt. In giving his reasons, Bartholdt presented a scenario in which a literate husband was allowed to enter the United States, but then "the thumbscrews are put to the wife." He depicted this potential illiterate wife as a "loving wife, a good mother to her children and a good cook for her family." Did it matter, he asked, whether she could read or write? Then he warned, "If this conference report is adopted, this worthy woman, this good wife and mother, will be ruthlessly torn from husband and children and sent back to the country whence she came, or else the whole family must return with her."[73] Thus for Bartholdt and other opponents of this measure, a woman's worth came from her simplicity and devotion to family. Her illiteracy did not make her a liability to the nation.

Some supporters of the literacy test actually extolled the virtues of women's education and literacy when they defended the change in the bill, but this praise was not an acknowledgement of the way that women in the late nineteenth century used education to carve out new opportunities for themselves. Instead, the congress-men linked the need for education to the duties of motherhood, harkening back to the ideal of the Republican Mother, who used her education to train her son to become a good citizen.[74] Senator William Chandler, Republican from New Hamp-shire, defended the importance of literate wives and mothers, saying, "If the father can read and write and the mother cannot, the children will grow up in ignorance. But if the mother can read and write, she teaches her children to read and write in the sanctity of her home." Continuing, he said that literate immigrant mothers "will make not the voters of this generation perhaps, but the voters of the next generation, whether they be all males or whether they be males and females alike, intelligent and fit to exercise the suffrage in this Republic of ours."[75] Even as he acknowledged that women may be voters in the future, the core of Chandler's argu-ment was that a woman's role as a mother made it essential that she be able to read. Like most other supporters of restriction—Lodge being an exception—Chandler did not concern himself with the racial characteristics of immigrant women.

In the end, a compromise was reached after the conference committee met again: Lodge backed down from his stand, and the final bill allowed that unmarried women would be subject to the literacy test, but wives of men admitted would not, thereby reinforcing the dependent status of wives.[76] In February of 1897, the bill easily passed in the House with a vote of 217 to 36 and more narrowly passed in the Senate, with a vote of 34 to 31.[77] Because Republicans dominated the House of Representatives and had a majority in the Senate, most of the votes in favor of the bill came from them, although a few Republicans voted against it.[78] A good number of Democrats did vote for the bill, but the vast majority of the opposition came from Southern Democrats who made up almost all the votes against the lit-eracy test in the House and the majority of votes against it in the Senate.[79]

The literacy test did not become law at this time. Grover Cleveland, who had shown sympathy for immigrants and had spoken out against mob violence against Chinese immigrants in the 1880s, vetoed the bill in March of 1897, one of his last acts as President.[80] He gave an extensive, point-by-point refutation of the bill and started by making the conservative argument that the bill was a "radical depar-ture" from the nation's past immigrant policies, and declared that all that should be required of immigrants was "physical and moral soundness and a willingness to work." Moreover, he cited what he saw as the traditional American values of open-ness and opportunity and called the provisions "unnecessarily harsh and oppressive." At the same time, he did give some legitimacy to Henry Cabot Lodge's argument. He agreed that "protecting our population against degeneration" was the best rea-son given for the bill's "racial restriction," but he disputed the notion that a literacy test would accomplish this goal.[81]

Lodge and the men of the Immigration Restriction League were disappointed by Cleveland's veto, but encouraged by other political winds. Even though the literacy test bill did not pass, the IRL celebrated the fact that the Republicans had adopted the IRL's exact language about immigration restriction in their 1896 platform, and that even the Democrats' platform contained language about restriction.[82] Prescott Hall wrote to the IRL membership and said that "no measure before Congress in many years has been so unanimously advocated and demanded by the country and the press regardless of section or party." He then vowed to keep fighting "until there is a law on our statute books which shall exclude the absolutely illiterate from this country." He explained that the League's first priority was to push for the introduction of a literacy test bill in the 55th Congress.[83] Since the bill passed in the 54th Congress, and the seemingly sympathetic Republican William McKinley was President, the IRL was confident that it was only a matter of time before the literacy test became law.

Hall and the men of the League would be disappointed. They had had great faith that McKinley would press hard for immigration restriction, but in fact the opposite was the case. McKinley owed considerable support to manufacturers, who wanted to continue having access to unskilled immigrant labor. Thus while the Senate passed a literacy test bill in 1898, the House, probably with the support of McKinley, quashed it.[84] By that time, popular support for the literacy test had diminished. The end of the depression had made the economic case less pressing as the demand for labor grew. Moreover, the United States' swift success in the Spanish-American War led to new confidence in the nation, and increased optimism about the ability to absorb immigrants.[85] By 1899, the men of the Immigration Restriction League lost some of their motivation, and in April of that year they voted to disband the organization.[86]

Conclusion

While Henry Cabot Lodge and the men of the IRL did not see legislative success in the 1890s, they established some key assumptions. They made the literacy test a test of racial fitness, one that would keep out undesirable immigrants from southeastern Europe. They also introduced the idea that the test would preserve Anglo-Saxon manhood and insure that Anglo-Saxon men would pass on strong bodies, strong minds, and strong character to their sons and future citizens. When the IRL reemerged in the twentieth century, its members would find themselves better equipped to make this argument. They would attach themselves to the growing popularity of the eugenics movement, and the threat of immigrant "breeding" would become the central motif of the League's fight for a literacy test. Further, the League would take advantage of another new political ideology of the early twentieth century—progressivism. They could justify the literacy test as both a test of racial advancement and a legitimate use of government power by the greatly empowered federal government.

Yet even as they found more receptive audiences for their arguments in the first decade of the twentieth century, the IRL would face new challenges. As the numbers of immigrants climbed to even greater heights, more Americans would use debates about immigration restriction legislation as a place to define the citizens of the new progressive state, and they wanted to make sure that the definition of those citizens included people like themselves. One group that saw particularly high stakes in this definition was white, middle-class, Progressive women. One of the most prominent organizations that arose out of this group self-consciously refuted the Immigration Restriction League by naming itself the Immigrants' Protective League. Led by Hull House denizen Grace Abbott, the women of the IPL used the debate over the literacy test to challenge the notion that citizenship was about Anglo-Saxon manhood, and instead offered a definition that acknowledged womanly qualities as essential. Both groups would get a chance to promote their visions at the highest level of government when they participated in the massive study of the Senate Commission on Immigration, also known as the Dillingham Commission.

–2–

Parents and Progeny

The Dillingham Commission Report

*I*n the first decade of the twentieth century, the parameters of the literacy test debate were transformed. The economic growth of the early twentieth century led to a huge demand for labor and, consequently, a spike in immigration. Over ten million immigrants arrived in that decade, the vast majority from southern and eastern Europe.[1] Overall wages increased and unemployment remained low, which weakened the restrictionists' case that immigration hurt working men. At the same time, the growth of the progressive movement had called into question much of the laissez-faire policies of the past, including policies about immigration. The presidency of Theodore Roosevelt shook up the established political order and Roosevelt justified the use of government power to curb the excesses of industrialization. More and more native-born Americans began to perceive the rising numbers of immigrants as perpetuating the social problems of the industrial economy, and the Immigration Restriction League (IRL), when it reemerged, continued to push the idea that a literacy test designed to rein in immigration was a logical solution. President Roosevelt spoke out publicly for the need for government action to solve what had become known as the immigrant problem, and in 1907 he called for a mammoth congressional study of immigration to the United States. The President charged the Immigration Commission, also known as the Dillingham Commission, to study the impact of immigration on all levels of society and to decide whether a literacy test was the best legislative approach to the immigrant problem. During this same time, new participants were entering the literacy test debate, including a new organization that had formed out of Hull House in Chicago: the Immigrants' Protective League (IPL).

When the leaders of the Immigration Restriction League and the Immigrants' Protective League were asked to submit statements to the Dillingham Commission, they saw it as an opportunity to have their views of the nation validated by national legislation. In true progressive form, they bolstered their arguments about immigration legislation with statistics, case studies, and testimony from scientific and social scientific experts. Their approaches were alike in other ways as well. The leaders of both organizations described the "immigrant problem" as one of fathers and sons, mothers and daughters, and they saw immigration legislation as a way to promote the strength of families, and thereby the strength of the nation.

Their view of strong families, however, differed. Robert DeCourcy Ward, a member of the executive board of the IRL, made the issue about the preservation of Anglo-Saxons, declaring, "The question before us is a race question. It is a question of what kind of babies shall be born."[2] Grace Abbott, the director of the IPL, did not see race at issue at all, and instead argued that the pressures of an industrial society had fractured the bond between mothers, fathers, and their children, thereby threatening the immigrant family's ability to become part of the community. "What is really needed," she declared, "is a re-establishment of the parents in the eyes of the immigrant child" in order for those children to "become the sort of men and women we want."[3]

Ward, Abbott, and other members of the IRL and the IPL also insisted that the federal government had to take a more active role to ensure that immigrants and their children were the sort of men and women the nation wanted. Abbott criticized the laissez-faire approach of the government to immigration issues, and asked Americans to consider "the cost to the community of spending neither time, thought nor money on the question of making Americans out of the million people who are coming to us every year."[4] In her work through the IPL, Abbott would argue that desirable outcomes would occur when there were protections in place to shield immigrant men and women from exploitation, and thereby allow them to be good husbands, wives, and parents. Ward agreed that the government had been too laissez-faire in its attitude about immigration. For him, however, the action the government needed to take was to establish eugenic restriction, preferably through a literacy test. "By selecting our immigrants through proper immigration legislation," he declared, "we have the power to pick out the best specimens of each race to be the parents of our future citizens."[5]

As both Ward and Abbott made arguments about the need for government action to deal with immigrant parents and their progeny, they were also making a larger case about who belonged to the nation and had a right to determine its future. At a time when the women's suffrage movement was gaining momentum, the men of the IRL insisted that citizenship was the purview of Anglo-Saxon, upper-class men like themselves. As they argued that innate racial qualities prevented immigrant men from living up to that standard, they linked those qualities to femininity, simultaneously making the case that women were incapable of citizenship. For the good of the nation, in their view, encroachments on Anglo-Saxon male privilege had to be rebuffed by the force of law. In contrast, Abbott and the members of the IPL, who were mostly women, stressed that the government needed to look to the reform work of middle-class women as a model for the types of programs that would protect immigrants; they thereby made the larger case that the rights and privileges of citizenship needed to be opened up both for immigrants and for women like themselves. As part of this strategy, they compared caring, feminine values with destructive, masculine values that led to the exploitation of immigrant families. Thus the literacy test debate also became a proxy debate about the role of women in the state.

Immigration Politics in the New Century

In the new century, debates over the place of immigrants in American society and the need for immigration restriction expanded, and the politics surrounding these issues became more complicated. The most significant change was that opposition to immigration restriction became more widespread. Businessmen, philanthropic organizations, religious organizations, and representatives from immigrant groups had organized to fight the literacy test and, in the process, had promoted the importance of immigrants in American life.[6] Moreover, the importance of immigrant votes had become more apparent, and Republicans in states with high immigrant populations had begun to compete with Democrats for them. The powerful Republican Speaker of the House, Congressman Joseph Cannon of Chicago, saw the importance of the urban immigrant vote and sought to dampen Republican support for immigration restriction.[7] At the same time, the growth of anti-Japanese agitation in the West increased the support for restriction among Western congressmen. Support for restriction among Southern Democrats also grew as the perception of the racial inferiority of southeastern Europeans began to take hold.[8] After he became President following the assassination of William McKinley in 1901, Theodore Roosevelt attempted to manipulate the situation to the best political advantage to himself.

In 1901, Roosevelt gave his message to the 57th Congress and said that, while the nation welcomed any immigrant who brought "a strong body, a stout heart, a good head, and a resolute purpose to do his duty," he wanted to keep out the ignorant and those "who are below a certain standard of economic fitness," a vague phrase that could denote those who did not have the ability to make a living or those who would not demand a decent wage.[9] Restrictionists in Congress took up his call and introduced a bill that expanded the classes of excluded immigrants to take account for the mentally ill, anarchists, and prostitutes; this bill became law in 1903. Before it was enacted, Representative Oscar Underwood of Alabama attempted to add the literacy test to the bill, but the amendment received little support. Henry Cabot Lodge fought for it at first, but backed away when it became apparent that the amendment would not receive adequate support.[10] He assured Prescott Hall that he would introduce the literacy test in the next session of Congress.[11]

Little happened with immigration restriction in the 58th Congress, but the 59th Congress produced a flurry of immigration bills. In 1906, Senator William Dillingham of Vermont introduced a bill that strengthened earlier provisions, increased the head tax, and called for the exclusion of the "physically defective."[12] Lodge added a literacy test provision for all aliens over age sixteen, except for wives, children, and parents over the age of fifty-five.[13] The IRL hoped, with some reason, that Theodore Roosevelt would become an enthusiastic backer of immigration restriction and the literacy test, because he had preached against race suicide and praised the glories of the Anglo-Saxon race. But the members would be disappointed. Roosevelt, as President, remained ambivalent about immigration questions, and in speeches he would both warn of the effects of "undesirable" immigration and praise the contributions of immigrants to American society.[14]

Furthermore, a new organization, the National Liberal Immigration League (NLIL), was formed for the express purpose of keeping immigration as open as possible. The NLIL particularly sought to protect the interests of Jews from Eastern Europe. Founded by a coalition of Jewish leaders and businessmen, as well as liberal progressives like Jane Addams, their intention was to thwart restriction measures and promote the positive contributions immigrants made to American society. In 1906, the NLIL organized letter-writing campaigns and mass rallies in Boston and New York to persuade congressmen and the President at least to study the problem before they supported a literacy test.[15] In the end, Roosevelt and moderate congressional Republicans, particularly Speaker of the House Joseph Cannon, maneuvered to quash the 1906 bill and pushed to form a commission that would study, comprehensively and scientifically, the "immigrant problem" before taking any legislative action. In 1907, Roosevelt signed into law the bill sponsored by Dillingham that increased the head tax on immigrants, remanded those who had tuberculosis to the excluded category, and legalized the "Gentleman's Agreement," which severely limited immigration from Japan. The bill also called for the formation of the Dillingham Commission to study immigration to the United States scientifically and come up with recommendations for government action.[16]

The Immigration Restriction League Regroups

When Prescott Hall, Robert DeCourcy Ward, and other members of the executive committee re-formed the Immigration Restriction League in 1901, they had to deal with this new political reality. They chafed at the rise in the opposition to immigration restriction and saw it as part of the challenge to the predominant place of Anglo-Saxons in the nation.[17] In particular, they resented the presumption of organized

Jewish groups, such as the NLIL and United Hebrew Charities, in claiming the right to speak for the good of the nation on immigration issues. In one letter, Hall complained that "the Jews in this country are bitterly opposed to any proper restriction of immigration laws, partly because many of their coreligionists are so poor, diseased, and generally unfit."[18] Even as they expressed frustration at the challenges to Anglo-Saxon dominance, the men of the IRL were pleased that immigration restriction had become part of a national debate and that some restrictions were passed in 1903 and 1907. As these different bills wound their way through Congress, the members of the IRL refined their arguments and built up new constituencies.

When Hall and Ward reestablished the Immigration Restriction League, they sought to present it as a professional organization, one that fit into the scientific, progressive mold of the day. Executive Committee members Richards M. Bradley and Joseph Lee oversaw a more sophisticated fundraising campaign that reached out to old-money Bostonians. Lee, who had spearheaded the movement for urban playgrounds (and became known as the "Father of Playgrounds") attempted to build sympathy for the IRL in the Boston reform and philanthropic communities. The leaders of the IRL also sought to broaden their connections by reaching out to organizations and individuals outside of Boston. While they had initially rejected the anti-Catholic sentiments of groups like the American Protective Association in the early 1890s, by the early twentieth century they had formed an alliance with the anti-Catholic Junior Order of United American Mechanics, a labor organization that was a holdover from the Know-Nothing party. Under the direction of the IRL, the members of the Junior Order formed branches in New York. The IRL kept its association with the Junior Order hidden from public view, but trumpeted the growing number of university presidents and distinguished academics associated with the League, including Lawrence Lowell, president of Harvard University; David Starr Jordan, president of Stanford University; and John R. Commons, a distinguished economist from the University of Wisconsin. The IRL also hired as its representative in Washington James H. Patten, a man with extensive knowledge of the workings of Congress who worked tirelessly, even fanatically, for the IRL for over twenty-five years. Patten had ties to numerous agricultural, labor, and business organizations, and patriotic societies, and encouraged the IRL to reach out to these potential allies.[19]

In the new century, IRL publications still argued that immigration was a problem for American workingmen and published pamphlets that offered statistics showing that undesirable laborers would be restricted through a literacy test.[20] But they also made their argument about the racial threat of immigration most predominant, in part because they had a terminology with which to do it. In the 1890s, no language existed to demarcate European "races," except for the vague terms "Anglo-Saxon" and "Hebrew." Others were referred to by nationality. This system began to change in 1899 when Harvard Professor William Ripley published *The Races of Europe*, in which he divided Europeans into three races—Teutonic, Alpine, and Mediterranean—and soon other sub-classifications emerged.[21] At the same time, there was no scientific or social consensus about how many races actually existed in the world, with some postulating as little as two and others insisting there were more than sixty.[22] Even with this confusion, the IRL adopted a new language to describe European races. While in the 1890s IRL pamphlets had described undesirable European immigrants by nationality, by the early twentieth century, they divided European immigrants into different racial categories. One pamphlet defined the "Teutonic Division" and "Keltic Division" as being from northwestern Europe, the "Iberic Division" as being from southern Europe, and the "Slavic Division" as being from Eastern Europe.[23]

Moreover, the IRL could rely more on racial arguments because of the growing acceptance of eugenics in the United States. The increasing popularity of eugenics after 1900 came with the rediscovery of the writings of a Moravian monk, Gregor Mendel, whose study of pea plants led him to postulate that heredity was determined by the combination of dominant and recessive traits.[24] As Mendel's theories took hold, Americans at first began to discuss how to use them to promote better agriculture and livestock, but the focus quickly turned to questions of how to promote the birth of children with desirable traits and prevent the birth of the undesirable. In 1904, the Department of Agriculture founded the American Breeders Association, a research station at Cold Spring Harbor, New York, under the direction of Harvard zoologist Charles Davenport. At first this group was made up of plant and animal breeders who were interested in keeping up with advancements in genetic science, but Davenport quickly turned to questions of human heredity. Davenport and others began to propose ways the government could promote "clean" heredity, known as "positive eugenics," and inhibit human reproduction that would lead to the birth of "defectives."[25] Overall, the ideas of science, government control, and the influence of experts involved in eugenics fit in very well in the Progressive Era.[26] By the early twentieth century, participants in the eugenics movement, according to Wendy Kline, intertwined race and gender anxieties. It became about which men and women actually had children and what kind of men and women would be the products of that reproduction.[27]

The men of the Immigration Restriction League used these eugenic ideas to argue that the qualities of ideal manhood were racial traits that could be passed on from father to son. They maintained that the Anglo-Saxon race created the nation, and that their descendants fell heir to the strength, hardiness, health, and mental vigor to preserve it. John R. Commons made his case plain in his 1907 book, *Races and Immigrants in America.*[28] Operating under the assumption that men were the practitioners of democracy, he argued that, for a democracy to succeed, the races that practiced it had to possess "manliness," which he described as "that which the Romans called virility, and which at bottom is dignified self-respect, self-control and that self assertion and jealousy of encroachment which marks those who, knowing their rights, dare maintain them." A quality like manliness was, according to Commons, "established in the very blood and physical constitution." Individuals could change religion, occupation, language, or form of government, yet "underneath all these changes they may continue to exhibit the physical, mental and moral capacities and incapacities which determine the real character of their religion, government, industry and literature."[29] Commons and other League members stressed that Anglo-Saxon men possessed greater strength, assertiveness, intelligence, and self control, and that the literacy test was a way for the State to use its power to preserve the superiority of American men by preventing the eugenic contamination of the nation's population by the weak, effeminate traits of southeastern European races.

In the first decade of the twentieth century, the men of the IRL put front and center their argument that those who possessed a stalwart, manly racial inheritance, like the Anglo-Saxon men of their organization, needed to stand guard over it by advocating for restriction to protect the nation's genetic quality. They also insisted that the ability or inability to read and write was an indicator of whether immigrants possessed other positive or negative heritable traits that would be passed on to their sons and future citizens. If immigrant races did not have qualities of manhood—that is, strength of body and strength of will to find the opportunity to learn to read—then these races would not only make poor citizens in the present, but their undesirable traits would enter the nation's bloodstream and corrupt the racial future of the nation.

The men of the IRL, then, made the literacy test into a proxy for a eugenic test. One way the League's literature did this was to argue that the presence of illiterate immigrants would deter Anglo-Saxon fathers and mothers from reproducing, and thereby allow immigrant children to become dominant in the population. A 1904 pamphlet first stated this claim, declaring that "there is another struggle between the newcomers and their children on one side, and the children of those already here on the other, in which the latter are defeated and slain by never being allowed to come into existence."[30] This kind of argument paralleled that made by sociologist E. A. Ross when he argued that open Japanese immigration would increase competition, drive down wages, and lead Anglo-Saxon men and women to have fewer children, since they would not want them to have to compete with those who could survive on less. Ross called this phenomenon "race suicide."[31] The IRL did not use Ross's term at this point, but they started to paint immigrants more decisively as a eugenic threat because they would outbreed the Anglo-Saxon race.

The IRL also began to suggest an even worse possibility than race suicide— that immigrants would *interbreed* with Anglo-Saxons, and thereby contaminate the

Anglo-Saxon race. Framing arguments in this way also allowed the IRL to play off the ways Americans linked sexual power to racial dominance, with an important indicator of sexual power being the ability of men to maintain sexual control over women and sire sons.[32] Historians, and particularly historians of African American women, have also shown that nineteenth-century white Americans consolidated their social power by linking racial power to sexual power.[33] After the Civil War, fears of miscegenation between blacks and whites, and particularly the fear of the black male rapist, provided much of the justification for the rise in the 1890s of Jim Crow laws, and became a standard lament in the scientific literature about race.[34] The control of all women's sexuality by white men was central to the dominant racial hierarchy, and sexual encroachment by lesser races would upset power balances.

Another key strategy the IRL adopted was to broaden the base of support for the literacy test by appealing to white Southerners. The League members realized that white male boosters of the New South wanted to tap into immigrant labor to build up Southern industries.[35] But they also realized that race trumped everything in the South, so they made a conscious effort to link the racial qualities of southeastern European immigrants to those of African Americans. Robert DeCourcy Ward, in a 1905 *Atlantic Monthly* article, wrote that the whites in the South accused blacks of being "less efficient than before the war; with incapacity, irresponsibility, and instability; with unfitness for and dissatisfaction with his work; with demanding too much pay and requiring too many holidays." He noted that white Northerners recognized these unmanly traits in immigrant laborers and servants, thereby linking the immigrants with the "Negro Problem."[36] In that same year, Prescott Hall sent out a survey to over five thousand white Southern men seeking attitudes about a literacy test and the head tax. Hall asked leading questions that linked positive qualities to northwestern European immigrants and negative qualities to southeastern European immigrants, and then asked which group Southerners desired.[37] Hall wrote to Henry Cabot Lodge about the results of this survey, and said, "In many quarters there was a distinct disposition to generalize from their experience with the introduction of the Negro as a solution of the Eighteenth Century labor problem and to declare that they did not wish to fly from 'present ills' to 'ills unknown.'"[38]

In their writings aimed at Southerners, IRL members tried to promote suspicion of immigrants by suggesting that southeastern European immigrants were racially closer to the "Negroes" than the they were to Anglo-Saxons, and likewise posed a sexual threat. Robert DeCourcy Ward suggested the threat of race suicide in a speech in Richmond, Virginia, in 1905. While advocating a literacy test, he admonished the attitude among Southern farmers who said, "we will take [the immigrant] with low vitality, poor physique, mentally deficient, unused to outdoor work, dishonest." Immigrants with these qualities, according to Ward, exposed the hardy country population to a conniving, unmanly element. Even more dire, the presence of these immigrants would cause "a decrease in the birthrate among the older portion of our population [i.e., Anglo-Saxons]" since this "older portion" would not want to bring children into the world to compete with the rabble of immigrants.[39] In his 1908 book *Immigration*, Prescott Hall pushed the point even further by playing upon the sexual anxieties of white Southern men, as he linked immigrants with African Americans. He declared the immigrant races to be "servile, like the Negro," but more of a threat, because they would be "certain to intermingle far more than [the Negro] with the native stock."[40] In other words, Hall implied that immigrant men were not only outbreeding native-born Anglo-Saxons but also interbreeding with them. He likened the sexual liaisons between Anglo-Saxons and immigrants to a kind of miscegenation that would upset the dominance of Anglo-Saxon men in the South. At this point, the miscegenation argument was muted, but it would become a more prominent one for the League in the future.

Starting in 1908, the IRL openly embraced eugenic reasoning and linked the sexual and racial threats of immigration. In that year, Prescott Hall wrote a pamphlet for the Immigration Restriction League called "Eugenics, Ethics and Immigration," in which he took on what he saw as a simplistic reading of Social Darwinism, and argued that those concerned about the American racial stock had to move beyond survival of the fittest. The fittest, by Hall's logic, were obviously the most manly, and the most manly races emanated from northwestern Europe, particularly from the "Teutonic Division." But industrial conditions in the United States, especially in cities, had begun to favor the servile, the weak-limbed, the destitute. Hall called for action, and the idea of pushing for reforms that might change the environment did not seem to occur to him. Instead, Hall made a circular case that would be repeated often by men affiliated with the IRL: to ensure survival of the fittest, the nation needed to keep out undesirables in order to make sure the race that was actually fittest, which he unquestionably believed to be Anglo-Saxons, would survive. Or, as he said: "We have seen, for example, both in biology and in history that individuals with traits of the highest value may disappear before the onslaught of lower types which in one way or another are better fitted to perpetuate themselves." He then pointed out that "the great recent influx of South Italians and Slavs has had a perceptible effect in checking immigration from Northern and Western Europe. . . . The admission of the less desirable means the exclusion of the better class. To which of the two does the future belong?"[41] He knew to which the future *should* belong, and believed the government needed to take steps to make it happen. Using the language of progressivism, he wrote that "we have begun to realize the control of man over nature, and to see that the highest results come from collective effort consciously directed toward that end."[42]

In a 1910 article for the *North American Review,* Ward also employed eugenic reasoning. In the article, he told a hypothetical story about a poor tailor and his puny son. He argued that sentimentalists might say, "the father's unhealthy occupation is responsible for the weakling child." But that kind of reasoning, according to Ward, was giving in to "our natural prejudices." Instead, he argued, his readers should recognize that "the father was probably physically so degenerate that he could not follow any occupation except that of a tailor and the poor physique of his offspring undoubtedly resulted from his own poor physique."[43] Ward believed that the government had a responsibility to prevent this kind of genetic material from entering the nation's bloodstream. By setting up a restrictive literacy test, he argued, "We in the United States, have an opportunity which is unique in history for the practice of eugenic principles."[44]

By 1909, when the IRL was asked to participate in the Dillingham Commission Report, it had made more political allies and inroads, and its leaders felt that their arguments were resonating with the public. There was, however, a rising source of opposition that the League did not see, or perhaps did not want to recognize: the political force of organized, white, middle-class, Progressive women.

The Founding and First Years of the Immigrants' Protective League

In 1908, as she was putting the finishing touches on her *Twenty Years at Hull House,* Jane Addams saw a growing need in the immigrant community. As the arrivals in Chicago from Ellis Island swelled, so too did the con artists, false labor agents, and sexual predators who met immigrants at the city's bustling train stations. She declared that those who worked in Chicago settlement houses "have keenly realized the need of some systematic and centralized effort on behalf of the immigrants living in Chicago," and she set out to create a bureau that would protect immigrants from economic and financial exploitation.[45] She was inspired by other women activists of the era. By the early twentieth century, the National Council of Jewish Women had pioneered work in protecting newly arrived immigrant girls and young women from sexual exploitation by setting up aid stations at Ellis Island and monitoring young women who arrived alone, and the Council was looking for a way to expand its work to inland cities. In Chicago, the Women's Trade Union League had formed an Immigration Committee to protect immigrant women in industrial jobs. Representatives from both of these organizations worked with Jane Addams to form the Immigrants' Protective League.[46]

When Sophonisba Breckinridge, a brilliant political economist at the University of Chicago, turned down the offer to be director of the IPL, Addams asked her if she knew of a "competent man" who could do the job.[47] Breckinridge instead suggested Grace Abbott, a woman who was part of the extensive network of university-educated social workers in which Breckinridge operated. The choice proved to be fortuitous. Abbott possessed a keen intelligence, a strong sense of organization, and an extraordinary energy, which she directed toward the field of social work. She and her sister Edith left Nebraska in the first decade of the twentieth century to study at the University of Chicago's innovative School of Social Work. Edith became an asset to Grace as an expert at economics and statistics and, like her sister, began to use her knowledge to produce studies of the working and living conditions of Chicago's immigrant communities.[48] Grace Abbott could also tap into the extensive network of Chicago's women social workers, such as Frances Kellor, Katherine Davis, Sophonisba Breckinridge, and Julia Lathrop.[49] Starting with this set of connections, Abbott built a membership composed primarily of white, middle-class, native-born women—mostly Protestant or Jewish—who were affiliated with either academic or charitable institutions. While the presidents of the IPL were always men of great influence, such as Judge Julian Mack and industrialist Alexander McCormick, it was the women of the IPL, and Grace Abbott in particular, who designed the programs, did the research, accomplished the tasks, and wrote the annual reports.

As soon as she took the position as director in 1908, Abbott moved to Hull House in a rapidly changing West Side neighborhood made up of immigrants, the most prominent at the time being Poles, Greeks, Italians, and Russian Jews. Abbott plunged into her work and defined the IPL as a strong, vital organization both in the immigrant communities and within the larger white, middle-class community of Chicago. She wore many hats in her position. The primary work of the League was to protect immigrants who arrived by train to Chicago from cheating expressmen, shady employment agents, and men who wanted to corrupt the virtue of immigrant girls and women. She oversaw a staff composed primarily of foreign-born women who served as translators when she visited train stations or looked for lost immigrants. Abbott soon expanded the focus of the IPL to include monitoring employment agencies and offering legal assistance. In her role as director, she also wrote detailed reports of the League's activities and published articles in academic and popular presses that explained the situation of immigrant communities and families in Chicago.

One reason that the Immigration Restriction League might have refused to acknowledge the IPL is because the women of the IPL, and Grace Abbott in particular, did not frame their arguments within IRL's parameters. Instead of portraying immigrants as threatening outsiders, the IPL participated in Jane Addams' project of building cross-class bonds as a way to ameliorate class and race tensions. Further, Abbott and the women of the IPL approached immigrants from a stance of sympathy rather than hostility. They acknowledged racial differences among

European immigrants, but avoided language that denoted innate racial inferiority. Finally, when they did address immigration legislation, they saw the role of the federal government in a decidedly different way. They argued that the government should focus its energies on promoting naturalization policies that would protect and nurture these future citizens, rather than set up barriers to block their entry. In other words, Abbott argued that the nation should do what the nonvoting women of the IPL were doing—nurturing immigrants and, in the process, making them into better citizens.

A story from an unpublished biography of Grace Abbott written by her sister, Edith, illustrates the different trajectory from which Grace approached immigration issues and gender roles. Edith told of how Grace learned that Carmella, a young Italian immigrant girl, was in a situation where her mother worked while the girl's father stayed home with the younger children. When Grace consulted the Bureau of Charities about this case, they told her that the father was "a typical Italian—he wants to sit around in the sun but he doesn't want to work." Edith wrote that "Grace did not accept the current stories about Italian men who 'did not want to work,'" and she went to the family's home to discover the truth. Grace wanted to examine the situation, because "relief might be needed to keep the mother at home, and anyway, the twelve year old Carmella must go to school." She found that the father was a carpenter, but he did not have the money to join a union, and Abbott, through the Immigrants' Protective League, provided the funds for the man to join. He then obtained a job, the mother stayed home with the children, and Carmella went to school.[50]

One obvious contrast to the practices of the Immigration Restriction League is the way in which Grace Abbott dismissed the stereotype of the "typical" Italian. She refused to fall back on simple racial typing, and sought to understand the specific circumstances of Carmella's family. Throughout her career, Abbott portrayed herself as a strong opponent of "race prejudice." As one of the dynamic group of early-twentieth-century social workers trained at the University of Chicago, she studied the works of anthropologists who disputed the biological certainty of race.[51] At the same time, her sister Edith made Grace into the engine of the story —she took the action that set Carmella's family on the right path. She also insisted on a traditional ideal for the family: the father needed to earn the wage; the mother needed to stay at home and care for the children; and the children, especially the daughters, needed to be in a secure and protected environment. Once the family secured themselves in these roles, they were on their way to becoming productive members of the community.

Grace Abbott used her work with immigrants and her participation in immigration restriction debates not only to make a case for the protection of immigrants, but also to prove the stellar citizenship qualities of people like herself—middle-class women reformers. She stressed that socially active, racially tolerant women represented the ideal of United States citizenship, not Anglo-Saxon nativists, the most vocal of whom tended to be men.[52] Yet even as she defended immigrants from the nasty insinuations of people like Prescott Hall, she also argued that immigrant women and men needed women like herself to get on the right path to citizenship. In a way, she set up what might be called a triangulation in modern political parlance, by placing activist white, middle-class women into positions as protectors of vulnerable immigrants and showing them to be ethically and morally superior to their restrictionist opponents.

In many ways, Grace Abbott's attitudes reflect the attitude that modern historians of women and gender have termed "maternalist."[53] Maternalism, in the words of Seth Koven and Sonya Michel, "transformed motherhood from women's *private* responsibility into *public* policy."[54] By invoking the language of motherhood, maternalists like Abbott hoped to increase the force of their arguments and gain the power to enact their proposals. Historian Linda Gordon has defined maternalists as women who believed that women's socialization as mothers made them uniquely able to be leaders of reform work in society. Gordon also maintains that maternalists constructed themselves as mothers to those they aided. Through this philosophy, they sought to skew the prevailing male-dominated power structure by articulating an argument against women's political, economic, and social subordination. In these arguments, they tied women, and particularly women of the lower class, to domestic duties and childcare, and then argued that these duties were vitally important for the nation.[55] But in this schema, according to Gordon, Koven, and Michel, lower-class women were not vital to the nation in the same way as middle-class white women. Poor women were supposed to remain passive and without a voice; they needed the middle-class women to speak for them. Gwendolyn Mink writes, for example, that certain women reformers believed that the relationship of lower-class, African American women to the state "was limited to their condition as subjects of maternalist social policy."[56]

But while Grace Abbott certainly positioned herself in a place of power in relation to immigrants, she was not simply expecting immigrant women to take a submissive role in the family as she, a white, middle-class woman, could seek out all the fulfilling work she wanted. Instead, she used her work to Americanize immigrant families as a way to articulate an innovative view of citizenship. As Suronda Gonzalez argues, "Grace Abbott forged a new discussion of social citizenship based on enlarged social entitlements and a more expansive democracy for all U.S. residents—immigrants and native-born, male and female alike."[57] Throughout their participation in the immigration restriction debates, Abbott and the members of the IPL insisted that citizenship was not gendered male, and that women were, in fact, central to the success of the nation. She modeled the relationship between the state and its citizens after the relationship between men and women in families. Instead of defining the family dynamic as independent men who took care of properly dependent women, she argued that both sexes needed each other, and that both men and women had roles of strength and weakness. At the same time, she made interdependent men and women in families the primary metaphor for how to conceptualize citizenship. Individuals in a nation did not thrive on their own, she argued, but in communities, and they counted on others for support and protection. Immigrants, as potential citizens, found themselves in especially vulnerable positions, and needed extra protections. But they also contributed their labor and culture to the community, thereby making the nation stronger economically and culturally. Thus, Abbott argued, the government needed to fortify immigrants, not impose strictures. The protection of both women and men in immigrant families was critical.

In order to put family at the nexus of citizenship, Abbott worked to take the concept of family out of the "private" realm and place it in the realm of the political and, in the process, she contributed a differently gendered viewpoint to the immigration restriction debates. First, she did not even address the question of the "breeding" of immigrants or talk about their "blood." Instead, she defined the problem as one of containing the sexuality of immigrants within the immigrant family. Further, she insisted that the problems faced by immigrant mothers, fathers, and children were not individual, but a result of the migration process, and argued that it was this transitional status that social workers and legislators needed to address. She also placed immigrant women at the center of the solution to the "immigrant problem." Abbott argued both that immigrant women needed more support and protections to become citizens themselves and that the citizenship potential of men depended on having a strong female presence in their lives. The way to produce good citizens was not to create independent men and properly dependent women, but to create men and women who were interdependent within families. In the first few years of the IPL's existence, Grace Abbott worked out some of these ideas in lectures and articles printed by popular and scholarly presses about the situation of immigrants in the Chicago area.

In the first article she wrote in her position as director of the IPL, titled "The Chicago Employment Agency and the Immigrant Worker," Abbott stressed gendered themes that would often be repeated in her writings.[58] As she leveled strong criticism at mostly immigrant-run employment agencies, portraying them as at best inept and at worst corrupt, she saw distinct differences in the problems for women and for men.[59] Abbott began her article by providing statistics about how employment agencies dealt with women. She downplayed economic exploitation and instead stressed the threat of sexual exploitation of immigrant girls and young women, especially if they were forced into prostitution. Like other middle-class women reformers at this time, Abbott blurred the lines between coercion and consent when dealing with the sexual behavior of young immigrant women.[60] She repeatedly stressed that these women entered into extremely dangerous surroundings when they arrived in Chicago, situations in which they could easily find themselves sexually exploited. In the article she declared, "No direct evidence of the moral exploitation of the immigrant girl was secured, although there is reason to believe that there is in a few instances actual cooperation between the [employment] agent and the keeper of the house of prostitution."[61] She believed that work in saloons could be just as morally bad for the "simple-minded and ignorant foreign girl."[62] And while she admitted that most of the time the problem with the agent had more to do with carelessness than maliciousness, she believed that the government needed to step in to regulate these employment agencies in order to secure for the immigrant girl "work where she is morally protected, work which is congenial, and in which she will learn English and become rapidly Americanized."[63]

Then Abbott turned her attention to the ways that employment agencies handled immigrant men. Abbott did not counter claims of the IRL and argue that immigrant men possessed a virile, muscular masculinity. Instead, she maintained that, while immigrant men arrived in the U.S. with the potential to be good providers for their families, they were at risk of being economically exploited. Being taken advantage of in this way would hurt them as breadwinners, and if they lost their ability to support a family, they would lose the uplifting influence of a wife and children. She often used a language of helplessness to describe their situation. When the immigrant first arrived in the United States, Abbott explained, he was "especially defenseless when he offer[ed] himself in the labor market."[64] She took her readers through many stories of immigrant workers' being stranded in rural areas or being promised one wage and then paid a fraction of that amount when they actually arrived at the worksite. She blamed the employment agencies for creating an army of seasonal laborers who became idle in the winter, and declared that the immigrant workers "become the material out of which a degraded working class is created."[65] The solution, though, was not to exclude these immigrants, but to create protections to make sure that immigrant men would not be financially exploited. She carefully spelled out the impossible situation in which these men found themselves, and always indicated that it was through no fault of their own.

Abbott also wrote articles that examined particular immigrant groups in order to explain to the general population the cultural context from which they emerged and the challenges and exploitation they faced in their new American environment. Again, she did not extol the manliness of these immigrant groups; she even tended to denigrate it. She stressed the various ways these men were exploited, discussing the way propaganda worked on "such a simple people as the Bulgarian peasants."[66] She defended Greek men by saying that it was unreasonable to expect them to live up to "the glory of ancient Greece and Byron's romantic championship," and, indeed, she admitted that this ideal would not be found in "the thrifty, good-natured and polite keeper of a fruit stand or a 'shoe-shine parlor.'"[67]

Yet Abbott continually stressed that these immigrant men had the potential to be excellent citizens because of their loyalty, intelligence, and work ethic. Bulgarian immigrants, she argued, were "splendid material for skilled workmen—strong, quiet, sober, intelligent and eager to work." In a swipe at literacy test advocates, she also emphasized the way Bulgarians, both at home and the United States, valued education. "An enormous amount has been spent on the public schools in Bulgaria," Abbott wrote, "every hamlet in Bulgaria now has a school building." The result, according to Abbott, was that, of a group of Bulgarians she studied, there was "only one who was unable to read and write in his native language, and several knew Turkish, Italian and French in addition to Bulgarian."[68] She also insisted that the Greek's loyalty to his homeland, while sometimes "exasperating," was also a "most desirable characteristic and one which the Anglo-American should readily appreciate."[69]

In defending Greeks and Bulgarians, she directly took on the notion that south-eastern European immigrants were somehow worse than other immigrants and a detriment to the community. Abbott declared that the government should not only consider an immigrant's "moral standards, his capacity for self-government and his economic value" but also "whether his development in these directions is being promoted or retarded by the treatment he receives in the United States."[70] A large part of the responsibility, in Abbott's view, settled on native-born Americans, and how they interacted with these immigrants when they arrived. It was that relationship, more than any racial qualities, which would determine whether immigrants would become good citizens. And it was that relationship that she believed the government should nourish with productive protective legislation.

While Abbott defended the political and economic contributions immigrant men could make, there were areas where she was decidedly critical. When it came to sexual morality and the treatment of women, she actually lobbed criticisms against Greek men and Greek culture. Greek immigrants stood out because of the large numbers of men who settled in Chicago without wives and children.[71] Abbott termed their cooperative housing arrangements "non-family groups" and she distinguished them from the "family group in which the wife or daughter does the housekeeping." Without family support, particularly from the women in their families, these men could sink into debauchery, and Abbott also made veiled references to homosexual behavior.[72] She found that the lack of "restraining influences" that came with "normal family relationships" led to the charges of immorality the Greek community faced, and believed that Greek men in many ways were worse off in the United States than at home "due probably to the demoralizing effect which living in a city's congested district, where invitations to vice are on every side and where there is no counter-claim or attraction of a home."[73]

As she continued to write about immigration, Abbott began to define the solution of the "immigrant problem": the wife and mother of each family. In fact, Abbott made the presence of a wife and mother pivotal to building all immigrants into good citizens. A main aspect of the "immigrant problem," in her mind, was that the immigrant mother did not hold a powerful enough place in the newly urbanized immigrant family. A strong wife would keep her man contained in a "normal family group" and thereby make him fit for citizenship. An attentive mother would keep her daughters away from the path of ruin, and in general keep her children protected. Of Greek women, Abbott wrote that they were "kept in almost oriental seclusion," although she did believe that they might be able to change their cultural attitudes and adapt to American gender ideals—despite "their eastern traditions and training," she wrote, "the Greek women adapt themselves quickly to American customs."[74] When immigrant women broke away from their oppression and asserted themselves within the family, they were better able to uplift the entire family and make it more fit for citizenship.

By the end of 1909, Grace Abbott and other members of the IPL's executive committee decided to put together the first annual report for their organization. This report allowed the leadership of the organization to document the various works and accomplishments of the League. Another possible incentive for this report was that the Dillingham Commission was requesting statements from societies and organizations, and Grace Abbott and the IPL wanted to have something impressive to add. Thus, their first official report became their report to the Commission.

Restriction, Protection, and the Dillingham Commission Report

By 1909, the members of the Dillingham Commission had already conducted extensive research on immigration to the United States. The 1907 Immigration Act called for nine commissioners, three appointed by the Senate, three by the House, and three by the President.[75] The men on the Commission spanned the spectrum of opinions about immigration, from sympathetic New York Republican Congressman William Bennet to hard-core restrictionists Henry Cabot Lodge and Congressman John Burnett, a Democrat from Alabama. All the commissioners, though, wanted to produce an accurate, solid report bolstered by statistics, a report that would provide a clear framework for government action.

From 1907 to 1910, the Commission oversaw an investigation that studied various levels of the impact of immigration. Six of the commissioners traveled through Europe to examine firsthand the activities of U.S. consulates, as well as the conditions from which immigrants came at European ports and in steerage.[76] In the United States, commissioners and their staff studied multiple aspects of the relationship between immigrants and labor conditions, as well as issues of urbanization, education, fertility, and crime. Conflicting understandings of race contributed to the complexity of the report, and participants in the Commission worked to produce a *Dictionary of Races* that sought to classify immigrant groups by physical and cultural attributes. In a different vein from the sociological focus of most of the studies, anthropologist Franz Boas researched the physical impact of immigration on the bodies of immigrants by taking cranial measurements, or the "cephalic index," of parents and children from Jewish and Italian immigrant families.[77]

In late 1909, the Dillingham Commission requested reports and recommendations from various societies in the United States that worked with immigrants. Like the members of the Dillingham Commission itself, these groups spanned the spectrum of opinion about immigration, from the restrictionist Junior Order of United American Mechanics and the Patriotic Order of the Sons of America to groups like the National Liberal Immigration League and the North American Civic League for Immigrants, which both advocated more open immigration policies. Jewish groups had a significant presence, with the National Council of Jewish Women, the American Jewish Committee, and the Jewish Immigrants' Information Bureau all submitting reports.[78] In the end, these reports would be sequestered to one volume of the final Dillingham Commission Report, and there is little evidence that the Commission gave much consideration to them when it made its recommendations.[79] Yet both the Immigration Restriction League and the Immigrants' Protective League took the invitation to participate seriously, and they saw the Commission as a means of legitimizing their arguments and policy recommendations.

The men of the Immigration Restriction League leapt at the chance to participate in the Dillingham Commission. They realized that it represented the ultimate source of authority of its time because of its insistence on statistical and scientific studies and its link to government power. Joseph Lee, one of the chief financial backers of the IRL, wrote in a letter to Lawrence Lowell, president of Harvard University, "if the report is negative, it will hurt us for many years, whereas a positive report, favoring especially the literacy test, would be a considerable help."[80] The men of the IRL strategized to determine how best to approach the report and came up with a plan: they would not only present a report that included statistics and arguments in favor of restriction, they would also cull responses from the "best men" of the nation to bolster their case. Prescott Hall wrote to over four hundred men listed in *Who's Who in America*, soliciting their views on immigration. Lee, in turn, wrote to Hall and, referring to the *Who's Who* men, spoke of "leading them along" to get them to write back advocating a literacy test.[81] Hall stated in his letter that the IRL was opposed to immigration that "lowers the mental, moral and physical average of our people." He also pointed out that 25 percent of immigrants could not read, and that 75 percent were from the "Slavic and Iberic races of southern and eastern Europe." He provided statistics that highlighted high rates of unemployment, criminality, pauperism, and insanity among the immigrant population, and pointed out that those "pecuniarily interested in lax immigration laws are strongly organized to influence legislation." Finally, he asked his readers to say whether they favored a literacy test, a means test, or a head tax.[82]

When it came to the actual writing of their report, the IRL experienced some internal debate on how much to emphasize race and eugenics. Prescott Hall and Joseph Lee consulted William Ripley, the Harvard economist who had written the 1899 *Races of Europe*, and asked him how they should state the dangers of "racial intermixture." Ripley responded that the data were uncertain, and that "the case for immigration restriction can be sufficiently treated from the economic standpoint without attempting to deal with this other phase of it."[83] But Prescott Hall could not help himself. While his final report did repeat many of the statistics about crime, poverty, and other social problems caused by immigrants, Hall did not hide the fact that he saw the literacy test as a means of protecting the racial heritage of the United States. He emphasized that Poles, Italians, Russian Jews, and other undesirables would never be able to meet the requirements of United States citizenship because they could not live up to the stellar standards of American manhood. He scoffed at those who argued that immigrants had not been given proper opportunities to succeed because of poverty or persecution, and insisted, instead, that many immigrant men had not inherited the traits necessary to create a literate society. As he put it, "their races have not made the opportunities; for they have had all the time that any other races have had; in fact, they often come from older civilizations." Their race traits had made them impotent to change their situations even in their European homelands, which were, in Hall's words, "backward, downtrodden, and relatively useless for centuries." These racially degenerate immigrants exhibited "low intelligence, poor physique," and were "deficient in energy, ability, and thrift." Hall pointed out that "a considerable portion of this class would be excluded" by a literacy test, because "ignorance and incapacity in general go together."[84] The literacy test, in other words, was not way to exclude illiterates, but a way to exclude those who did not possess the genetic traits necessary to maintain the high quality of American manhood.

In a section of the report titled "Restriction Needed from a Eugenic Standpoint," Hall made eugenics the most pressing reason for exclusion.[85] Using one of his favorite phrases, he warned that immigration would lead to "'that watering of the nation's lifeblood' which results from [immigrants'] breeding after admission."[86] A literacy test, in Hall's mind, would provide the most effective method of protecting the nation from this threat. He wrote: "Education can develop what is in an immigrant, but cannot supply what is not there. Assuming what is by no means proved, that a mixed race is a better race, we should do as we do in breeding any other species than the human, viz., securing the best specimens to breed from."[87] The literacy test, then, would test more than the immigrants' ability to read. It would also test the quality of their race and their ability to breed quality future citizens.

To bolster his authority, Hall submitted with his report to the Dillingham Commission statements culled from his survey of prominent men listed in *Who's Who in America*. In the report, Hall boasted that, out of 403 professional men surveyed, 375 supported restriction, and 81 percent favored the literacy test.[88] He included the men's letters in his report, and many of them echoed his own contention that immigrant races would lower the quality of citizenship. Most of the letters portrayed southern and eastern European immigrants as deficient in manly self-control, independence, and strength; and many referred to immigrants as "paupers," "criminals," and "scum," and as "hordes swarming over our borders."[89] David Starr Jordan, the president of Stanford University, remarked that the nation had a right to test immigrants for manly qualities of "character, initiative and physical and mental force," and implied that a literacy test would be a way to do so.[90]

Further, while the original letter Hall wrote to the men of *Who's Who* did not mention race suicide, many of his respondents declared that immigrants were hindering the Anglo-Saxon man's ability to father future citizens. A former Senator, Fenimore Chatterton, exhorted that "we now have a sufficient breeding stock on hand; it is time to pay attention to breeding the best human being possible."[91] Retired Admiral John H. Upshur implored, "In God's name, let us have increase of population by the incubation of Americans, and not hasten to welcome all the offspring of foreign countries."[92] Allen G. Braxton, a lawyer, warned that "unless some check is put upon the unrestricted outpouring upon us of these . . . members of unassimilable races, I believe that posterity will rise up to curse us for our folly and neglect."[93] These men and others who responded to Hall's survey expressed concern about the future citizenry, and who would be the fathers of those citizens. They also agreed with the IRL that a strong legislative solution in the form of a literacy test was necessary, or the United States might become, in the words of author James Dinkins, "a nation of beggars and organ grinders."[94]

Luther Burbank, a naturalist from southern California, also responded to Hall's request, saying that there should be "a more thorough sifting of the foreign-born population which come to our shores." Burbank then expanded on his thoughts in a way that seemed to disturb at least one member of the IRL. He wrote: "I would go further and say that there is not a greater disgrace existing in the world today than that our women should not be allowed to vote while foreigners, who know nothing of our government or our institutions . . . should be allowed to vote. . . . That such a condition exists in a civilized country is astounding beyond belief." In the margin of Burbank's letter, an unidentified member of the IRL clearly wrote "omit" beside this paragraph, although in the end the entire letter appeared in the report to the Commission.[95] Even though suffragists might have made good allies, Hall and the men of the IRL did not want to appear to be in sympathy with women's suffrage, and no other letter mentioned this argument. Yet women would not be silenced, and the members of the Immigrants Protective League would use their report to the Dillingham Commission to challenge the IRL's vision of how to understand immigrants and their progeny.

When Grace Abbott wrote her report for the Dillingham Commission, she was not directly addressing the IRL's report. Yet, like her earlier work, her report attacked the type of logic used by the IRL and offered a different vision of the government's responsibility to immigrants and to the nation as a whole. "The Federal Government," she argued, "in emphasizing constantly developing the restrictive features of [immigration] legislation has allowed the equally important function of protection to fall into comparative insignificance and disuse." She insisted that "a moral duty rests upon the Federal Government to reinstate the protective aspect of immigrant control in its proper place."[96] Overall, the IPL used its report to argue that the immigrant problem was not one of too many immigrants or the wrong kind of immigrants, but instead the exploitation faced by immigrants once they arrived in the United States, a situation that could potentially degrade them, and their children, as future citizens.

Abbott began her report with a list of ten cases in which young, vulnerable immigrants—almost all under the age of eighteen—either disappeared or found themselves under some threat while en route to Chicago or once they arrived in the city. Eight of the cases concerned young women or girls who were unable to find relatives, were approached by strange men, or who totally disappeared. Abbott pointed out that often nothing happened to these girls, but emphasized that they "were for a short time in quite a dangerous position." "The immigrant man," Abbott said, "while not in danger of moral exploitation suffers from the same petty financial exploitation on the journey to Chicago as the girl."[97] The government, in Abbott's view, needed to focus its efforts on preventing this kind of exploitation.

After she laid out these ten case studies, Abbott made the central theme of her report her vision about the government's responsibility to immigrants. She related the history of immigration legislation from 1848 to the Act of 1907, and showed that all of the measures, to date, had contained clauses that allowed for some form of protection of immigrants. This history, she argued, showed both that "the protection of the immigrant is not an accidental or secondary matter, but embodies one of the vital policies of immigration legislation," and that "the present law seems to contain ample powers for this purpose which have not been properly developed."[98] She further argued that Congress had the authority to pass legislation protecting immigrants by comparing it to Congress' power to spend tax funds and control interstate commerce. Another justification that she offered for protective legislation was based on the government's power over naturalization. She contended that immigrants should be "treated as potential candidates for citizenship," and that, if the government claimed the power of deportation, then "surely conditions less far-reaching in character, relating to conduct, residence, occupation or education may likewise be imposed."[99]

Having employed history, policy, and concrete cases of potential abuse, Abbott then explained that the government should use its power to do what the women of the IPL did—to monitor immigrants at vulnerable points to make sure their transition into American life went smoothly. Specifically, she recommended that the government build a federal immigrant aid station in Chicago, a logical location for providing this type of assistance not only because Chicago was an important destination for immigrants, but also because it was the central transfer station for railroads. If the proposed aid station worked in Chicago, the concept could then be extended to other cities as well. In arguing for the establishment of such a station, Abbott laid out seven aspects of the work its bureau would perform, including making sure arrivals corresponded with departure lists from New York, giving aid and information to arriving immigrants, providing temporary accommodations, regulating expressmen and others who worked with the immigrants at the stations, studying the conditions of immigrants, and working with local organizations to prevent exploitation. She argued that the chief inspector of the aid bureau should be a "man of intelligence, familiar with the problem," but that "at least half of the [assistant inspectors] should be women."[100]

"Exhibit A" for the IPL's report was their 1909–10 Annual Report, which articulated the gendered nature of the immigrant problem and spelled out the successes that the IPL had had in tackling it. The contributors to this report portrayed the IPL's initiatives as vital to both immigrants and the community, and as worthy of government emulation. In an introductory letter, Jane Addams concluded that the IPL was "fast proving to be one of the most effective instruments for social amelioration in Chicago."[101] Julian Mack, the president of the organization, specifically stated that the government should model itself on the IPL, which approached every immigrant with the full realization that his or her "future loyalty and patriotism to the country that is going to be his home may be seriously affected by his first contact with its men and women." Mack maintained that it was not simply a matter of humanity, but also essential to the future of the nation to "overlook the differences of race and creed and habits," and to "guard the foreigners against the perils to which they, more than the average man, are subject, and to open up to them opportunities for . . . patriotic citizenship." While he allowed that there would always be a place for private philanthropy, he also stated that "a large measure of assistance can, however, be and in judgment should, be rendered by the municipal, state, and federal authorities."[102] In another part of the annual report, Sophonisba Breckinridge, secretary of the IPL, reviewed Abbott's ideas on the proposed federal aid station for immigrants. In her review, Breckinridge declared that "women need the information and protection such a bureau could give in order to safeguard their morals. Both men and women need it to avoid exploitation." She continued, saying, "The country is disadvantaged by the number of those who become sources of peril or burdens on its philanthropic resources."[103] Both Mack and Breckinridge singled out Grace Abbott's work and praised her dedication. Thus a theme developed in the report—that the reform-minded women of Hull House, and Grace Abbott in particular, offered a model approach to immigration for the government.

Abbott's own report detailed specific incidents the IPL confronted and actions they took. She divided her statement into two main sections, "The work with immigrant girls" and "the work with men."[104] The problem of girls was clearly the main focus of the IPL's work at that point, and the section on girls dwarfed the section on men eight pages to two. In it, Abbott attempted to draw connections between middle-class, native-born women and immigrant women, saying that "any woman can understand the nervous apprehension which the immigrant girl must feel as she comes into one of Chicago's bewildering railroad station."[105] At the same time, she established herself and other middle-class women reformers as the ones who had the knowledge to protect defenseless immigrant women.

The major theme of Abbott's section on immigrant girls was that these girls were potential victims of sexual exploitation, which would result in a girl's being "ruined."[106] Abbott saw the journey to and arrival in Chicago as the most dangerous times for these young women, and she told numerous stories of girls' being approached by strange men, finding themselves in saloons, or being abandoned, alone and at night. In one story, a seventeen-year-old Polish girl arrived at three o'clock in the morning at the wrong address. She had no money and "wept disconsolately," yet the expressman refused to bring her back to the train station. Fortunately, a kindly saloon keeper took her in, and she stayed there until her sister eventually found her.[107] This story and others like them, Abbott argued, could have had much more sinister endings.

Abbott then turned to the issues of employment and home life once a girl was in Chicago, and emphasized that groups like the IPL had to guard these young women against exploitation, and even against their own lack of self-control. She noted how girls from different "language groups" faced problems particular to their situations. Polish girls, for instance, often arrived without parents or specific protectors, and found themselves working in restaurants among unscrupulous types. Abbott commented, "Knowing that her whole mode of life is to undergo a great change in America, we are fearful that some of the safeguards on which she relies will fail her."[108] Jewish, Bohemian, and Slovak girls, according to Abbott, faced a different problem. Because they associated more frequently with English speakers, they risked a "too rapid Americanization" which could lead them to disregard traditional notions of sexual purity. As a young woman tries new foods and clothes, Abbott argued, she "often wrongly concludes that all her old-world ideals are to be abandoned and that in America she is to live under a very different moral code from the one her mother taught her."[109] This particular assertion, of course, gets back to Abbott's contention that parents, and mothers in particular, needed to be present and respected if daughters were to remain morally safe.

A further problem of "too rapid Americanization" came when immigrant girls sought recreation in dance halls. As Kathy Peiss argues, the sexual fears of many middle-class women reformers centered on dance halls, where young women experimented with their own sexuality and socialized freely with young men away from chaperones.[110] When she addressed dance halls, Abbott blurred the issue of responsibility and victimization, and focused instead on the results of the problem. On Saturday nights, Abbott wrote, immigrant girls needed some sort of excitement after a hard week of work; however, the girl's "physical and nervous exhaustion and her demand for acute sense stimulation" would lead her to become "an easy victim for the unscrupulous." Abbott saw nothing good in these dance halls. At best, they added "to the nervous demoralization which began with the girl's over fatigue," and at worst they left the immigrant girl "disgraced and ruined."[111] The dance hall furnished another place where the citizenship potential of young immigrant women could be endangered, because it could further remove them from the path of home and family.

Abbott believed that middle-class women's active involvement was essential to protecting immigrant daughters from exploitation; if left unprotected, these girls would face social ruin that would, in turn, degrade the citizenship potential of both the girls themselves and their families. In one of its first projects, the IPL placed agents at a train station in Chicago to monitor immigrant girls who arrived alone and to make sure they ended up in the proper hands. Workers would take the names, addresses, and nationalities of the girls who arrived, as well as the names of the persons to whom they were to be released. They would then follow up each initial interview with subsequent visits, to make sure the girl lived in a proper boarding house and was signed up for English classes. Abbott saw the IPL as offering motherly assurance to immigrant girls while at the same time guiding them on the right path to becoming good American women. Abbott also stressed that the government needed to follow the IPL's lead and take a more active stance to prevent the evils of exploitation. She maintained that "the girlhood of those who work in restaurants and in stock yards, as well as those who work in 'factories, laundry and mechanical establishments' must be protected by the state."[112] These measures were not solely for the benefit of the individual girl. By protecting an immigrant girl, Abbott argued in other writings, the government would be protecting a wife and mother of the future—a woman who would not only be a citizen, but would also enhance the citizenship of those around her.

Abbott next turned her attention to the situation of immigrant men, and she painted them, much like her depiction of immigrant women, as potential victims, but of economic rather than sexual exploitation. Much of the information in this section of Abbott's report repeated what she had written in earlier articles, and she iterated how the immigrant man "suffers" at the hands of unscrupulous employment agents and bosses.[113] As in earlier articles, Abbott did not make lofty claims about the manhood of immigrant men; in fact, she often described them as "helpless" and "ready prey for the scoundrel."[114] She argued that, when faced with the economic power of employers and their agents, immigrants had no recourse but to go along with sub-standard wages and living conditions. She stressed the vulnerability of immigrant men in this situation, writing that "the immigrants themselves are powerless to correct these evils."[115]

The evils of the system went beyond economic exploitation. Abbott contended that improvement of immigrant workers' labor conditions was "a matter of concern to the entire community," because the economic exploitation that debased immigrant men would reverberate through the entire immigrant family and then through the larger society. Abbott accused labor camps of placing the immigrant man in unsanitary conditions, mistreating him, and taking him "away from his family and all normal, wholesome contact with society." When men who had worked under these conditions returned to Chicago, they would bring with them "those diseases and vices which come with such living conditions," and which would degrade them as husbands and fathers.[116]

As in her discussion of immigrant girls, Abbott used her section on men to show the necessity of the IPL's work and make a case that the government should be doing more. She said that immigrant men were "often in need of the help of the league," she explained how IPL workers mediated in disputes about employment agency fees, issued complaints about unsanitary working conditions, and did studies into the situation of workers both in Chicago and in rural areas. She boasted that, because of a report issued by the IPL, the Illinois legislature had provided protections for immigrant men who entered into labor contracts to work in lumber camps or ice camps, or as farm laborers.[117] But she also reported that another bill that would have provided for state-run employment agencies had so far failed, leaving still more work to do.

Overall, in its report to the Dillingham Commission, the IPL used many of the same tools as the Immigration Restriction League—statistics, testimony of experts, and appeals for greater government involvement. Yet, through the IPL's report, Grace Abbott and her colleagues sought to reshape both the meaning of the immigrant problem and the role of the federal government in solving it. The active involvement of the government, according to Abbott, should center on making sure that immigrant men and women could fulfill their roles as wives, husbands, and parents; the way to insure this was to protect them from the exploitation they faced when they were at their most vulnerable. By providing some safety checks at this point in the citizenship process, Abbott argued, immigrants would in turn become strong contributors to the American economy, polity, and, most important, the community.

Reactions to the Dillingham Commission Report

In December of 1910, the Dillingham Commission issued a brief statement about its findings. The Commission made a series of recommendations, including improving steerage conditions, expanding federal supervision of immigrant aid institutions, expanding coordination with individual states, and implementing legislation to prevent exploitation. But its main recommendation, and the one that gained the most public attention, was a call to restrict immigration, with a literacy test being "the most feasible" method.[118] While some of the commissioners, particularly Henry Cabot Lodge and John Burnett, saw this test as a way to curb the racial threat of immigration, the final report emphasized that restriction was needed to protect the nation's economic and social standards from low-wage immigrants. Yet, as historian Robert Zeidel points out, the perceived threats caused by southeastern European immigrants were not backed up by the actual data in the reports, which showed that the social and economic conditions of immigrants actually improved over time.[119] Even more strikingly, Franz Boas' report to the Commission, titled *Changes in Bodily Form of Descendants of Immigrants*, found that after one generation, almost no difference in cephalic index (a ratio of head width and length) existed between the children of east-European Jewish immigrants and the so-called American type. From this evidence he concluded that environment had much more to do with the physical development of bodies than fixed racial characteristics.[120]

The men of the Immigration Restriction League were made ecstatic by the recommendation of a literacy test in the Dillingham Commission Report. In a jubilant letter to Lawrence Lowell, Joseph Lee wrote, "Senator Lodge has simply done the trick . . . I mean the achievement of having the Immigration Commission not only unanimously recommend restriction . . . but also got all but [Senator William S.] Bennet to say specifically that there should be an illiteracy test."[121] But even though the IRL got its way in terms of a literacy test recommendation, the Commission did not frame it in the way the League would have chosen. In another letter to Lowell, Lee said that the IRL would stress economic and practical arguments to support the literacy test, although he declared that the racial argument "is my favorite one, which makes the position difficult."[122] A few weeks before Lee wrote this letter, Richards M. Bradley, the secretary of the IRL, wrote to Lee, arguing that emphasizing the race issue would be a tactical mistake, since it put the "races involved" on the defensive, and those races were becoming "numerous and influential in pivotal states." Bradley instead advised putting "the thing on economic and sociological grounds, other than the race issue, which seems to me much better for all purposes, including fighting purposes."[123]

In an article that appeared in the liberal journal the *Survey* in support of the Commission's recommendation of a literacy test, Lee took this advice, emphasizing the harm immigrants did to the American working class, saying that "practically unlimited immigration of unskilled workers keeps the unskilled class of labor in this country permanently below the American standard of living."[124] Yet he could not help taking a swipe at Franz Boas' findings about the changes in bodily form of immigrants. Adopting a tone of reasonable impartiality, Lee called the findings "hopeful," but then warned, "Until the Negro, who was imported very much earlier and has been subjected to American conditions now for many generations, has become more fully assimilated in form, color, and perhaps more important attributes, to the white race, any conclusions drawn from changes in bodily structure of other immigrants cannot be accepted as indicating a reasonable hope of early social assimilation." He then argued that a literacy test would exclude the immigrants who were least likely to assimilate, physically or socially, pointing out that 35 percent of new immigrants from southeastern Europe were illiterate, while only 3 percent of "old" immigrants were.[125]

In the same issue of the *Survey*, Grace Abbott reacted to the Commission's recommendations with a tone of frustration. She complained that the Commission recommended a literacy test because it claimed immigration led to lower standards of living. Yet, she said, the Commission never actually showed this, and furthermore, immigrants "would never intentionally underbid in the labor market." She blamed labor agents and employers who "take every advantage of [the immigrant's] ignorance of American conditions," and then said, with some disgust, "Protective measures could, of course, be devised to prevent these practices, but the public unfortunately continues to be more interested in restriction than in a means by which these immigrants may be saved from industrial exploitation."[126] She then criticized the literacy test, saying, "The ability to read and write has never been regarded as a means of determining character. It is not even a test of ambition, for the immigrants come without this meager educational equipment because they have been given no opportunity to attend schools in the countries from which they come." Thus she stressed that environmental conditions, and not innate racial capabilities, were responsible for illiteracy, and that immigrants should not be punished for it. In any case, she asserted, a literacy test or head tax or any other test would not change the fact that millions of immigrants had already come, and would continue to come, to America. The nation's energies, in her opinion, should be directed at how to create citizens out of immigrants once they were in the country. The real issue, she concluded was "how the industrial, social and political adjustment of the immigrant may be accomplished with the least possible loss to himself and the community."[127]

As the 62nd Congress took up the recommendations of the Commission's report in 1912 and 1913, Abbott would continue to oppose a literacy test and press for legislation that would protect immigrants in the process of adjustment, while the members of the Immigration Restriction League would continue to press their eugenic reasoning for the literacy test. But even as they entered the new decade with great confidence, both the IRL and the IPL had to contend with new challenges to their arguments. A new group—the American Association of Foreign Language Newspapers—entered the fray to offer a spirited defense of immigrant manhood.

Muscle, Miscegenation, and Manhood

The Literacy Test at the Height of the Progressive Era

*B*y early 1912, literacy test legislation was front and center in the American political landscape, and the men of the Immigration Restriction League (IRL) were delighted. After the Dillingham Commission's findings, they believed that a literacy test was just around the corner. At long last, the nation would be protected from weak and dependent immigrants dragging it down. The year 1912, however, was also a time when interest groups from across the political spectrum felt empowered to participate in debates about the scope of government power and the role of immigrants in American life. Thus, even after the Dillingham Commission validated its call for a literacy test, the IRL faced more intense opposition than ever. One group that aggressively entered the fight in 1912 was the American Association of Foreign Language Newspapers (AAFLN), a group of foreign- and native-born men who became fierce opponents of the literacy test. Yet the AAFLN combated the arguments of the IRL on the IRL's own terms by linking the desirability of southeastern European immigrant races to the manliness of those who belonged to them.

On January 11, 1912, Louis Hammerling, the charismatic president of the AAFLN, brought a group of his Association's editors to testify before the House Committee on Immigration and Naturalization. They spoke out against HR 22527, an immigration bill that included a literacy test for restriction of immigration. Hammerling declared that he and the men of his organization attended the hearings to "protest against any new laws that would prohibit desirable and worthy immigrants from entering this country."[1] The desirability of immigrants, according to Hammerling, was proven by the work they did once they arrived in the U.S. "The prosperity and development of the nation is due to the sturdy immigrants we have received during the last 30 years," he asserted. Then he warned congressmen that "if you gentlemen were to pass the educational test today we would be deprived of the men we need."[2] Rev. C. L. Orbach, president of *Slovak v. Amerike,* a

Slovak semiweekly from New York City, also testified that a literacy test would bar excellent men, arguing that, "the best men can not get the education they would like. They will come here and bring you clean and good hearts and strong arms and everything else this country needs."[3]

When it came to the literacy test, the AAFLN and the IRL came down squarely on opposite sides, but both groups returned to the same questions. What did the transformations of the early twentieth century mean for white American manhood? Would the literacy test ensure that the nation would get fit, hardy men who could meet the challenges of the present and propagate the right kind of traits to future American citizens? In answering these questions, both the IRL and the AAFLN offered mirror-opposite views of native-born Americans and southeastern European immigrants. The IRL defined the true Americans as those who belonged to the races of northern Europe. Members of the IRL insisted that the racial superiority of Anglo-Saxons emanated from the greatness of their race's manhood, which had been proven by the deeds of their ancestors, who conquered forests and mountains. These arguments played into fears of decline by warning that the low-wage, tedious, subservient work done by southeastern European immigrant men proved their inability to live up to the example of the strong, independent Anglo-Saxon men of the past. In other words, the relegation of southeastern European immigrants to the lower classes was caused by their racial inferiority. The AAFLN, in contrast, embraced southern and eastern European immigrant men as the key to *future* American greatness. Hammerling and others of the AAFLN insisted on the white racial identity of those immigrants and argued that immigrant muscle would transform the nation into an industrial power and contribute to the expansion of American power in imperial ventures.

The IRL and AAFLN also took mirror-opposite views on the eugenic contribution of southern and eastern European immigrants. By 1912, the men of the IRL had ramped up their eugenic arguments about immigrants by painting them as a sexual threat to Anglo-Saxon men. They decried sexual relationships between southeastern European immigrants and those of northwestern European descent as miscegenation and a threat to the future American race. The AAFLN used eugenic reasoning to assert the opposite. They adopted the views of those like Theodore Roosevelt who insisted that racial hybridity—the mixing of different aspects of the white race—made for a more hardy and accomplished race.[4] They declared that the sexual relationships between immigrants and native-born Americans—and the sons they produced—would be the salvation of the nation by adding vigor and hardihood to the degenerating native-born stock.

In addition to their opposing views on immigrants and native-born citizens, the IRL and the AAFLN offered divergent ideas about the power of government to shape the nation's population, particularly through a literacy test. The IRL promoted the government as a defender of the interests of the superior race and argued that it needed to require a literacy test in order to ensure that the right sort of men would survive and thrive. The AALFN decried this view of government not only as paternalistic but also as an impediment to future progress. They advanced an ideal of laissez-faire government that would reject a literacy test and allow for the building of the American people through natural processes.

Ironically, though, the visions of the IRL and the AAFLN contained many parallel understandings about the archetypical American. Both depicted the ideal American as unquestionably male by emphasizing the physical bodies, work, and virility of men. Both organizations ignored class distinctions between men and instead made race the primary marker of difference. They assigned gendered qualities to races, positing that superior races possessed qualities that were linked to manhood and asserting that the white race was the most manly. Furthermore, these groups promoted an idea of citizenship based on racial identity, rather than on natural rights or shared political values.[5] IRL writers framed immigration restriction as a means of preserving the political, economic, and sexual power and privilege of those who truly belonged in the United States—Anglo-Saxons—and they offered the superior manhood of Anglo-Saxons as proof of their superior status. The men of the AAFLN did not challenge the connection between citizenship and manhood but instead insisted that southeastern European immigrant races met the test of manhood and that citizenship should be broadened to include all the races of Europe, not just Anglo-Saxons.

Moreover, the IRL and the AAFLN linked the sexual power of the nation's male citizens to national power. They both used eugenic language to argue that the future of the nation depended on ensuring that the right kind of sons were being born, sons who would possess physical vigor and the abilities to protect the nation's racial interests and perpetuate desirable racial traits into the future. When they discussed the struggle for racial dominance, members of both groups portrayed women in a passive role—females were to be attractive to men and give birth to sons who would perpetuate racial superiority. Neither group gave credence to the growing calls made by progressive women reformers for women's equal citizenship. Ultimately, when the men of the IRL and AAFLN looked at themselves in the mirror, they saw the ideal American. Both groups made the success or failure of the literacy test into a means by which they could confirm their understandings of the nation and of themselves as white male citizens.

Congress and the Literacy Test, 1912–15

In the wake of the Dillingham Commission's recommendation, many congressmen were eager to get a literacy test bill passed, but the national debate over the literacy test was becoming more complex and widespread. In the election of 1912, all the major party candidates sought immigrant votes, and none came out in favor of restriction. At the same time, support for restriction had become more widespread in Congress, as more Southern Democrats and Western congressmen from both parties joined New England Republicans in support of a literacy test bill.[6] Both Senator William Dillingham of Vermont and Representative John Burnett of Alabama introduced literacy test bills in their respective houses, and in 1912 the Dillingham-Burnett bill (most commonly known as the Burnett Bill) wound its way through Congress.[7] This bill called for the exclusion of immigrants ineligible for citizenship—that is, Asian immigrants—and increased the head tax on all immigrants. But the main, and most controversial, feature of the bill was its requirement that all immigrants (except those from the Western Hemisphere) over the age of sixteen had to be able to read thirty to forty "ordinary" words in English or the language of some other country. The bill was careful to mention that literacy in Hebrew or Yiddish counted. Adolph Sabath, a Jewish Czech immigrant and fiery Democrat from Chicago, rose up during this debate as one of the leading opponents of immigration restriction.[8] He introduced an amendment proposing that only male immigrants had to take the literacy test, but it was defeated. The final bill, however, did allow any immigrant man to bring to the U.S. his illiterate wife, mother, grandmother, or unmarried daughter, as well as his illiterate father, provided his father was more than fifty-five years of age. It passed both Houses by wide margins, and in January of 1913 it reached the desk of President William Howard Taft, who had to decide whether or not to sign it.[9]

By the time he was presented with this bill, Taft had become a lame-duck president. He had lost the 1912 election after facing both Woodrow Wilson and Theodore Roosevelt. At the beginning of his presidency, Taft had looked upon a literacy test with some favor, but over time he had begun to express more reservations. Most influential on his thinking was his Secretary of Commerce and Labor, Charles Nagel, who convinced the president that a literacy test would deprive American industries of needed workers and that it was actually a poor predictor of the a quality of an immigrant. Taft's veto message was written by Nagel. He rejected the bill by arguing that it would unfairly exclude immigrants who came to do work that "the natives are not willing to do."[10] The Senate voted to override the veto by a large majority, but in the House supporters of restriction could not get the two-thirds majority of votes needed, and the veto stood.[11]

During the 63rd Congress of 1913–15, John Burnett introduced another immigration bill that was almost identical to the one from the previous Congress.[12] The new president, Woodrow Wilson, had given mixed signals as to whether he would support a literacy test bill. In his 1901 textbook *History of the American People*, Wilson sharply criticized the "new" immigrants for being "the men out of the ranks where there was neither skill nor any initiative to quick intelligence."[13] Yet when he was president of Princeton University and governor of New Jersey, Wilson had been affiliated with the National Liberal Immigration League. When he ran for President in 1912, he reached out to immigrant leaders, declaring that immigration benefited the nation.[14] When presented with the Burnett Bill in 1915, he vetoed it, contending that literacy tests were "not tests of quality or of character or of personal fitness but tests of opportunity." He continued, claiming that many immigrants, through no fault of their own, did not have the opportunity to receive an education. A literacy test, therefore, was an unfair requisite for entry into the United States.[15] The House was only four votes shy of the two-thirds majority needed to override the veto.[16]

As the literacy test bills wound their way through Congress, the question of what to do about immigration became a topic of vigorous national debate. More and more groups from across the political spectrum organized letter-writing campaigns, distributed petitions, or wrote editorials and magazine articles in order to sway public opinion in favor of or against a literacy test.[17] The Immigration Restriction League continued to take the lead in this work, and sought new allies and strategies in its continuing battle to turn the literacy test into law.

The Immigration Restriction League and Progressive Social Science

These were heady times for the IRL, full of hope and frustration. In 1912, they rejoiced when the literacy test passed by wide margins in both houses of Congress, and they began a campaign to induce Taft to sign the bill by sending out circular letters encouraging influential men across the country to write to the President.[18] Taft's veto infuriated them, and they blamed Charles Nagel, whom they saw as controlled by both business interests and the immigrant lobby.[19] The veto also led the leaders of League to reevaluate their organization. Robert DeCourcy Ward even proposed that they dissolve the League and form a new organization called the National Committee for Regulating Immigration, then get members of the "influence list" to become associates in order to use their names for fundraising.[20]

Although the IRL was not dissolved, Prescott Hall and Ward sought to raise the stature of the organization by associating themselves even more with men they considered prestigious, particularly those in academia and science.[21] They expanded their connections with Charles Davenport and his eugenics work at Cold Spring Harbor by working with him to form an Immigration Committee of the Eugenics section of the American Breeder's Association.[22] The League added to its National Committee distinguished scientists and social scientists, like New York University sociologist Henry Pratt Fairchild, University of Wisconsin economist John R.

Commons, and Cornell University economist and political scientist Jeremiah Jenks, who also coauthored the summary of the Dillingham Commission's conclusions.[23] These men not only wrote popular books and pamphlets about immigration restriction, they also took part in lobbying for the literacy test.[24] The IRL's greatest new allies, though, were two men who would provide stirring rhetoric in support of the literacy test: E. A. Ross and Madison Grant.

Both of these men had massive egos, but they employed them to different ends. E. A. Ross grew up in Iowa among Scotch-Irish Presbyterian farmers, but left rural life for his academic pursuits, eventually receiving his PhD in sociology from Johns Hopkins. In the 1890s, he made passionate speeches in support of worker's rights, and in 1900 he was fired from Stanford for using extreme language at a labor rally calling for the exclusion of the Japanese.[25] He then began his career at the University of Wisconsin, and by the early 1900s he had begun to warn that immigration hurt the ability of native-born working men to support themselves, thereby forcing them to have fewer children. As he had done with Japanese immigrants a decade before, Ross linked the specter of race suicide to southern and eastern European immigrants.[26] Ross also commented on the declining number of children middle-class women had. While, in part, he saw the decline as a sign of progress, springing from a society that was "democratic, individualistic, feminist, secular and enlightened," he worried that the "same individualizing influences . . . [would] prompt some couples to a selfish evasion of all duties to the race." This neglect of duty would leave an opening for immigrants to impose themselves onto American society and threaten the Anglo-Saxon race with extinction.[27]

Madison Grant, in contrast, had no interest in promoting the rights of workers or linking individualistic, feminist qualities to progress. Heir to a large fortune and a life-long bachelor, Grant attended Yale and Columbia Law School. Instead of practicing law, he spent his life pursuing his many intellectual interests, particularly zoology, genealogy, anthropology, and environmental conservation, as well as immigration restriction. Common to all of his writings was an aristocratic tone and a call for the preservation of a patrician social order. He saw unions and other attempts to organize workers as akin to socialism, and he was dismissive of activist women, at one point intoning, "All women are queer."[28]

Ross and Grant believed in the Progressive Era ideal of government action as a means to reshape society, even as they disagreed about what that society should look like. They also both believed that a literacy test designed to restrict immigration would serve the public interest. By 1912, both were firmly ensconced in the IRL, and they used their clout to petition major political figures to support the literacy test, including Woodrow Wilson and Theodore Roosevelt.[29] Ross and Grant also published books meant for popular audiences that expounded on the dangers of immigrant races to the future of the nation. E. A. Ross's 1914 *The Old World in the New: The Significance of Past and Present Immigration to the American People* condemned both servile southeastern European immigrant races and the cynical industrialists who hired them.[30] Madison Grant published *The Passing of the Great Race, or the Racial Basis of European History* in 1916. In this book, he popularized a new racial term—Nordic—to describe tall, blond, fair-skinned peoples of northern Europe. He used his book to warn that this superior Nordic race was on the verge of extinction caused by the war in Europe and immigration in the United States.[31]

Both of these books used eugenic reasoning to bolster their claims, and like other writings connected with the IRL, neither Ross nor Grant were consistent in how they applied what they considered scientific arguments in favor of their cause. At times, they emphasized the physical environment as the determining factor of racial superiority and inferiority. Using Lamarckian ideas, they argued that the ways in which Anglo-Saxons conquered the forests of Northern Europe and the American continent developed in them superior, manly qualities which they could pass down to their descendents, while southeastern European races wallowed in their homelands, denied the opportunity of surroundings that allowed them to toughen themselves.[32] At other times, Ross and Grant adopted Mendelian ideas, claiming that superior and inferior racial traits were inherited from fixed "germs," which were unaffected by the environment.[33] Ross, Grant, and other members of the IRL were not striving for scientific consistency. Instead, their goal in using the scientific language of eugenics was to naturalize their social arguments about the inferiority of immigrants and the superior claims to American citizenship of Anglo-Saxons or, in Madison Grant's language, Nordics.

Certain people, however, did continue to question these arguments, and the members of the IRL, as well as their social scientist allies, projected a sense of embattlement even as the literacy test was gaining support politically. They felt assured that their position as Anglo-Saxon men meant that they should wield the most power in determining the nation's future. Yet they worried that their opponents would get the upper hand. In one circular letter urging the membership to lobby for Taft to sign the Burnett Bill, Prescott Hall warned that "certain foreign-born interests are opposed through selfish, pecuniary or racial interests to this provision and have been seeking to persuade Mr. Taft that its enactment would alienate voters from his support."[34] One group of "foreign-born interests" was indeed using its political muscle to push Taft. By 1912, the members of the American Association of Foreign Language Newspapers had propelled themselves into the literacy test debate, ready and willing to take on the arguments of the IRL.

Louis Hammerling, the AAFLN, and the *American Leader*

The American Association of Foreign Language Newspapers operated on many levels, as a marketer of advertising, an apologist for big business, a political arm of the Republican Party, a vehicle of self promotion for its founder, and a staunch defender of immigrant rights. The AAFLN sprang from the vision of Louis N. Hammerling, a charismatic, Polish-speaking immigrant from Galacia, a section of modern-day Poland that had been occupied by the Austro-Hungarian Empire. Biographical information on Hammerling is sketchy, but by all accounts he lived a rags-to-riches story, working in the mines of Wilkes-Barre, Pennsylvania, and eventually using his skill at languages and writing to develop publicity materials for the United Mine Workers.[35] By 1908, however, Hammerling had abandoned the union movement and shifted his attention to advertising and the newspapers. He worked to ingratiate himself with businessmen and promoted foreign language newspapers as both an untapped advertising market and a vehicle for Americanization.

Louis Hammerling founded the AAFLN in 1908 as a way to coordinate advertising in foreign language newspapers. The organization began with a membership of 250 foreign language newspapers and magazines, and by 1912 this membership had grown to 508 newspapers representing twenty-nine languages.[36] Hammerling became a member of the National Liberal Immigration League in 1908 and, in cooperation with them, he distributed articles about the evils of immigration restriction to the foreign language press.[37] In February 1912, one month after Hammerling testified against the literacy test in Congress, the AALFN started publication of its English-language journal, the *American Leader*, which republished translated articles from foreign language papers as well as articles, speeches, and political tracts from native-born Americans that could then be translated for foreign language newspapers. After 1912, the AAFLN continued to grow; membership in the organization reached its height in 1916, with 813 newspapers as members. To bolster its business and political cachet, the AAFLN claimed that it appealed to large numbers of foreign language readers; the Association insisted that, at its height, AAFLN advertisements and writings reached 32 million foreign language speakers. This figure, however, was based on U.S. census data about various nationalities in the United States, and was no doubt quite inflated.[38]

While Hammerling had begun his career in the union movement, he was seeking to ingratiate himself with business interests by the time he started the *American Leader*. The AAFLN began primarily as an advertising distributor for the *Leader*, and articles in the *Leader* portrayed the business function of the AAFLN as important work for Americanizing.[39] Alan C. Reiley, an advertising manager of the Remington Typewriter company, argued in an article for the *Leader* that while race and language were "congealing factors" in America's melting pot, the most potent melting factor was business, which, he stated, was "more powerful in the end than the congealing factors because it is *the only practical factor*. While the others are matters of training and sentiment, business is a matter of the stomach and the pocket. It is by that which we live." Advertising, he maintained, served as the prime method of introducing immigrants to business.[40] Another *Leader* article, called "The Educational Value of Reading Ad Pages," declared that advertising was the "textbook for advancement" in the United States.[41] Critics of Hammerling and the AAFLN were not so idealistic. They claimed that Hammerling distributed "boiler-plate" articles of "little or no intrinsic value, political or commercial."[42] There is no doubt a good deal of truth to this charge. The *Leader* published many articles lauding the value of the phone company, corn syrup (made by a subsidiary of Standard Oil), postal savings organizations, and various other businesses whose advertising they also sold. Spokesmen for these organizations were honored at AAFLN banquets.[43]

Hammerling also used the AAFLN to further his political ambitions and promoted himself and his organization as the Republican Party's link to the immigrant voter. Many in the Taft administration were suspicious of Hammerling, but he did make allies, particularly with Secretary of Commerce Charles Nagel, who would eventually become a regular contributor to the *Leader*.[44] During the 1912 Presidential campaign, Hammerling himself published a pamphlet, "From Lincoln to Taft: 1854–1912, The Republican Party: A Record of Nearly Sixty Years," a propaganda piece that documented the growth of the Republican Party and was intended for translation in foreign language newspapers.[45] The *Leader* printed many articles praising the Republican Party and Taft; they particularly printed articles that demonstrated Taft's and Nagel's praise of immigrants as good workers and good citizens.[46] The *Leader* also published attacks on Taft's opponents, Theodore Roosevelt and Woodrow Wilson.[47] Once Wilson was elected, however, the AAFLN began to see him as an ally; after 1913 the *Leader* rarely criticized him, and instead praised his stand against the literacy test.[48]

Moreover, Hammering made the *Leader* and the AAFLN into a vehicle for self-promotion, and he never lost an opportunity to publish praise of himself. He was lauded in one article, republished from a Syrian-language newspaper, as "one of the best citizens, who is an admirable example of the immigrants who are doing as much good to this country as possible," and a Serbian editor praised him for reaching "one of the greatest positions that any man could wish to attain today, that of President of the American Association of Foreign Language Newspaper editors."[49] Other articles— generally with no author, so possibly written by Hammerling himself—described the banquets in honor of Hammerling and the awards he received. One article, with a picture, was solely about a pair of "diamond studded gold metal cuff links" Hammerling was awarded.[50] In the pages of the *Leader*, Hammerling was held up as an exemplar of productive immigration work and endlessly praised as an ideal citizen.

Despite their practical motives, Hammerling and the men of the AAFLN also promoted themselves as the most important institution in making immigrants into upstanding citizens. At one banquet of foreign language newspaper editors, Hammerling declared that "the entire foreign language press of the country is animated with the laudable motive of inculcating the principles of good citizenship among its readers."[51] The members of the AAFLN claimed that their newspapers were essential vehicles for educating the foreign-born about civic duties, voting, workplace mores, and American ideals of capitalism.[52] A subtext to many of these articles was that the AAFLN encouraged workers to be uncomplaining and resistant to radical ideologies. The members of the AAFLN further viewed themselves as an organization that would not only help immigrants become good citizens, but would also build racial tolerance, at least among Euro-Americans. One article declared that "America is in the making . . . and we believe that not a little of the credit of uniting and solidifying this great body of races will be given to the editors of the foreign language press, who have ever sought to lead their people to the knowledge and practice of sound Americanism and who have ever striven to combat prejudice and ignorance."[53]

Yet even as the mission of the AAFLN was based on the idea of promoting goods, services, and the American way of life to newspaper *readers*, when Hammerling and other members participated in the literacy test debate, they extolled the virtues of *illiterate* immigrants. In articles, testimony, and other lobbying efforts, they promoted brawny, hard-working immigrant men as the foundation for an industrial nation hungry for labor. In its first years of publication, the *Leader* presented a vision of citizenship that echoed the one used by congressional opponents of the literacy test in the 1890s, who had argued that immigrants proved their citizenship and racial fitness by their manly work both in factories and on farms. As eugenic reasoning gained more persuasive power, however, writers in the *Leader* pushed their arguments further, arguing that the virile blood of immigrants would improve the white race, thereby strengthening the nation. Throughout, though, they insisted that testing the ability of immigrants to read and write would bar the type of men the nation needed to man factories and father strong sons and future citizens.

Factories, Frontiers, and Farms

Between 1912 and 1916, as the IRL and the AAFLN made their cases about the literacy test, members of both organizations made immigrant labor a central focus. Neither group, however, said much about issues such as wages, industrial productivity, or even the benefits of a literate workforce. The leadership of the IRL made alliances with labor unions, but only for utilitarian purposes, as can be attested in a letter Joseph Lee wrote to a friend. In the letter, Lee explained that John Mitchell of the United Mine Workers and Samuel Gompers of the American Federation of Labor had agreed to support the IRL's call for a literacy test, and then commented, "I don't know whether you will rejoice over these especial allies, but they can be very effective."[54] Writers for the *Leader* continually distanced themselves from labor leaders and labor unions, especially from Gompers and the American Federation of Labor.[55] Rather than promote themselves as the champions of working-class men, writers for the *Leader* instead attempted to erase the issue of class altogether and focused their concern on the physical bodies of both native- and foreign-born men and whether those bodies could help build up the nation.

In their common focus on the immigrant male body over immigrant intelligence or immigrant initiative, both the IRL and the AAFLN exposed their deep-seated and often contradictory feelings about industrial, urban society and the changing place of men in it. The vision promoted by the men of the IRL reached into the past, and their focus became the preservation of the preindustrial male body that their Anglo-Saxon ancestors had perfected. The AAFLN, in contrast, focused on the American man as a work in progress, heading toward a future perfection, and asserted that brawny immigrant male bodies offered the right kind of bodies for the nation to use in expanding its industrial power.

The social scientists affiliated with the IRL, particularly E. A. Ross and Madison Grant, developed the most expressive paeans to the ideal American male body, which they described as Anglo-Saxon or Nordic. Both Ross and Grant were influenced by the thesis of Ross' University of Wisconsin colleague Frederick Jackson Turner, who, in his 1893 address "The Significance of the Frontier in American History," had argued that the "crucible of the frontier" made the American people great. Ross and Grant emphasized how this ideal body was developed by the deeds of men of the past, the pioneer ancestors who had ruled Europe and conquered the American frontier.[56] For instance, Ross credited the American frontier for producing a race of "great physical self-control, gritty, uncomplaining, merciless to the body through fear of becoming 'soft.'"[57] Madison Grant depicted Nordic pioneers in North America as "a powerful and racially homogeneous people, and . . . one of the most gifted and vigorous stocks on earth, a stock free from the diseases, physical and moral, which have again and again sapped the vigor of old lands."[58] When describing the superior Anglo-Saxon male body, the men of the IRL saw environmental influences as key to manly qualities. Instead of focusing on their current-day environment, however, they focused on the environment in which their ancestors lived. They drew on the Lamarckian belief in inheritance of acquired characteristics, and argued that their Anglo-Saxon ancestors had not only built up their own bodies through the physical endeavors of colonization and frontier conquering, but also the bodies of their descendants, who fell heir to their strength, hardiness, health, and mental vigor.

The contrast with the immigrant male body, according to these authors, was stark. E. A. Ross told readers that if they observed immigrants, they would be "struck by the fact that from ten to twenty per cent are hirsute, low-browed, big-faced persons of obviously low mentality."[59] Moreover, Ross emphasized that just as the frontier environment had allowed Anglo-Saxon men to develop superior bodies and pass them on to their descendents, so too had the languid response of immigrant men's ancestors to the backward environments of southeastern Europe determined the quality of present-day immigrants' bodies. Ross argued, "These ox-like men are descendants of those *who always stayed behind*. Those in whom the soul burns with the dull, smoky flame of the pine-knot stuck to the soil, and are now thick in the sluice ways of immigration."[60] Madison Grant continued this theme, saying that the Slavic race had "been everywhere conquered and subordinated by Celtic- and Teutonic-speaking Nordics," which caused it to sink into "the subordinate and obscure position which it still largely occupies."[61] As was the case with the Anglo-Saxon race, the manhood of immigrant men had derived from what their ancestors did and the environment in which they did it. Staying behind in peasant Europe, rather than conquering the wilderness, had doomed their sons and grandsons to inferior bodies and minds.

Even as commentators from the IRL spouted self-confidence about the manly bodies they had inherited from their pioneer grandfathers, their writings contained a strong undercurrent of fear. Frederick Jackson Turner had declared in his 1893 address that the frontier was closed, and Ross, Grant, and others in the IRL worried that the environment that had produced the hardy Anglo-Saxon stock was disappearing while the new, industrial landscape favored the inferior bodies of immigrants. Grant, like others in the IRL, adopted the Social Darwinist belief in superior races, but also distrusted the Darwinian process of selecting races, declaring that it was the "heavy, healthful work in the fields of northern Europe" and the act of "clearing the forests, fighting Indians, farming the fields and sailing the seven seas," as American Nordic men had done during colonial times, in which the Nordic race's manhood thrived. In Grant's day, however, "the cramped factory and the crowded city" more and more typified the environment in which the average American lived. "The little brunet Mediterranean," Grant wrote, "can work a spindle, set type, sell ribbons or push a clerk's pen far better than the big . . . Nordic blond, who needs exercise, meat and air and cannot live under Ghetto conditions." He continued: "The survival of the fittest means the survival of the type best adapted to existing conditions of environment, which today are the tenement and factory, as in Colonial times were the clearing of forests, fighting Indians, farming the fields and sailing the seven seas. From the point of view of race it were better described as 'survival of the unfit.'"[62]

Linked to this focus on natural selection was a fear that immigrant men were proving to be more virile than Anglo-Saxon men. E. A. Ross had coined the term "race suicide" in 1901 to describe the racial competition between native-born Euro-Americans and Chinese immigrants, and by 1914 he had extended the term to southern and eastern European immigrants as well. In his book *The Old World in the New*, Ross noted the declining birthrates of native-born white women and argued that "the competition of low-standard immigrants is the root cause of the mysterious 'sterility' of Americans."[63] He also included pictures of what he termed "dependent" Italian and Slovak families who had large numbers of young children (see fig. 3.1; he noted in one picture that two of the children were absent).[64] His goal was to shake Anglo-Saxon Americans out of their complacency and spur them to do their duty and have more children. In making this argument, however, Ross was playing on incongruous assumptions. The immigrant men who were the heads of the families in the photos might have been "dependent," but they were also virile, as shown by the large numbers of their children. The question was, were they more virile than most Anglo-Saxon men? Ross did not hide his anxiety that Anglo-Saxon Americans would lose out in sexual competition to lesser races. He decried those who would let in more immigrants while letting their own children "perish unborn in the womb of time." He ended his book by saying that "a people that has no more respect for its ancestors and no more pride of race than this deserves the extinction that surely awaits it."[65]

The men of the AAFLN found ways to twist the fears expressed by the men of the IRL to their advantage as they argued against the literacy test. In 1912, they leapt into the literacy test debate with a full-throttle defense of immigrant men's ability to prove their racial fitness through feats of strength and through the fathering of sons. The writers in the AAFLN's journal, the *American Leader*, agreed that strong, virile men were necessary for the nation to thrive, but instead of focusing on the past, they embraced the industrial present. They portrayed immigrant men, with their taut muscles and willingness to work, as conquerors of a new, industrial frontier. These men, and not the effete descendents of long-dead pioneers, had become the foundation of· the nation's power.[66] In the formula of the AAFLN, a restrictive literacy test undermined the purported goals of men like Grant and Ross—the propagation of superior white manhood.

In a speech at the annual banquet of the AAFLN, former Congressman William S. Bennet of New York, who claimed to be one of those who could "trace their lineage back thirty generations of English-speaking people, to the Magna Carta,"[67] vividly depicted his belief in the importance of strong male immigrant bodies. He described a visit to Ellis Island, where he saw a "room full of men, on more than one occasion, stripped stark naked and examined by not one but by three surgeons to ascertain any defects that might exist in those men which might unfit them for the work which they are to do in this country." From this experience, he concluded that the nation was getting nothing but "good, strong, sturdy, healthy men, and that is

Dependent Italian Family, Cleveland. (Two Children Absent)

Dependent Slovak Family, Cleveland

Figure 3.1. As a way to illustrate the threat of race suicide, E. A. Ross included these photographs in his book *The Old World in the New*. He made sure that his readers knew that these large immigrant families were, in his words, "dependent." (Photographs by E. A. Ross. *The Old World in the New: The Significance of Past and Present Immigration to the American People* [New York: Century, 1914], facing page 249.)

what we ought to have."[68] J. George Frederick, the financial officer of the AAFLN, stressed the physicality of immigrant men's bodies, speaking of them as "muscle and bone" and "brain and sinew."[69] Even though Frederick included "brain," most depictions of immigrants by native-born men stressed the physicality of immigrant men, rather than their intelligence, and Frederick and others warned that the nation would deny itself this brawn if a literacy test were introduced.

The foreign-born contributors to the *Leader* provided less vivid descriptions of male immigrant bodies, but they did write with pride about how the men of their races contributed their physical strength to the country. Peter S. Lambros, publisher of the *Greek Star* of Chicago, wrote that Greek immigrants were mostly "young men at the height of their productive capacity," and were "excellent in physique, earnest, well-meaning and hardworking," and a net gain for the United States. Of the "new" immigrants in general, one *Leader* editorial said they were "willing to perform rough and disagreeable kinds of labor, [and] can work harder and better under conditions that would kill off a large percentage of those who speak slightingly of them."[70] N. L. Piotrowski, a Polish immigrant who became the City Attorney of Chicago, also said the nation would suffer if it debarred immigrants. He claimed, "This country's immense growth is largely due to the millions of sturdy men who work in the mines, in the mills, in the forests, and on the farms. . . . Should able-bodied, thrifty and morally sound men . . . be prevented to enter [*sic*] our land because of lack of educational opportunities through no fault of theirs?"[71]

The view of immigrant men as solid, if somewhat stolid, workers in factories and mines served many purposes for the AAFLN. This description of immigrant manhood could assure factory owners as well as other native-born Americans that illiterate immigrants would be men who simply wanted the opportunity to work, and would not be swayed by unions or, worse, by radical political ideologies. Many editorialists in the *Leader* argued that educated immigrants caused greater problems than the industrious and uncomplaining immigrant worker. Armour Caldwell, in a list of reasons opposing the literacy test, insisted, "Able-bodied, moral work-men, even if they cannot read and write, constitute the safest ballast in the ship of state."[72] At the same time, authors in the *Leader* countered attacks by groups such as the IRL, which often portrayed immigrant men as puny weaklings who detracted from the nation. Immigrant men, writers in the *Leader* maintained, proved their manhood and fitness for citizenship by what they actually did in the here and now and what their sons would do in the future—provide the muscle that an industrial nation needed. As Ira Bennett, an editor of the *Washington Post* and a contributor to the *Leader*, put it, the literacy test would admit the literate radical while an illiterate father of "a family of fine, healthy boys" would be debarred.[73]

Other depictions of immigrant manhood that appeared in the *Leader*, however, contradicted the portrayal of the immigrant urban industrial worker as an ideal

man. Some authors argued that the way to preserve the manly qualities of immigrant races was to distribute them to the rural areas of the United States. This
tension among different perceptions of immigrants in the *Leader* arose in part as a
result of competing business interests that were affiliated with the AAFLN. Certain businesses that advertised in the *Leader*, particularly railroads, had an interest in
immigrants' migrating to rural areas.[74] Others also used the portrait of immigrant
men living as rugged individuals off the land, including foreign language newspaper
editors whose articles were reprinted in English in the *Leader*.[75] This view of immigrants did have some utilitarian purposes, such as promoting railroads as a way to
get to rural areas. Yet it also contested restrictionist views like those of the IRL
who believed only men who descended from Anglo-Saxon pioneers could benefit
from the rugged life of the countryside.

A message in many of the *Leader*'s pieces about rural life was that immigrants had
the racial ability to meet the challenges of life on the rural frontier. The cartoonist
for the *Leader*, Edward Kemble, drew a cartoon on the theme of immigrant distribution in which he showed that, in the country, immigrants could become like a
normal, white rural American family—the father takes up a hoe, the mother loses
her babushka in favor of a bonnet, and the son trades his cap for a straw hat (fig.
3.2).[76] Ira Bennett most explicitly countered this portrayal by drawing a connection
between the whiteness of the immigrants and their manhood. He emphasized that
the United States needed "able-bodied, healthy, white immigrants of good character," or "strong, healthy, moral, white immigration." The nation, he argued, would
forever regret it if they impeded this "wholesome stream," for "the open spaces
of the West are crying out for such men, and if they are to be attracted to Austra-
lia and Canada, the demand will be still stronger for new blood from Europe."[77]
In other words, southeastern European immigrants would not racially corrupt the
countryside; they would, in fact, protect and preserve it for the white race, a race
that included all of European descent.

Indeed, according to writers in the *Leader*, the open spaces of the West needed
immigrants from southern and eastern Europe to counteract a greater threat in the
eyes of the AAFLN—Mexican immigration. While people of Mexican descent
had lived in the Southwest since the United States' acquisition of those states in the
Mexican-American War, the revolution in Mexico that began in 1909 led hundreds
of thousands of Mexicans to migrate to the United States.[78] In one *Leader* article,
an author explained that Arizona, not eastern states with high rates of European
immigration, had the greatest "immigrant problem" because of the migration of
Mexicans, who were "the most undesirable race which enters our borders, about
50 percent of them being illiterate and their general working ability very low."[79]
Leader writers also emphasized the undesirability of Mexicans and attacked congressmen from the South and Southwest who supported the literacy test. One

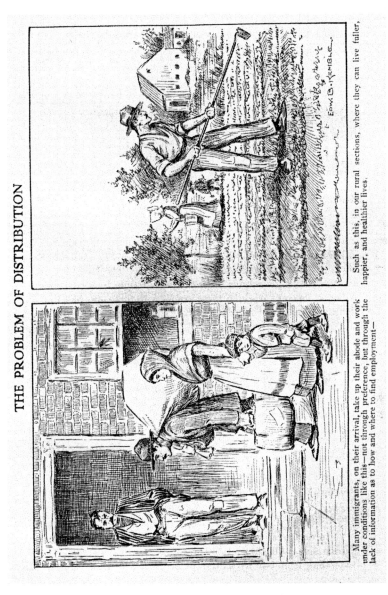

THE PROBLEM OF DISTRIBUTION

Many immigrants, on their arrival, take up their abode and work under conditions like this—not through preference, but through the lack of information as to how and where to find employment—

Such as this, in our rural sections, where they can live fuller, happier, and healthier lives.

EDW. B. KEMBLE.

Figure 3.2. This cartoon appeared in *The American Leader* as a way to illustrate the benefits of immigrants' moving to the countryside. Kemble remarks that, in rural areas, the immigrants can live "fuller, happier lives." (Illustrations by Edward Kemble. "The Problem of Distribution," *The American Leader* 6 [September 10, 1914]: 281.)

editorial explained that the only Southern state with high immigration rates was Texas, but this state got "the unenviable accession of Mexicans." The editorial argued that Texas should instead promote European immigration, "where it would form a valuable asset both from the economic and racial point of view."[80] Thus the *Leader* linked southeastern European immigrants to white, manly laborers, and tried to separate them from nonwhite Mexican immigrants.

The argument that immigrant men should move to rural areas as a means of fortifying their manhood and the countryside particularly disturbed the men of the IRL. They constructed the farms and fields of the United States as repositories of pure and superior Anglo-Saxon men and, at the same time, insisted that this racial haven was delicate and unable to withstand an onslaught of lesser races. While members of the IRL argued that the rural and frontier environment had built up the Anglo-Saxon race, they also maintained that this environment could not possibly change immigrants because their racial inferiority was innate. In fact, the presence of these immigrants could actually degrade the environment that had been the crucible for Anglo-Saxon greatness. In a letter to the editor of the *Hartford Post*, Prescott Hall critiqued a distribution plan that the paper had proposed, saying that it would not only lead to the "displacing of native Americans," but that immigrants' inferior bodies and minds were indelible and would "not at all be changed in character by this move and [would] be likely to cause the formation of a great many small slum districts all over the country."[81] In 1913, Madison Grant wrote to Hall, expressing his distaste for any "schemes for the distribution of immigrants," and framed these "schemes" as a direct challenge to Anglo-Saxon manhood. "Cities," he wrote, "are consumers of men and the countryside producers of them. So we still have some chances for the future if we are able to keep the blood of the countrymen pure." But, Grant warned, "The Jews would like nothing better than to divert the flood of East side Jews to the country side, and poison the blood there."[82]

"They Are Beginning to Take His Women"

Madison Grant's fear of Jewish immigrants' intention to "poison the blood" of Anglo-Saxon farmers echoed a larger fear of the IRL—that of racially inferior immigrants' outbreeding or, worse, interbreeding with the Anglo-Saxon race. Arguments had alluded to race suicide and miscegenation in earlier years, but by 1912 the rhetorical gloves were off. The men of the IRL put these threats front and center in their case for the literacy test, warning that immigrant men threatened to outbreed Anglo-Saxon men. Even worse, immigrants could interbreed with Anglo-Saxon women, thereby corrupting the Anglo-Saxon race with degenerate traits.

These sorts of arguments, though, exposed contradictions in the thinking of the men of the IRL. For them, the sexual dominance of Anglo-Saxons, expressed in their ability to sire strong sons and keep sexual control over their women, was a sign of their superiority. Yet they portrayed immigrants, with their weak muscles and groveling dispositions, as a direct sexual threat. Not only, then, did immigrant men threaten to triumph over Anglo-Saxons in the factories and farms, but they also threatened to debilitate Anglo-Saxon men through sexual competition.

Interestingly, the men of the IRL pushed the idea that Jewish immigrant men, whom they invariably portrayed as unmanly, posed a particular sexual danger to the racial future of the nation.[83] By the second decade of the 1900s, the men of the IRL began to express anti-Semitism much more blatantly in their public and private writings, often in ways that demonstrated their insecurity about Jewish power in the United States, with references to how the "chosen ones" were behind opposition to literacy test legislation.[84] In 1912, the leaders of the IRL found themselves in direct confrontation with a prominent Jewish academic, namely Franz Boas, the man who had challenged the notion of acquired racial traits in the Dillingham Commission Report. Robert DeCourcy Ward and Prescott Hall had formed the Immigration Committee of the Eugenics Section of the American Breeders Association (ABA), and, to their chagrin, Boas was also placed on the committee by the directors of the ABA. Ward and Hall, however, excluded Boas from the actual writing of the report, giving as their excuse that the committee was too dispersed to have formal meetings.[85] In the report, the stated goal of the committee was to "ascertain in what particulars the present laws governing the admission of aliens are defective or inadequate and whether the administration of those laws . . . can be effective to shut out those elements of immigration which are dangerous to the well being of the nation for eugenic reasons."[86] The report concluded that the present laws were not stringent enough and were in fact a "detriment to . . . the eugenic future of the race."[87] It listed a series of resolutions that called for limiting the number of immigrants who would be allowed to enter, although this first report did not directly call for a literacy test, probably in an attempt to be politic.

Boas' reaction to the report infuriated the men of the IRL. He officially dissented from the conclusions and recommendations of the committee, saying, "If a serious draft report is to be drawn up, I am ready to attend a meeting, but I cannot approve, much less sign your draft."[88] In reporting Boas' dissent to James Field, another member of the committee who had signed the report, Hall wrote how he had known that Boas would be trouble from the start, because "very few Jews have any manners." Continuing, he said that Boas had received "some shekels and much kudos" for his Immigration Commission Report, *Changes in Bodily Form of Descendants of Immigrants*, but that "Madison Grant tells me the biologists are all laughing at his measurements of school children's skulls.[89]

Hall and other members of the IRL certainly *wanted* Boas' study to be laughable, because it struck at the foundations of one of their arguments against immigrants. When his findings demonstrated that almost no difference existed in the cephalic index of the children of European Jews and native-born Americans, Boas concluded that the environment in which individuals lived had much more to do with the physical development of bodies than inherited racial characteristics.[90] Members of the IRL, on the other hand, insisted that neither time nor place would ever change the fact that southeastern European immigrants would always be inferior to Anglo-Saxons. Boas' rejection of the IRL's carefully constructed racial ideology—in which he asserted, in effect, that weakling Jewish immigrants could become as sturdy as Anglo-Saxons in the American environment—made the men of the IRL see red, particularly Madison Grant.[91] After the publication of the Report of the Immigration Commission, Grant wrote to Senator F. M. Simmons to explain Boas' true motive—an assertion of racial equality between Anglo-Saxons and Jews. "Dr. Boas, himself a Jew," Grant wrote, "in this matter represents a large body of Jewish immigrants, who resent the suggestion that they do not belong to the white race, and his whole effort has been to show that certain physical structures, which we scientists know are profoundly indicative of race, are purely superficial."[92] It was this claim of racial equality that rankled IRL members the most. Boas' challenge highlighted how the men of the IRL saw their status in the nation being challenged by upstart immigrants, particularly Jewish immigrants.

In the minds of the men of the IRL, Boas' claim of the whiteness of Jewish immigrants would justify the seduction of Anglo-Saxon women by racially defective Jewish men. The most vivid expression of the IRL's struggle to maintain their racial superiority emerged in their arguments about sex, specifically the way they portrayed a threat of miscegenation posed by racially inferior immigrants.[93] E. A. Ross warned that "pleasure-loving Jewish business men spare Jewesses but pursue Gentile girls," while Madison Grant complained that Jewish immigrant men "adopt the language of the native American, they wear his clothes, they steal his name and they are beginning to take his women."[94] This pursuit of gentile women by Jewish men directly threatened not only Anglo-Saxon male sexual power, but also the physique of future American men. E. A. Ross decried the "poor physique" of Jewish immigrants, saying, "on the physical side the Hebrews are the polar opposite of our pioneer breed. Not only are they undersized and weak-muscled, but they shun bodily activity and are exceedingly sensitive to pain." He quoted a settlement worker: "You can't make boy scouts out of the Jews. There's not a troop of them in all New York."[95] Yet these weak-muscled Jews would infect and ruin the Anglo-Saxon race for, as Madison Grant emphatically argued, "Whether we like to admit it or not, the result of the mixture of two races, in the long run, gives us a race reverting to the more ancient, generalized and lower type. The cross between a white man and an Indian is an Indian; the cross between a white man and a Negro is a Negro . . . and the cross between any of the three European races and a Jew is a Jew."[96]

Madison Grant's grouping of Jews with African Americans was a way to link southeastern European immigrant races to the ultimate miscegenation threat—that of interracial sex between black men and white women. Prescott Hall furthered the point, warning that southeastern European races themselves were the product of miscegenation between European and non-European races. In a 1912 article for the *North American Review*, he wrote, "The South Italian, which constitutes the largest element in our present immigration, is one of the most mixed races in Europe and is partly African, owing to the negroid migration from Carthage to Italy."[97] Hall broadened the threat by invoking the stereotype of Italian immigrants as emotionally unrestrained and asked, "what would happen if a large Mediterranean population should be colonized in our southern states and should interbreed with the Negro population it finds there?" The consequences, he warned, could be dire: "Will the descendants of the emotional, fiery Italians submit to the social judgment that a man with a sixteenth or a thirty-second part of Negro blood is a colored man who must occupy a position socially, if not politically, inferior? Absolutely not."[98] Hall implied that this future mixed-race man of "fiery" Italian and Negro blood would not respect the sexual boundaries placed on black men. If this dire scenario occurred, the threat to white womanhood, and by extension the power of white men, would rise exponentially.

Thus challenges to the IRL's racial ideology, particularly from Jews like Franz Boas, had to be countered with all the weapons, rhetorical and otherwise, at the IRL's disposal. After Boas openly opposed the organization, the men of the IRL tried to discredit him at every turn. They made sure he was removed from their ABA committee and even attempted to get him fired from his post at Columbia University.[99] By 1914, the committee, now made up entirely of sympathetic exclusionists, had issued a second report declaring that, for "the physical soundness of our race," Congress needed to ignore special interests like immigrant associations, philanthropists, and steamship companies, and pass a law requiring a literacy test.[100] Boas continued to contest the IRL's racial ideologies and would eventually succeed in marginalizing its views in the field of anthropology.[101]

By 1913, writers for the AAFLN realized that it was no longer enough to show that southeastern European immigration provided the nation with ideal men who continually proved themselves in both factories and farms. Instead, they had to address directly what effect immigrant virility would have on American manhood and racial dominance. Instead of denying the possibility of sexual relations between the native- and foreign-born or challenging notions about racial superiority and inferiority, they embraced the idea of intermingling southeastern European immigrants and Anglo-Saxons and argued for it as a positive good. They invoked the idea, propagated by Americans such as Theodore Roosevelt, that racial hybridity would enhance the population of the United States and create a stronger nation.[102] In making this argument, the AAFLN reasserted the notion that southern and eastern Europeans were safely white and, therefore, the "interbreeding" between native-born and immigrant whites was not miscegenation.

Henry Mann wrote articles for the *Leader* that epitomized this developing focus on eugenics by the AAFLN. In an article "Common Sense and Immigration" he upheld the IRL's contention that interracial sexual relationships affected manly traits, but he challenged the idea that it would lead to a deterioration of the nation's manhood. Immigration, according to Mann, was "a vital element in our American life, ever supplying fresh vigorous blood to the beating heart of the nation," and immigrants would supply a "sturdy, wholesome strain to invigorate the older population."[103] Trying to preserve Anglo-Saxon racial traits by restricting strong, healthy southeastern Europeans, the AAFLN argued, would only lead to racial stagnation and the degeneration of the nation's manhood. To make this argument, the men of the AAFLN began attacking the racial qualities of Anglo-Saxons, insisting that pure Anglo-Saxon blood led to stagnation in the population. Yet while they challenged the idea about a racially pure nation, they left intact the idea of a white nation and citizenry. In fact, the whiteness of southeastern European immigrants was demonstrated by the very desirability of interbreeding. Thus, while using arguments about sex to expand the boundaries of whiteness, the members of the AAFLN reinscribed the boundaries of whiteness more firmly around Europeans and their descendants.

Articles in the *Leader* suggested that, if left to upper-class Americans of Anglo-Saxon heritage, the nation would become weakened, and some authors openly attacked what they saw as the decadence and frivolousness of the Anglo-Saxons. Rossiter Johnson, who also claimed Anglo-Saxon heritage, complained about the "idle and useless persons" who appeared in the society pages.[104] These types of criticisms became more common by 1913, as many writers in the *Leader* sharpened their criticism of Anglo-Saxons as a race incapable of doing the work of the present or producing the type of men the nation would need in the future. Charles Nagel, who began writing articles for the *Leader* once he left office, declared, "We may have men enough in our country to do our work, but we certainly have not men enough willing to do it. . . . When we ourselves fill the places, men will cease to come to seek them; not until then."[105] The *Leader* also emphasized that race suicide among the Anglo-Saxon races was leaving a dearth of workers and citizens. One editorial asked, "Where the gentlemen of Congress expect in the future to get laborers for our great constructive works is beyond our guess. We only know that they are not rearing their sons for such tasks, and all their sons combined would not number enough to tackle a good-sized job."[106]

Armour Caldwell took a different tack by promoting the idea of racial mixing between Anglo-Saxons and southeastern European immigrant races. He held that "judicious intermarriage" led to "the renewal and rejuvenation of the very life-blood of the community. It is like adding yeast to dough."[107] This point—that interbreeding between Anglo-Saxon Americans and southeastern European immigrants would improve the white race—was one that writers of the AAFLN became even bolder in making. Harry Olson, a Swedish immigrant, AAFLN supporter, and Chief Justice of the Municipal Court of Chicago, firmly believed that eugenics could solve the problems of society, but he also insisted that southeastern European immigrants meet the qualification of good breeders.[108] He argued that the illiterate "peasant stock" of Europe, "from the standpoint of the biologist and the eugenicist, is preferable, from which to propagate the future American, to the descendants of some of the inhabitants of the congested cities of Europe," who would more likely be able to read. Olson cited Gregor Mendel's ideas about dominant and recessive genes and claimed that "it is better for the future generations to admit to our land the dominant, who cannot read, than the recessive, who may come with the diploma of the best University of Europe in his hands. The sons of the former will be presidents to our universities; the sons of the latter, inmates of the alms-house, insane asylum and penitentiary."[109] The "peasant stock," he maintained, would add this dominant element, not the over-educated, neurasthenic classes. George L. Dyer, who explained that his family had been in the country fourteen generations, still held the belief that he could see "the need for this new blood in our national arteries." Where immigrants mixed with the native-born population, he argued, "we find health, energy, industry. And where there is no foreign language population we find stagnation, retrogression, obstruction—a disposition on the part of the people not to do anything themselves."[110]

Thus the AAFLN sought to expand the boundaries of whiteness in the most fundamental way—by insisting that sexual relations between Anglo-Saxons and southeastern Europeans were not only acceptable but also desirable. Yet for writers in the *Leader*, whiteness still had boundaries, and they ended at Europe's borders. Different writers in the *Leader*, and particularly Louis Hammerling, declared their support for the imperial projects of both the United States and Great Britain, and explained that all people of European descent—including southeastern European races—should take part in these undertakings. By expressing their desire to conquer and rule over those they considered nonwhites, these writers sought to reinforce the whiteness of immigrants.[111]

In a 1913 article, Hammerling wrote about the "Centenary of Peace" celebration between Britain and the United States, and tried to draw a connection between southeastern European immigrants and the civilizing mission of both British and American Anglo-Saxons.[112] He explained that, like the United States, Great Britain "perhaps more than any other country except our own, has throughout the centuries received streams of immigrants of different nationalities and succeeded in blending them with her own native stock." The United States, like Britain, was stronger because of its immigrant blood, and able to take on the challenges of Empire. For, as Hammerling argued, "the problems of Asia and of the Pacific are the 'white man's burden,' which the two 'white men's' empires, the United States and the British Empire, have got to bear in common."[113]

In his rush to praise the idea of a white American empire, however, Hammerling undercut his own argument against the literacy test. In commenting on the U.S. occupation of the Philippines, he explained how American freedoms were not extended to the peoples of those islands, "and wisely so." He insisted that liberty depended on "self-restraint," and that "self-restraint is the product of education, and can no more be imparted to man by law than any other virtue. Savage, or semi-savage peoples are notoriously devoid of self-restraint, hence their incapacity for self-government."[114] So, at the same time as he made the case that education did diminish the racial quality of southern and eastern European immigrants, Hammerling also argued that education proved the racial superiority of white Americans over the Filipinos. In his eagerness to link himself and southeastern European immigrants to imperial power, he made a similar argument as that used against southeastern European immigrants by restrictionists.

The IRL, the AAFLN, and Women

A different article in the *American Leader* contradicted the arguments of AAFLN members in the literacy test debate. Instead of dealing with imperialism, though, this article, titled "Illiteracy and Sex," editorialized that the rates of literacy among women were too low to allow them to vote.[115] Thus as the members of AAFLN sought to define their whiteness by identifying with the U.S. imperial project, they also sought to define their manliness by criticizing women's push for greater rights. And they were not alone. The IRL also perceived the strengthening of the women's movement to be a threat to their arguments about male dominance. By 1912, the women's suffrage movement had achieved solid victories, and a coterie of educated women—many coming out of Hull House—had emerged as leaders in defining the major issues of progressive reform. The idea of women setting the political agenda rankled the men of the both IRL and the AAFLN, and it also undercut their position that white manhood represented the apogee of national power.

One way the members of these organizations dealt with this challenge was to ridicule the methods and goals of women reformers. The men of the IRL rarely mentioned women, but by the second decade of the 1900s, they had started to complain about "sentimental" opponents to the literacy test, including women's groups that sought to help immigrants. In one 1912 letter urging the President to sign the literacy test bill, Joseph Lee warned against those who acted from "sentimental consideration for the oppressed and unsuccessful of other lands." Madison Grant, in writing to Senator Elihu Root, complained about "sentimental clap trap opposition."[116] While the men of the IRL did not deign to mention women's suffrage in their public writings, the men of the AAFLN did, and often in derogatory ways. Rossiter Johnson, in an article in the *Leader* noted that women already had property protections and protection in the workplace, so they could only want suffrage in order to fight for "special privileges." He warned that women's suffrage was like putting "a flame near a powder keg" and painted a dire picture of women serving on juries and demanding civil offices "to be bestowed upon women who have led them continuously in a long and strenuous campaign."[117] AAFLN members also offered more general critiques of the arguments women made about increased government regulation, which they often termed "paternalism." One article praised a speech by Charles Duschkind, a New York district attorney who denigrated the champions of paternalism in gendered terms as "narrow-minded, long-haired men and short-haired women."[118]

Further, when the men of the IRL and the AAFLN spoke of race-mixing, women were present only as the objects of sexual conquest and the vessels for the future sons of the nation. Madison Grant was most explicit about this, declaring that women were the key to Anglo-Saxon racial purity, but only because of their wombs. He referred obliquely to the issue of slave owners impregnating enslaved women, calling it a "frightful disgrace," but then claimed that "its effect on the Nordics has been negligible, for the simple reason that it was confined to white men crossing with Negro women and did not involve the reverse process, which would, of course, have resulted in the infusion of Negro blood into the American stock."[119] As Grant saw it, the child of a sexual liaison between a white man and a black woman was automatically black, and thereby did not affect the white race. He realized with some trepidation, however, that sexual relationships between Anglo-Saxon men and southeastern European immigrant women would be considered white, and could thereby pass on inferior race traits to future generations. He made the comparison of ancient conquerors who did not bring their women with them. "If the conquerors are obliged to depend upon the women of the vanquished to carry on the race," he declared, "the intrusive blood strain of the invaders in a short time becomes diluted beyond recognition."[120] Control over Anglo-Saxon women, for Grant, was key to maintaining racial power.

Others in the IRL and AAFLN mentioned women only sporadically as compliments to men, not as independent citizens. One aspect that members of both organizations emphasized was the importance of protecting a woman's place in the home and family. In his book *The Old World in the New*, E. A. Ross chastised immigrant men for allowing their wives and daughters to work in factories, for "engaging in such masculine work not only prevents immigrant women from rising to the American woman's sense of self-respect, but it hinders their men from developing the American man's spirit of chivalry."[121] Writers in the *American Leader* made similar arguments as they promoted the migration of immigrant men to the countryside. One editorial insisted that sending immigrant men to the countryside would allow farm women to do less work in the fields and more in the home. "As a nation," the editorial declared, "we have always taken a great and just pride in the high position in which we hold women. Are we going to endanger the lives of farmers' wives because a handful of lawmakers in Washington wish to curtail and limit our most valuable national asset—immigrant labor?" The author then reported that a mother of six was killed while working in the fields, and asked, "Are such mothers so plentiful and so unnecessary that we can afford to sacrifice them when the trained peasant farmers of Europe stand ready to do the work, if only Senators from Vermont, Massachusetts, Kentucky, and Alabama do not object?"[122] Those Senators who supported the literacy test, he argued, were ripping women from their homes and children and forcing them to do work for which only men were suited.

In the rare instances when writers for the IRL and AAFLN addressed the affects of miscegenation on future women of the nation they focused on how it would affect women's beauty and desirability as mates for men. E. A. Ross lamented that interbreeding would adversely affect the "good looks" of American women, and remarked that "among the [immigrant] women, beauty, aside from the fleeting, epidermal bloom of girlhood, was quite lacking. In every face there was something wrong—lips thick, mouth coarse, upper lip too long, cheek-bones too high, chin poorly formed, the bridge of the nose hollowed, the base of the nose tilted, or else the whole face prognathous." Finally he arrived at the crux of his point, saying, "It is unthinkable that so many persons with crooked faces, coarse mouths, bad noses, heavy jaws, and low foreheads can mingle their heredity with ours without making personal beauty yet more rare among us than it actually is. So much ugliness is at last bound to work to the surface." He continued: "It is noteworthy that the beauty which has often excited the admiration of European visitors has shown itself most in communities of comparative purity of blood.... It is in the less heterogeneous parts of the Middle West, such as Indiana and Kansas, that one is struck by the number of comely women."[123] Armour Caldwell, on the other hand, not only argued that mixing races would make better men, but also that it would produce more lovely women. "Mixed races," he insisted, "are not only the most virile and progressive, but . . . the highest beauty of feature and form is also evolved out of the amalgamation of many divergent nationalities. The fusion of races with the opposite characteristics makes for a symmetrical and balanced race."[124] The women of mixed races, he held, would be much more attractive than purebreds, and therefore more pleasing mates for white men.

Conclusion

The literacy test arguments made by both the IRL and the AAFLN were replete with ironies and contradictions. On one hand, the highly educated professional and academic men of the IRL, most of whom had never done a day's work of manual labor, wanted to exclude illiterates not because they valued intellect but because they valued muscular bodies. The men of the AAFLN belonged to an organization that served literate populations, yet they argued that the nation needed strong, uneducated peasants to do the dirty work. Neither side exposed or even seemed to see the inconsistencies of the other side when they debated the literacy test. This neglect in itself reveals that, for these men, the literacy test debate was not about whether immigrants could read or write, the virtues of literacy, or the need for a literate citizenry. Instead, both groups used highly sexualized language to express more visceral power struggles about who had power and authority in a nation that was experiencing massive economic, political, and social transformations. The overall goal of both sides was not only to get their way on legislation, but also to legitimize their view of the ideal American, a view that placed men like themselves at the center.

This imperative allowed both sides to plow through other contradictions in their arguments for or against a literacy test. The men of the IRL portrayed themselves as members of a dominant race, but then warned that their manly, vigorous race was under sexual threat by weak, degenerate men. They extolled environmental factors as the producer of manly traits and yet insisted that those traits were inherent to a race and unchangeable by surroundings or time. The AAFLN at times promoted burly immigrant factory workers as the ideal, and at other times encouraged immigrants to move to rural areas as a way to build up their bodies and prove their racial desirability. Its members argued for racial openness by defending southeastern European immigrant races as desirable breeders for the future American stock, and they promoted racial exclusivity by insisting that only men of European descent met the test for racial fitness. Despite their conflicting rhetorical strategies, the members of the IRL and the AAFLN continued to insist that white manhood formed the basis of citizenship and automatically justified claims to power. The men the nation wanted, they all asserted, were just like the men they were.

While the men of IRL and the AAFLN sought to portray themselves as ideal men and citizens, the political ground was shifting under their feet. They had to come to terms with women activists who had exploded onto the political scene and challenged the notion that citizenship was reserved for men only. The men of these organizations wanted to relegate women to positions as pretty, petted objects, as creatures to be protected or admired by men, not as workers or independent citizens. But women as political actors were becoming harder to ignore. During this same period, Grace Abbott and the women of the IPL would insist that women had to be front and center in understanding immigration, citizenship, and the power of government to shape the population.

–4–

Practical Aid and Sympathetic Understanding

Grace Abbott's Alternative to the Literacy Test

When testifying against the Burnett literacy test bill in 1912, Grace Abbott refused to be baited. Everis Hayes, a California Republican and member of the House Immigration and Naturalization Committee, pushed Abbott to admit that the racial composition of immigration had changed, and not for the better.[1] Abbott acknowledged that more immigrants had come from southeastern Europe, but she also challenged the notion that they were racially inferior. "Anyone who knows the family life of the newly arrived immigrant," she claimed, "sees very little menace in the situation." She spoke of the sacrifice young men and women made to save money and bring over relatives, and then concluded, "I have often wondered what the average American boy or girl could teach the foreign boys and girls in the matter of that fundamental Americanism—devotion to one's family."[2] For Abbott, proof of whether an immigrant was desirable was neither established in the manly conquest of a frontier nor in germ plasma that fathers passed on to sons. Instead, it emerged in the family and community, where men and women, husbands and wives, sons and daughters fulfilled their obligations to each other and to the larger society. A literacy test, she argued, was a false indicator of whether an immigrant could become a good citizen because it did not test whether immigrants could realize that "fundamental Americanism."

It was not as though Grace Abbott devalued literacy. In fact, she promoted literacy as a positive good, much more so than the men of the Immigration Restriction League (IRL) or the American Association of Foreign Language Newspapers (AAFLN). In 1911, she, along with Jane Addams, wrote to Democratic Representative Oscar Underwood of Alabama, a restrictionist member of Congress, and acknowledged that education was desirable among the citizenry, and that "much could be said in favor of an educational test as a requisite for naturalization."[3] For Abbott, though, using literacy as a test for admission was an improper use of government resources and did not get to the root of the "immigrant problem." Immigrants, she argued, came to the United States with a value system that could make them good Americans, but those values could be corrupted by their interaction with the harsh industrial economy. Instead of instituting a literacy test, she argued, the government needed to do what she and her fellow members of the Immigrants' Protective League (IPL) already did—facilitate the transition of immigrants into the community. By following the IPL's program of shielding young immigrant women from exploitation, helping immigrant men find work, and providing all immigrants with advice in navigating the urban environment, the government could help ensure that "practical aid may be more intelligently rendered and a more sympathetic understanding developed."[4]

In articulating her practical and sympathetic approach to immigration, Grace Abbott offered an alternative logic to the debate over the literacy test and restriction, one that challenged assertions of white male power by groups like the IRL and the AAFLN. Instead of citing scientific theories or relying on vague gendered or racial assumptions, Abbott told stories based on her firsthand experience with the immigrants she encountered, documenting struggles and triumph, exploitation and resolve. In telling these stories, she accomplished several things. First, she used them to dampen the perceived threat of immigration by portraying immigrants as members of families instead of inferior races. She also upended patriarchal notions of independent men and dependent women by putting immigrant women at the center of stories, portraying them as vibrant and capable potential citizens. At the same time, she often portrayed immigrant men as exploited victims of industrial society. Further, Abbott's stories challenged the idea that immigrants posed a sexual threat to Anglo-Saxons by showing that the real sexual threat came from the predatory behavior of men, whether foreign- or native-born.

Abbott's stories, however, did more than argue for an inclusive view of immigrants. In accentuating her firsthand experience with immigrants, she claimed her own right to partake in the debate over immigration restriction. Her stories promoted a vision of immigration policy that was shaped by white, middle-class, reform-minded women, a policy through which the government provided immigrant men, women, and children the proper supports so they could fulfill their obligations to their families, present and future. While Abbott pushed lawmakers and the wider public to view immigrants as citizens in the making, she also made it clear that the ones doing the most work in creating these citizens were the women workers of the IPL. Women like her, she argued, had a superior vision for how the government should address immigration, and she therefore claimed her place as an equal to any man in this debate.

Grace Abbott, Progressive

By 1912, Grace Abbott was coming into her own as an activist, an immigrant advocate, and a progressive. She adopted many of the same progressive ideals as groups like the Immigration Restriction League, such as relying on a scientific, statistical approach and on a belief in the need for expanded government power. At the same time, she insisted that true progressive action required "sympathetic understanding" by individuals and the government in order for society to advance. Abbott cultivated a reputation as a pragmatic yet sympathetic spokesperson for the liberal immigration cause, one who could handle herself in the rough and tumble of political debate. Jane Addams pushed her protégée into the spotlight, describing her as someone who "speaks very clearly and logically and always makes a fine impression on men."[5] Years later, Marshall E. Dimock, who was the Assistant Secretary of Labor at the time of Abbott's death, confirmed this judgment in his praise for Abbott. In his eulogy at her 1939 memorial service, he explained why Abbott transcended the labels of "liberal" and "humanitarian" and achieved the title of "progressive." The liberal, he declared, "disciplines himself to see both sides" and the humanitarian "feels a deep bond of sympathy and helpfulness for human kind," but Abbott "was more than both together," for she added "a hard-headed program of action."[6] Between 1912 and 1915, Abbott worked to establish her political credentials as a progressive political actor as she sought to protect exploited immigrants.

During these years, Abbott published fewer scholarly and popular articles, but she intensified her study of the immigrant problem and expanded the work of the IPL. In the fall of 1911, she took a solo trip through eastern European countries to study immigration at its source. She saw this trip as essential to her work in Chicago, arguing that it is "quite impossible" to "assist people in making their adjustments to American conditions ... without seeing their normal home life." During her trip, she visited "Polish, Slovak, Bohemian, Croatian, Magyar and German-Hungarian villages" in Eastern Europe because those areas supplied the heaviest immigration to Chicago.[7] She paid particular attention to travel conditions, the labor situation for men and women, and racial tensions.[8] Upon her return to the U.S., she continued to expand the work of the IPL, assisting immigrants at train stations, tracking down lost immigrant girls, reporting abuses by employment agencies, aiding in deportation cases, and encouraging school attendance and English classes for immigrant children and adults. Abbott also expanded the IPL's work by investigating immigrant-run banks and increasing their aid in deportation cases. The raw numbers of immigrants the IPL helped increased exponentially, from 1,903 travelers aided in 1910 to 41,322 in 1913.[9]

Abbott and the IPL also began to get greater recognition from federal and state government agencies. In 1913, they worked with Chicago Representative Adolph Sabath to get Congress to pass a bill that established federal immigration stations at railway stations in the city. Abbott's reputation as an immigration expert continued to grow, and in 1914 the Massachusetts legislature asked her to run a special commission to study the status of immigrants in the state. She completed a detailed study of the problem, finished the report under budget, and was commended for writing, in the words of a commission member, "the ablest State paper ever issued in the Commonwealth."[10] While the presidents of the IPL continued to be prominent men—industrialist Andrew McCormick and Judge Julian Mack, for example—and the board and financial advisors included prominent male academics and community leaders, Abbott emerged as the spokesperson of the group.

When Abbott spoke out on immigration restriction, she did so with an air of one who felt validated to participate in public political debates. Despite the attempts made by male-dominated groups like the IRL and the AAFLN to deny it, the Progressive movement had empowered women across class, race, religious, and political spectrums to claim a political voice.[11] Those involved in Hull House, and Jane Addams in particular, were at the height of their political influence in 1912, as their vision of an activist State that sought to protect the weak and valued the expertise of women had begun to take hold.[12] Women activists, led by Lillian Wald and Hull House alumna Frances Kellor, saw success in their fight for a female-run agency in the federal government, and in 1912 William Howard Taft approved the formation of the Children's Bureau, run out of the Department of Labor and directed by another Hull House alumna, Julia Lathrop.[13] The four major candidates who ran for President that year—Taft, Theodore Roosevelt, Woodrow Wilson, and Eugene Debs—all advocated, in one way or another, the ideas of Addams and other Progressive women of using scientific methods and activist government to control the excesses of industrialization and protect individuals.[14] Furthermore, the women's suffrage movement was on the upswing; by the end of 1912, nine states had granted women full suffrage, and many more had the issue on the ballot.[15] By the time of that year's presidential election, women's suffrage was front and center, and all Progressive politicians had to figure out where they stood on the issue of women's citizenship rights.

Throughout her career at Hull House, Abbott had been excited about the political possibilities for women in the United States, and when she returned from her European trip at the end of 1911, she threw herself into the election of 1912.[16] Her sister, Edith Abbott, wrote that Grace "was born believing in women's rights," and that she "believed in politics as the way to get things done, and she enjoyed every moment of it."[17] Grace joined Jane Addams in backing Theodore Roosevelt's bid for president, and met with him to discuss the party platform. Their embrace of Roosevelt was not unproblematic for the Hull House women. His platform called for a buildup of the Navy, which went against their pacifist philosophy. Moreover, the organizers of the nominating convention refused to seat African American delegates from the South, a political stance that disturbed the racially tolerant Addams and Abbott. Moreover, Roosevelt himself had linked suffragists with race suicide, saying that suffrage could cause "appalling consequences . . . for hosts of absolutely innocent women and for the unborn."[18] By 1912, though, he realized that he needed the support of Progressive women in order to sway others involved in reform movements to back him. He reached out to Addams and other Hull House women, and they helped draft the social and industrial planks of his party.[19] In the end, Roosevelt spoke out publicly about women's suffrage at the 1912 Progressive Party Convention in Chicago, mentioning Grace Abbott by name and declaring that he hoped to see the day when women like her could vote.[20]

Abbott was drawn not only to Roosevelt's (eventual) public support of suffrage, but also to the liberal stance he took on immigration issues. While all political parties rejected restriction in 1912 in order to court the immigrant vote, the Progressive Party made a strong statement about the need to protect immigrants. Their platform, which labor advocate Florence Kelley helped to write, condemned "the fatal policy of indifference and neglect which has left our enormous immigrant population to become the prey of chance and cupidity." It then demanded that the government take a role in immigration distribution, in monitoring immigrant agencies, and in promoting immigrants' "assimilation, education and advancement."[21] This platform echoed what Abbott had been saying for years—that the government needed to be active in promoting immigrant welfare. Although Roosevelt did not go on to win in 1912, Abbott continued to work for the Progressive Party, serving with Florence Kelley, Emily Green Balch, and Jacob Riis on the party's Committee on Immigration.[22] Because of this affirmation from those in power, Abbott and other members of the IPL had reason for having confidence that their approach to immigration would become the model for the government's approach.

Overall, Abbott embraced a role as a public defender of immigrants. Edith wrote that Grace "became a serious supporter of liberal immigration policies and she was in demand as a speaker in behalf of the so-called new immigration."[23] In her Annual Reports for the IPL and her testimony before Congress, Grace sought to counter negative portrayals of immigrants and to promote protective measures the government could take. Her writings about immigration became a way for her to make a larger argument about how an activist government could protect men, women, and children from industrial excesses and exploitation. This kind of protection would, in turn, protect families, thus ensuring that all Americans, immigrant and native-born, could become strong, productive women and men.[24]

Grace Abbott's Representation of Immigrant Men and Women

When Abbott testified against the literacy test bill in 1912, she saw quite clearly that supporters of the literacy test did not value literacy as much as racial exclusion. She lamented "the discussion about inferior races" and dismissed the literacy test as "a departure from American traditions" and "no guaranty of character."[25] But beyond these issues, Abbott believed the literacy test missed the essence of the problem. A literacy test would not magically improve society, she argued, "because all the problems of a complex industrial and social life will remain, no matter what basis of exclusion is adopted."[26] In her view, instead of focusing on a literacy test, the government should protect immigrants as they made the transition into American society. She explained that an immigrant man needed to learn about "labor laws designed for his protection" so he would be able to support a wife and children.[27] Immigrant women and girls needed protection from "dangerous" travel and work situations in order to be upstanding wives and daughters.[28] Solving these problems, Abbott argued, would allow immigrants to thrive in the United States and make positive contributions to their communities.

What is more, Abbott's stories highlighted the struggles and triumphs of immigrants in the industrial landscape and, in the process, challenged assumptions about male economic, social, and sexual power. In the IPL's report for 1915, for instance, Abbott declared, "These men and women when they come have met the requirements of the entrance tests that they be sound in mind and body; their coming was a proof of their continuing ambition."[29] Notably, she characterized women as well as men as having sound minds, sound bodies, and ambition. Indeed, as Abbott defended immigrant races, she also disputed the notion that hard-driving, independent men and passive, dependent women constituted the American gender ideal.

Abbott used her stories to praise immigrant women who found independence from the Old World patriarchy, allowing them to thrive in the American environment. In one report, for instance, she told the story of a young Russian woman who had been brought to the U.S. to marry another immigrant. When the girl arrived, Abbott reported, she was "unwilling to consider" that man as a husband "when she found she could support herself in America."[30] In another testimony, Abbott told of a German-Hungarian girl who had managed on her own to save $500. When the girl married, she asked members of the IPL to hold her bankbook, "until she learned by experience whether her husband was going to allow her some economic independence."[31] At the same time Abbott also insisted that immigrant women were dedicated to family. She declared that they were "pioneers" who were "practicing the most rigid self-denial in order to send money home regularly or to save enough to bring over, one by one, the sisters and brothers and finally the old father and mother they have left at home."[32] The immigrant women heroines in Abbott's stories represented a womanhood that could be committed to family and still refuse to be subject to men.

Abbott also put immigrant women in the center of stories meant to challenge the notion that immigrant illiteracy proved their inferiority. During her congressional testimony, when a few congressmen pushed Abbott to address the question of immigrant literacy, she did so by telling the story of a young Lithuanian woman who had run away from her aunt's "disreputable" saloon. The Immigrants' Protective League helped the young woman find a job, then found out that she had left it a few weeks later. Abbott continued the story: "Further investigation showed that having saved $30 she had found a place to board and had enrolled in the public schools. Her only explanation was that she had come to America to get an education and that she was going to have $30 worth of education anyway." Abbott declared that that particular woman had shown an especially strong desire for an education, and said that her story was an illustration of the "great many men and women who make the same sort of sacrifice, who come expecting to get an education."[33] In her annual reports, Abbott also illustrated immigrants' strong desire for education by using women as examples. For instance, she reported the case of a Russian Jewish girl who lived with her brother and his wife, who both found her "mean and sullen" and wanted to throw her out of their flat. The members of the IPL found the girl a job, which provided her a room and a chance to go to school. The story had a happy ending. "From the time she entered school," Abbott recounted, "her depression and sullenness disappeared. At the end of the first term she had learned to read, write and speak sufficient English to be passed into the third grade."[34] Abbott's stories personalized the issue of immigrant literacy, and did it by using the experiences of immigrant women, and young ones at that, whose determination for education demonstrated their potential to be excellent citizens.

When Abbott described the situation of immigrant men, her approach contrasted with other defenders of immigrants, like the writers for the AAFLN journal the *American Leader*, and even one of the presidents of her organization, Alexander McCormick. In late 1913, McCormick appeared before the House Committee on Immigration and Naturalization to testify against the literacy test bill put before the 63rd Congress, and as he did so, he echoed the kind of language that writers in the *Leader* used. He praised the strength and hardihood of the "clean, fresh-faced, honest peasants" who migrated to the United States, and complained more than once that the literacy test would not "test a man's character or his muscle." McCormick also praised the eugenic contribution that immigrants made, arguing that they would "save this nation from degeneration . . . and race suicide."[35]

Abbott, in contrast, felt no need to bolster immigrant manhood by praising their muscles, fortitude, or virility. More often than not, in fact, she portrayed men as victims of economic exploitation.[36] She pointed out that the scope of industrial society made it impossible for men to cope with the economic downturns, unexpected injuries, and unscrupulous people willing to take advantage of ignorance without some sort of help. In her report for the year 1913, Abbott wrote that the immigrant man who came to the IPL for help "usually wants work, or has suffered from an industrial accident, or asks help in collecting the wages that are due him;

sometimes an employment agent has accepted money and then failed to give him work, or a banker has not forwarded the money he left to be sent to his wife, or he discovered that his lawyer is not to be trusted."[37] Abbott continued her focus on immigrant-run employment agencies, but a spate of bank failures starting in 1912 led her to focus on the exploitation that emerged from poorly regulated immigrant-run banks. In her report for 1914, she told the story of a Russian banker who disappeared, leaving the depositors, whom Abbott described as "little Russians," helpless.[38] The largest problem that came from such failures as this was that the men involved lost the abilities to support their families. "It is impossible to say," wrote Abbott, "how much of the dependency which has come during the past year of unemployment has been due to loss of savings which would have tided families over the winter."[39] She offered the victimhood of these men and their families as clear proof of the need for protections that would allow immigrants to navigate the treacherous industrial landscape to support their families.

Abbott also offered an alternative way of interpreting immigrant sexuality. In her annual reports, Abbott did not deign to address the IRL's grousing about the threats of race suicide and interbreeding or the AAFLN's praise of immigrant male virility and how immigrants provided "fresh, vigorous blood" to the American "stock." Instead, she argued that the greatest sexual threat came from male preda-tors, both native- and foreign-born, who seduced or forced immigrant girls into premarital sex or prostitution. In her argument, she offered an ambiguous view of immigrant sexuality, both male and female. She saw definite sexual misbehavior among immigrants, but did not see the problem as the fault of the immigrants themselves. Instead, the circumstances of urban industrial life most threatened the virtue of immigrant men and women. Overall, then, she used depictions of immi-grant men, women, and sexuality to critique the abuses in the industrial system and to challenge male dominance.

Abbott filled the pages in her annual report with suggestive stories about the sex-ual threat to young immigrant women who fell victim to both sexual abuse and the impersonal industrial environment that offered insufficient protections. She never mentioned prostitution by name, but made it clear that there were consequences to the lack of oversight of young immigrant women. She told one story of "failure" involving an eighteen-year-old Lithuanian woman who gave a bogus address when she arrived in the U.S. Upon investigation, the IPL discovered that the woman had been "called for by a notoriously disreputable man." Even though this young woman had provided deceptive information, Abbott muted her individual respon-sibility and instead emphasized that she was lost to the system, saying, "Everything pointed to the conclusion that the girl either voluntarily or by deception was lead-ing an immoral life but neither we nor the agencies to which the case was reported could locate the girl."[40] In 1914, Abbott reported the story of one immigrant girl whose aunt found her "unmanageable": the girl left her aunt's house and "all trace of her had been lost for some time." Abbott emphasized that, although the girl may truly have been unmanageable, she had nonetheless become undeservingly caught up in a web of sexual exploitation. She was found as she was "being transferred from one disreputable house to another. In this case, the man and woman responsible for her ruin were both convicted."[41] Moreover, Abbott presented the threat of sexual exploitation as extending beyond prostitution. In one instance, she told a story of a girl "who went to board with a cousin or a friend who lived with his family and five or six men boarders in a four-room flat." Abbott claimed that the girl "innocently did not appreciate that because of this congestion and the consequent lack of privacy and the restraints which privacy exercises," she could be in moral danger. Abbott again muddied the issue of responsibility, saying that the situation, caused by the economic circumstances in which the immigrants found themselves, left the girl "unprotected against herself and the people with whom she lived."[42]

An immigrant man, in Abbott's view, could also find himself at moral risk if his sexuality was not contained within a family structure. Yet the circumstances of industrial life worked against this desired state. Abbott continued to express worry about working-class Greek men who lived only with other men, in what she continued to call "non-family groups."[43] She pointed out that other immigrant men, particularly Russians, had "not saved sufficient money to send for their wives" and therefore also lived in "non-family groups."[44] She warned that "because of the absence of normal family life, [the men] are open to many temptations" that threatened their moral fiber.[45] In another story, she explained how hard and unremitting unskilled labor had not only caused an educated immigrant man to suffer a physical breakdown, but "perhaps more seriously has narrowed his mental outlook and weakened his self-control." Although Abbott was vague about what happened to the man, she described his plight as a "moral breakdown," implying some sort of sexual impropriety. She was afraid not only of the moral but also the economic consequences of this man's situation, saying that "he, and perhaps the entire family, would never be able to attain the standard which they knew at home."[46] This result—the degradation of the family—was the ultimate consequence of male sexual misbehavior.

Abbott argued that while immigrant women and men were victimized by charlatans, predators, and the vagaries of the industrial workplace, they could still be the kind of men and women the nation wanted. They were desirable as potential members of the nation not because they conformed to some sort of patriarchal social order but instead because of their intentions to better themselves in order best to fulfill family obligations. To keep those intentions from becoming thwarted, Abbott argued, the nation needed to work on creating safeguards instead of arbitrary and cruel restrictions. She offered a vision of integrating immigrants into the larger community and thereby making the whole community stronger. More-over, by positioning herself as a spokesperson for vulnerable members of society, Abbott asserted her right to participate in the debate as an unquestioned citizen. In the process, she validated her position—and the position of middle-class women reformers in general—as a political actor whose alternatives to the immigration restriction deserved an equal hearing.

Interpreting the Immigrants to the Community

During her testimony in Congress against the literacy test in 1912, Grace Abbott took the opportunity to promote her own tolerance of immigrants. She contrasted the negative perception many native-born Americans had of "new" immigrants from southeastern Europe with her own views. "When you come in daily contact with these new arrivals," she declared, "you find that they are men and women just like the rest of us, some good and some bad, and it is impossible to discriminate against them as a whole." She told her audience of congressmen that she did not worry that these "new" immigrants did not Americanize fast enough because "it took several generations to Americanize my Puritan ancestors."[47] Later she compared the supporters of the literacy test to one sanitary engineer who argued for immigration restriction based on his observation that epidemics of typhoid fever usually began in a "foreign colony." Abbott reported that this man had declared that immigrants were more susceptible because they "were accustomed to a pure water supply at home and therefore were more quickly affected by impure water than the Americans, who represented the survival of the fittest, as far as the effect of contaminated water was concerned." Abbott ridiculed the engineer's contention that the solution to this public health problem was that "some new basis of exclusion should be worked out" instead of improving the water supply for everyone.[48]

These statements in Abbott's testimony accomplished several things. First, the fact that she lived and worked among immigrants allowed her to present herself as an immigrant authority, one who was intimately familiar with the different immigrant groups and could act as a representative of their interests. As she wrote in one annual report, the mission of the IPL was to "interpret to the community those problems which have special significance for foreign groups."[49] Further, she demonstrated her great tolerance for immigrants, as compared to restrictionist men—like the sanitary engineer described in her report and, by extension, men like those in the Immigration Restriction League. While these men illogically made exclusion the solution to all problems, she offered sympathetic and logical solutions based on real-life observations to improve the conditions of immigrants and thereby strengthen the entire nation. At the same time, she also made it clear that she shared the racial pedigree of the restrictionists, letting it be known that she had Puritan ancestors, thus ensuring that her Americanism was beyond question. Overall, Abbott continued to place herself and other members of the IPL in a position of authority, not only as spokespersons for exploited immigrants but also as policy experts who offered a more practical and sympathetic approach to the so-called immigrant problem.

In her annual reports over the next few years, Abbott developed this triangulation as a way to claim political authority for herself as a white, middle-class woman. Abbott's advocacy for immigrants focused on tolerance—on allowing immigrants to be part of the community and to contribute their special gifts to the larger whole. The spunky young immigrant women she described had potential to be good Americans and should therefore be supported, she argued. At the same time, women's right to be considered full, equal citizens, in Abbott's rhetoric, was beyond question. While she focused on tolerance for immigrants, then, she simultaneously insisted on equality for white, middle-class women.[50] She continually promoted the work she did as head of the IPL as a model for the government and, by extension, as a justification for women and women's vision to be a central part of government action. Women like herself needed an equal voice in deciding government action on immigration in order to promote a vision of tolerance that would strengthen the whole community. This action did not mean a literacy test or other restrictive measures, but rather engaged government action that did what the women of the IPL did on a larger scale.

In the IPL annual reports, Abbott and other IPL leaders promoted their broad-mindedness about immigrants both as an argument for acceptance of immigrants by native-born Americans and as evidence of their own virtue. At the end of the report for the year 1914, for instance, Abbott stated that "the League was organized not only to serve all nationalities and all creeds, but to try to break down the forms in which racial injustice so frequently appears in the United States. All the members of the League have in a sense subscribed to the doctrine of Garrison that 'our countrymen are all mankind.'"[51] Others in the IPL echoed the theme of tolerance, making sure to note how Abbott and other members of the organization led the way in ameliorating tensions between the native- and foreign-born. Sophonisba Breckinridge, writing as the secretary of the IPL, praised Abbott and other members for "leading the way towards fuller understanding by the community of the problems presented by foreign groups, capable as they are of enriching and ennobling American life."[52] Moreover, while Abbott worked to interpret immigrants to the community, she also served as a positive representative of the community to immigrants. Judge Julian Mack, the president of the IPL, gave a speech in 1915 in which he said that "if that contact with Americans is of the kind that the workers in this League aim to bring to [immigrants], if they see that the spirit of America is helpful and hopeful, they will be started on the right road in that self-development that will enable them to give this growing American nation the best of their ancestry and their tradition."[53]

Abbott agreed with this sentiment, and she believed that the IPL accomplished some of its most important work when it showed immigrants that the community, as represented by the League, was pulling for them. For instance, while Abbott emphasized her work protecting immigrant men from crooked employment agencies or banks, she also wrote that immigrant men would visit the IPL's offices just to share their problems or triumphs: "they want to tell the visitor who is their only friend in America that they are home-sick, and discouraged, or almost equally to say that things are going much better now and sometimes in the glory of an entirely new outfit, happy and prosperous, to ask if we would ever recognize them for the same person that we had known in misfortune."[54] While Abbott believed that protecting immigrant girls from sexual exploitation was the IPL's most important function, she also pointed out that she and her staff offered "the encouragement which the girl so much needs in her first few years in America," such as in the case of a Russian girl who had found success in the United States but still visited the League "to let us know whether she has or has not heard from her mother, whether she likes her new job or whether she has been able to save enough to buy a new coat."[55] In these simple ways, Abbott argued, she and her staff served as surrogate mothers or sisters, listening and providing womanly assurance and sympathy—the kind of work that showed the immigrants the best of America.

Key to this work was Abbott's staff, composed of workers, almost all women, who in 1912, in the words of Sophonisba Breckinridge, "represented the Bohemian, Polish, Italian, Jewish, Russian, Bulgarian and American nationalities."[56] In her reports, Abbott made clear that the IPL needed these workers in order to connect to the immigrants in a way she and other middle-class, native-born women could not. They were, Abbott wrote, "sympathetic" visitors for the immigrants because they "spoke their language and understood their racial psychology."[57] The foreign-language-speaking employees of the IPL worked in the office translating the immigrants' tales of woe, and explaining to those immigrants the steps they needed to take. They also worked in the field, visiting immigrant families in their homes, tracking down lost immigrant girls, and checking out unsafe work sites. Yet while these workers' names were listed under "staff" in the annual reports, when Abbott wrote her stories about immigrants, she did not mention the specific skills staff members brought to their jobs or even their names, simply referring to them as "visitors." Instead she discussed the steps "we" took to correct a case of labor exploitation or how an immigrant turned to "us" to find a lost family member. Abbott obviously valued the work of the "visitors," but in her public reports she stood out as a citizen-advocate for immigrants, protecting their interests and at the same time demonstrating her own political acumen and model citizenship.

Grace Abbott, the IPL, and Immigration Policy

Grace Abbott used the political capital she claimed for herself to offer new models for understanding the relationship between immigration and government power. In the IPL's annual reports, she criticized government failures and offered alternative programs for the local, state, and federal governments. Abbott and others in the IPL argued that their ideas for immigration policy and government action were scientific, practical, and humane, and that they strengthened the whole community. Between 1912 and 1915, IPL members not only vigorously opposed the literacy test, but they also insisted that their vision of aid and protection should be the one the government followed. Therefore, Abbott insisted that not only immigrants needed her, but the men who ran the government did too.

A constant refrain from IPL leaders was that the kind of work they did in protecting immigrants from both economic and sexual exploitation belonged in the hands of the federal government, and their main goal during these years was to have government-run stations along the main railways traveled by immigrants after their arrivals in the U.S. The main purpose of these stations, according to Abbott, would be to ensure that young immigrant women found their families or friends instead of falling into the clutches of morally questionable people. When describing the problem of lost immigrant girls, Abbott declared that "there is no possible way of reducing the danger which this giving, either by intention or mistake, of incorrect addresses is to the girl and the community except through the federally supervised release of those who arrive."[58] The main threat to the immigrant girl was sexual exploitation but, as Abbott pointed out, the threat was not to the girl alone. The whole community suffered when girls were "ruined," but the community benefited when girls' virtue remained intact; therefore, the larger national community needed to take action.

When Congress finally established the Federal Immigration Station in Chicago in 1913, Abbott rejoiced "that this work shall be done for those who arrive at all the depots of the city by the United States Immigration Inspectors."[59] More than these concrete changes, though, members of the IPL trumpeted the fact that those in power had begun to adopt their philosophy about the power of government to protect individuals—in this case individual immigrants. In 1912, the president of the IPL, Alexander McCormick, pointed out that Senator Dillingham, who had recommended restriction in the Senate Report, had redrafted the immigration bill in a way that "amplified the provision on which we based the right of the government to undertake this work," providing "ample authority to establish the station not only here but in other cities."[60]

While Abbott did see some success for the IPL's vision of government action and immigration policy, she also continued to express frustration at the inefficiency of the government in fulfilling its duty, and became discouraged about the administration of the Federal Immigration Station in Chicago. At the end of 1915, she complained about the lack of use of dormitories, bathrooms, and laundry rooms in the facility, and declared it "an illustration of the way in which an administrative department of the government can refuse to carry out the laws passed by Congress. It should be interesting to students of political science." She continued to maintain that the "duty of protecting and caring for the immigrant on his journey belongs to the federal rather than the local government."[61]

Thus, even when she critiqued the literacy test and other government programs for immigrants, Abbott offered a positive program of government action. In 1915, when Congress was again considering a literacy test, she acknowledged that a large percentage of immigrants were illiterate, but that illiteracy was a failure of broader institutions rather than individuals. In her report for that year, she addressed charges that immigrants failed to learn to read and write English once in the United States, declaring that there was a logical reason: "even superficial investigation would have indicated the real difficulties. The men who are employed in steel mills of South Chicago work 12 hours a day for one week on a day shift and the next week on a night shift, while the classes that the city offers these men meet four evenings of every week throughout the term of twenty weeks." By failing to understand the circumstances immigrants faced, Abbott argued, the city government hurt the Americanization of immigrants and, by extension, the whole community. She declared that the government and the community needed to provide "an opportunity [for immigrants] to learn the English language and secure such a working knowledge of our laws and institutions as will enable them to join with us in making the United States a real democracy."[62] Again, the duty of the government and the community was the duty that Abbott and others in the IPL were working to fulfill.

The members of the IPL saw validation for their vision of the relationship between government action and the immigrant problem in early 1916, when Charles Nagel, former Secretary of Commerce and frequent contributor to the AAFLN's *American Leader*, spoke at their annual dinner. When Judge Julian Mack, that year's president of the IPL, introduced Nagel, he praised his stand against the literacy test, saying that Nagel agreed with the IPL's members "that exclusion measures— whatever they may be—ought to not to be based on literacy [and] that test ought not to be used to keep out the sort of men and women who from the beginning of the government have come in and made this country what it is."[63] In his speech, Nagel framed the immigrant problem much as the IPL did. Like the members of the IPL, he criticized the "race prejudice" of Anglo-Saxon exclusivists like the IRL who advocated the literacy test. He explained that, while "there were those who wanted me to consider the law technically—to keep out, 'to save us,' from the consequence of certain races," he had instead adopted the outlook of groups like the IPL, saying, "I thought that I would serve my country better if I interpreted the law fairly and humanely, and helped to make good citizens of those who were successful in coming in."[64]

Nagel also explained how he came to adopt the viewpoint of the IPL about expanded government power. He said that he had been suspicious when he had first heard the IPL's plan for the Immigrant Station in Chicago, because he was "a little afraid of paternalism." But, he declared, "it was your committee, and more especially Miss Abbott, who at a later date satisfied me that my argument was without value; that if the federal government assumes the right to determine at the ports what citizens shall come into this country, or what people shall be permitted to come . . . then that federal government must also assume the duty of protecting those people until they get to their destination."[65] More broadly, he offered an idea of government action that affirmed the IPL's beliefs. "In past years," he said, "many a fine opportunity has been lost in this country because people thought there was nothing between individualism and socialism, when the fact is that the real field of operation, of activity for the future, lies just in that space."[66]

Conclusion

That space for action that Nagel praised was one that Grace Abbott had helped to open up as she offered it as an alternative to restrictive measures like the literacy test. It was a space that recognized the interdependence of citizens—men and women, foreign- and native- born. It was also a space that gave power to women like Abbott, who modeled for the government humane and pragmatic ways to deal with the problems of immigration. She argued that individuals in a nation did not thrive on their own, but in communities, and that they counted on others for support and protection. Immigrants, as potential citizens, found themselves in especially vulnerable positions, and needed understanding and extra protections. The role of government, according to Abbott, was not to let immigrants forge their ways on their own, or to shield some sacred Anglo-Saxon remnant from infection, but to establish safeguards to protect families and to help in building understanding between different classes and races.

At the height of the Progressive Era, Abbott and other members of the IPL assumed that those in power had begun to see the "immigrant problem" the way they did—as an issue that needed positive, activist involvement rather than rhetoric of racial division or manly independence. Abbott and the IPL were proud of the leadership role they played in opposing the literacy test and suggesting alternatives. They believed that they played an essential role in making immigrants into better citizens, a task that proved their own exemplary citizenship. Like the men of the IRL and the AAFLN, however, Abbott and her colleagues had to face new political realties that would challenge their communal vision of the nation that recognized women as vital political actors. After World War I began in Europe, and as it started to pull the United States into its horrifying orbit, growing numbers of people in the U.S. questioned the loyalty of "hyphenated" Americans, privileged "preparedness" over protection, and disparaged the attempts of women who advocated peaceful, sympathetic approaches to the problems of the nation and the world.

−5−

World War I and the Literacy Test

In January of 1916, the House Committee on Immigration and Naturalization began hearings for yet another literacy test bill. Like the bills vetoed in 1913 and 1915, this bill called for immigrant men and unmarried immigrant women over the age of sixteen to pass a literacy test in order to gain admittance to the United States.[1] Prescott Hall, Louis Hammerling, and Grace Abbott entered statements into the record that reiterated the arguments they had developed over the years. Prescott Hall submitted a report from the Immigration Restriction League (IRL) which concluded that a literacy test would exclude those who would pass on their "poor physique" to future generations.[2] Louis Hammerling reiterated the typical argument of the American Association of Foreign Language Newspapers (AAFLN) about contribution of immigrant manhood to the United States, saying that "the fundamental development, continued growth and great prosperity of this nation have always been and are today due, in no small measure, to the sturdy, virile immigrants who have come to these shores in the past 35 years."[3] Grace Abbott, representing the Immigrants' Protective League (IPL), explained that the nature of the "immigrant problem" was "one of adjustment and protection against exploitation." Abbott went on to declare that her organization led the way in "trying to get those who are here well taken care of," and that "restricting immigration will not accomplish that end."[4]

Abbott also brought up a logical point. "We ought to postpone the question of further restriction of immigration," she declared, "until we know what conditions are going to be after the close of the war."[5] Indeed, the outbreak of war in Europe in 1914 had led to the decline of European immigration to the United States by some 400 percent.[6] Why waste time debating restriction, Abbott argued, if there were so few immigrants coming to the United States? By 1916, however, Abbott's practical point of view did not resonate in the larger American society. The momentum for the literacy test had grown, even as immigration declined, and the European war strengthened the hand of restrictionists.

As the armies in Europe began to slaughter each other, Americans reconsidered the desirability of racial and ethnic diversity, the role of women in society, the way that the government should exercise its power, and the meaning of citizenship. In this shifting political climate, the IRL, the IPL, and the AAFLN all had to fit their arguments about the literacy test into a new mold. The AAFLN and the IPL, who had both sought to broaden Americans' understanding about immigrants' capabilities for citizenship, saw their arguments losing ground as the war loomed. They found themselves not only having to stand up for immigrants, but they also had to justify their own place in the nation and their right to speak up in public debate. At the same time, the anti-immigration sentiment espoused by the IRL gained ground and, along with it, the IRL's conception of the nation as the province of white, Anglo-Saxon men.

The Great War and the United States

When the war began in Europe in 1914, President Woodrow Wilson proclaimed the neutrality of the United States, asking Americans at home to be "neutral in thought as well as action."[7] The war, however, set off intense political battles within the United States as Progressives debated how the government should respond to the growing conflict. Should they respect England's blockade and not trade with Germany? How should they respond to German attacks on shipping? Should American industries sell arms to all the belligerent powers or only England and France? Should the United States build up its own military forces, or should it serve as a peace broker in the conflict? As Americans struggled to answer these questions, they turned a more critical eye on immigrants within the United States and wondered whether they would remain loyal or whether they would reenact the violent ethnic struggles in Europe and bring war within the nation's borders.

German Americans bore the brunt of these suspicions. Even though President Wilson declared the nation neutral, he and many other native-born Americans felt a kinship with England. The Wilson administration declared that the United States would respect the blockade of Germany while still trading with England. Early on in the war, German Americans, who had been used to being viewed as a positive racial addition to the nation, still felt safe enough to insist that the United States follow a truly neutral stance. In January of 1915, representatives from almost all of the major German-American organizations met in Washington to protest the fact that the United States continued to sell munitions to Great Britain while respecting the British blockade of Germany. One month later, though, German Americans would find themselves on the defensive. On February 4, 1915, on the same day that the House of Representatives failed to override Wilson's previous veto of the literacy test bill, Germany announced its policy of unrestricted submarine warfare against British shipping, even vessels coming to the United States. Suspicion of all German Americans, whether native- or foreign-born, rose to new heights.[8]

Part of this backlash came in the form of the antihyphen campaign. By 1915, large numbers of native-born Americans, including Theodore Roosevelt and Woodrow Wilson, spoke out against "hyphenated Americans," who, in Wilson's words, "put selfish group interests blindly above national interests."[9] Theodore Roosevelt called for immigrant groups to stop thinking of themselves as German-American, Italian-American, Russian-American, or any other hyphenated American. Instead, they should drop the identity before the hyphen, and become, in the language of the time, 100 percent American. Roosevelt argued in public speeches around the country that those immigrants who maintained cultural ties to their homeland had divided loyalties, which he likened to "moral treason."[10] Many in the social reform movement, including Hull House alumna Frances Kellor, joined Roosevelt in insisting upon a homogeneous American culture to which immigrants needed to conform.[11]

This position on immigration, however, was not the kind of critique made by the IRL. They and other racial nativists wanted to exclude the southeastern European immigrants whom they saw as racially inferior, and certainly did not want them to assimilate to the point where they would "breed" with native-born Americans. In contrast, those who participated in the antihyphen campaign called for immigrants—Euro-American immigrants, in any case—to blend completely into American life. For the antihyphen agitators, being an American was something that could be achieved by thoughts and behaviors, at least for those considered white. In the ideal, the antihyphen campaign exhibited a "tolerant kind of civic nationalism" that allowed for all Euro-American immigrants to become part of the nation, if they were willing to give up all ties to their homelands. The execution of the antihyphen campaign, however, led to coercion of and outright discrimination against immigrants.[12]

Even as leaders like Roosevelt and Wilson called for national unity through conformity, the war had begun to cause political divisions in the nation, especially among Progressives. People from across the Progressive spectrum saw World War I, and the possible U.S. entry into it, as an opportunity to erect, in the words of historian Michael McGerr, "a model of the middle-class utopia on a far greater scale."[13] But which model of Progressive reform would be erected? While Progressivism had always contained multiple strains, the war turned the tensions within the movement into fractures. A struggle for the heart of Progressivism broke out around a central question—should the United States apply its resources to bring peace and aid the helpless at home or should the nation prepare for the worst, build up the army, and ready its citizens for war?[14] The antiwar Progressive position, championed especially by prominent women activists like Jane Addams and Lillian Wald as well as Grace Abbott, insisted that the United States should serve as a peacemaker in the conflict and at the very least do everything possible to prevent being drawn into the war. They saw peace as key to social progress.[15] The other side advocated what became known as "preparedness," and Theodore Roosevelt again led the charge. He and others called for a build-up of military forces, even compulsory military training, and an aggressive stance toward Germany.[16] Woodrow Wilson played both sides. While he used the slogan "He kept us out of war" for the 1916 election, he eventually came down on the side of preparedness.[17]

While some men became prominent antiwar Progressives, it was women who dominated the leadership of the pacifist movement. Women pacifists wanted Progressive reforms and government resources devoted to helping laborers, mothers, and children, and regulating the excesses of big business, not building warships. In January of 1915, a number of women activists, including Jane Addams, founded the Woman's Peace Party, whose goals included opposing militarism and sale of armaments, working for economic sanctions and economic reform, and advocating women's suffrage, which they saw as key to lasting peace. Addams declared that women's voices and political influence were essential since women were better at "treasuring life." These women framed their political views around their identity as nurturing women—the "mother half of humanity"—and saw the impulse for military expansion as a form of destructive masculinity.[18] Moreover, while calling for "an end to the bloodshed," these peace activists saw an opportunity to counter destructive militarism by advocating the political participation of women through universal suffrage.[19]

Advocates of preparedness, on the other hand, dismissed these women's pacifist arguments as unrealistic, sentimental claptrap. Men, they argued, had a greater understanding of national security issues because of their traditional role as soldiers. More than that, preparedness advocates like Roosevelt warned that peace activism, along with heterogeneity, would lead to a decline in "national manliness."[20] He believed that "mortal combat sharpened a people's racial instincts and strengthened its character," and scorned the "flabby pacifism" of his political opponents.[21] Women who became involved in the preparedness movement also used gendered rhetoric. Groups like the Daughters of the American Revolution and the Women's Section of the Navy League promoted a patriotic motherhood very different from that of the Woman's Peace Party by entreating women to encourage their sons to prove their manhood by defending their nation.[22]

In the spring of 1916, in the midst of these tensions, Representative John Burnett, an Alabama Democrat, introduced HR 10384, and the Immigration Restriction League, the American Association of Foreign Language Newspapers, and the Immigrants' Protective League again geared up to make their cases. The war, however, changed the political dynamic in the United States, and participants in the immigration restriction debates had to adjust accordingly. Between 1915 and 1917, when Burnett's bill finally passed, these groups had to confront questions about the hyphen, pacifism, preparedness, and the changes in Progressivism. They would also adapt their arguments for or against the literacy test to the new political and cultural realities.

Race, Manhood, and War

In November of 1915, Madison Grant wrote to Prescott Hall about his efforts to convince Theodore Roosevelt about the need for immigration restriction. Grant reported that they had had a positive meeting, but that Roosevelt remained non-committal. "He is terribly worked up over the question of the 'hyphen,'" Grant reported, "and is going to devote his energies to preparedness."[23] Grant's letter reflects an ambivalence shared by others in the IRL. The men of the IRL could sense they were on the cusp of their greatest victory, but as World War I began to shift American politics, they had some cause for concern. While they appreciated the increased suspicion of immigrants, they also worried that the debate over the hyphen would distract from their eugenic argument: the main danger was not that immigrants failed to assimilate, but that they might assimilate too much. For the men of the IRL, this kind of assimilation meant that the distinctive and largely inferior southeastern European immigrant races would breed into Anglo-Saxon or Nordic American races and thereby drag down the whole society.[24] A check against this, in their view, was a literacy test.

During the years leading up to U.S. entry into World War I, the IRL continually attempted to keep the focus on the eugenic threat that immigrants posed through race suicide.[25] In the statement the group submitted to the House Committee on Immigration and Naturalization, University of Wisconsin sociologist E. A. Ross and Yale sociologist Henry Pratt Fairchild both insisted that the question about restriction revolved not around whether immigrants *could* be assimilated but whether they *should* be. Ross declared that the case for the literacy test hinged on "posterity," the future men and women of the country who "will curse us if we do not have in mind their welfare in this matter." Fairchild echoed this sentiment, saying that policy makers had to keep in mind not only "the interests of the humanity of this generation but of the humanity of generations to come."[26] In another pamphlet for the IRL, Fairchild insisted that the future of the race had to be considered and that an immigrant who could read "furnishes better material, all things considered, for building up the American people, than one who cannot."[27] Both Ross and Fairchild argued that the offspring of undesirable, illiterate immigrants would pose the greatest threat from immigration, and implied that assimilating those immigrants to the point where they had children with Anglo-Saxons would produce a future race that would drag down the entire nation.

The hyphen debate posed another challenge to the IRL that was mostly directed at German Americans, whom the IRL had spent years promoting as racially desirable and literate immigrants. The mighty Nordic Germans, however, had started sinking U.S. ships and killing women and children, and committing atrocities in Belgium. The members of the IRL sought to distance themselves from its former defense of Germans, and Madison Grant, in his 1916 book *The Passing of the Great Race*, took on the chore of backpedaling. As he laid out the racial history of Europe, he allowed that the Germanic regions had been made up of strong Nordics, but argued that the Nordic race had declined in that region. The Thirty Years War of the seventeenth century was particularly to blame, according to Grant, because it "bore most heavily on the big blond fighting man" and thereby led to racial degeneration.[28] He also emphasized that in the eastern sections of Germany there had been so much intermixture with "Alpine," or Slavic, blood that the Nordic elements had been bred out, leaving squat, round-headed men in its place.[29] While he admitted that there were still many Nordics in Germany, Germans overall were not a pure race, and he commented on "the rarity of pure Teutonic and Nordic types among the German immigrants to America."[30] These newly racially impure Germans, then, could fit right into the IRL's argument about the racial threat of immigration to the American bloodstream. At the same time, IRL members kept up their arguments about the literacy test keeping out the most racially undesirable immigrants, even though Germans had some of the highest literacy rates in Europe.

Unlike the IRL, the men of the AAFLN took on the hyphen issue directly. They saw the agitation over hyphenated Americans as a threat to their status in the nation, and early on they felt secure enough in their political position to challenge the antihyphen campaign vigorously in the *American Leader*. In May and June of 1915, the *Leader* sought to legitimize the idea of dual loyalty by explaining that a true man would not abandon his loyalty to his homeland so quickly, and that, in fact, the nation did not want men whose allegiance to their native lands was so fleeting that they would quickly abandon it. Peter Lambros, editor of the *Greek Star* of Chicago, said that staying faithful to the land of their birth enhanced immigrants' loyalty to the United States, "for he who is loyal to his parent country is bound to become loyal to any other land, and he who is not loyal to the land that gave him birth is bound to be a disloyal and undesirable citizen in other lands."[31] Even as late as 1916, some articles spoke approvingly of hyphenated Americans, even Germans. One editorial from July of that year declared that "the hyphen may weld—and not separate—two nationalities," thus claiming that immigrants could be steadfast Americans even as they continued to identify with the lands of their birth.[32]

By the summer of 1916, however, the AAFLN's defense of the hyphen became much less tenable, as they began to feel the growing anti-immigrant pressure. By mid-1916, the *Leader* jumped onto the bandwagon of preaching the need for immigrants to conform. They also ratcheted up criticism of the hyphen. One editorial from June 1916 argued that an immigrant who lived in the United States should be compelled to become a citizen, and that "if his loyalty is to another country, he belongs there and not here."[33] The next month, Percy Andreae, a vice president of the AAFLN, echoed this theme, saying that "a man can only have one country. He who divides his allegiance between two countries is not worthy to be a citizen of either."[34] The *Leader* also published an editorial by United States Attorney General Thomas Gregory, who declared outright that "the hyphen has no place in American life. . . . There may have been a time when the hyphen could be used to designate the lineage of a citizen of this country, but as an outgrowth of recent events the use of the hyphen is an insult to the sincerity of a naturalized citizen."[35] The AAFLN had become sensitive to the "recent events" of the war, and they scrambled to situate themselves as loyal Americans.

To highlight their loyalty, the members of the AAFLN came down firmly on the side of preparedness, and almost all the authors in the *Leader* advocated military training and an aggressive foreign policy. Rabbi Abram Hirschberg, when discussing the possibility of war in 1916, argued for preparedness by saying that "American manhood can always be trusted to stand unflinchingly on the firing-line and come forth from the heated battle with honor unscathed and unsullied."[36] Jewish immigrants, he emphasized, despised "a weak-kneed and supine diplomacy that would purchase immunity from war at the loss of manhood and sacrifice of principle."[37] Thus Hirschberg and others in the AAFLN sought to link themselves to the preparedness campaign as a way to prove their credentials as manly defenders of the nation.

The AAFLN's embrace of preparedness allowed them to make new arguments against the literacy test and in favor of southeastern European immigrants. Authors in the *Leader* promoted the manliness, whiteness, and citizenship of immigrant men by praising their potential to be vigorous defenders of the nation—to be soldiers. By connecting immigrant men to the military, they were taking advantage of a powerful, entrenched understanding of traditional manhood.[38] While earlier articles in the *Leader* had argued that the literacy test kept out southeastern European immigrant men as a sturdy, muscular—and obedient—workforce, they now claimed that the literacy test would do something even worse—keep out sturdy, muscular men who would unquestioningly obey orders in defense of the nation. This focus on immigrant men as soldiers had been present before the First World War. Prior to the war, the *Leader* had argued that the wars of the past were not fought solely by Anglo-Saxon men, and authors in the *Leader* presented immigrants as having fought in all the nation's wars, particularly the Revolutionary War. This argument also appeared in the *Leader* when the United States entered a skirmish with the revolutionary government in Mexico in April 1914, when Edward Kemble drew a cartoon for the *Leader* that featured big, square-shouldered men lining up to enlist in the Army (fig. 5.1).[39]

AMERICANS—ALL

The foreign-born and their sons were among the first to volunteer their services in defending the honor of the flag of their adopted country

Figure 5.1. This cartoon appeared in *The American Leader* and made the case that immigrants were eager volunteers in the United States armed forces. The caption explained that "the foreign-born and their sons were among the first to volunteer their services in defending the honor of the flag of their adopted country." (Illustration by Edward B. Kemble. "Americans—All," *The American Leader* 5 [May 14, 1914]: 597.)

After the war began in Europe, Ira Bennett posed a hypothetical question: if a literacy test had been in effect during the previous fifty years, ten thousand of the U.S.'s enlisted forces would not be in the military. The literacy test, Bennett maintained, "would reduce the human material available for the national defense."[40] In 1915, when a letter to the *New York Times* accused foreign-born men of "frailty of fidelity," Louis Hammerling fired back a reply, saying, "From the time of the Revolution through every crisis in the life of the nation, citizens of foreign birth . . . have been in the foremost ranks of the nation's defenders."[41] Another article, in defending illiterate immigrants, asked of restrictionists, "Do they fear the illiterate Balkan, the race which can defy the Turk, standing as a unit in defense of their firesides and exhibiting the American spirit of 1776?"[42] The question was meant to be rhetorical, since the AAFLN believed that the fighting ability of these immigrants more than made up for any illiteracy.

The men of the IRL, however, did fear the Balkan race, as well as other southeastern Europeans, and used the European war to insist that the nation needed the literacy test more than ever. One tactic, particularly used by Madison Grant, was to denigrate southeastern European immigrant races as puny, weak-muscled, and unable to meet the challenges of war.[43] When Grant spoke with Theodore Roosevelt in 1915, he tried to get the former President to back the literacy test by focusing on military readiness. Grant singled out Jewish immigrant men as lacking the manly physical bodies to be soldiers. "You can walk down Fifth Avenue," he told Roosevelt, "and see literally hundreds of dwarfed and undersized Jews totally unfit physically, even if they had the moral courage, for military service."[44] In *The Passing of the Great Race*, Grant advanced this point further, and saw even more pernicious implications. He remarked that, when watching the parades of soldiers heading off to the Spanish-American War, one noticed "the size and blondness of the men in the ranks," whose appearance contrasted with that of "the complacent citizen, who from his safe stand on the gutter curb stayed behind to perpetuate his own brunet type."[45] Grant used this strain of argument to illuminate the major point of his book—that the Nordic race, the most virile, muscular, and productive race known in human history, was on the verge of destroying itself, leaving short, darker-skinned men to breed the future race. He maintained that Americans needed to do everything possible to protect Nordics in the United States if the race was going to survive.

The idea that the war would cut a swathe through the manly Nordic race in Europe and leave behind puny, dissolute men became the crux of the IRL's wartime arguments in support of the literacy test. In a May 1916 article for the *Scientific American Monthly*, Robert DeCourcy Ward said that, because of the war, the imperative was clear: "We need new immigration legislation. We need it at once."[46] He quoted an anthropologist who argued that the constant roar of the battlefield would "result in a more or less defective mental or nervous state in the progeny" of those who fought. Ward summed up the findings in his own words: "The weakling fathers . . . and the improperly nourished, overworked and harassed mothers of Europe, are handing on to their children who are now being born an inheritance of physical and mental unfitness which will mark not only this generation but future generations, through the long vista of time to come."[47] Considering, he said, "the probable effects of the war upon the character of future immigrants . . . it is for the best interests of our future race . . . to prevent as far as may be possible, the coming to this country of the mental and physical derelicts of the war."[48] Ward, like others in the IRL, kept bringing the issue back to the threat of immigrant breeding and its implications for the future American race and manhood. For Ward, the war only exacerbated the threat of immigration, since yet more degenerate men would be part of future migrations out of Europe to the United States. For him, the literacy test was the best solution to this threat.

In the years leading up to the war, the AAFLN and the IRL continued to offer mirror-opposite views of immigrant and native-born manhood in the literacy test debate. They both operated on the assumption that the war was a testing ground for manhood, and that the ideal American citizen would be one who not only faced military duty without shirking, but who, in fact, relished the duty. They framed their arguments around the idea of preparedness and spoke of the need for a strong fighting force, but they differed in their interpretation of whether immigrants could meet the challenge of military service, with the AAFLN providing a stout defense of southeastern European immigrant manhood and the members of the IRL scoffing at the idea of immigrant soldiers. The IRL's message, though, played more effectively into the growing environment of fear and suspicion caused by the war, and those whose loyalty was called into question would find their political effectiveness blunted—as Grace Abbott was also going to find out.

"A Reckless Squandering of Ideals"

As Grace Abbott argued against the literacy test in the lead-up to the U.S. entry into World War I, she continued to emphasize the themes she had developed—that the value immigrant men and women provided to the nation came from their dedication to their families, and that the government should worry less about restriction and instead concentrate on building structures to support immigrant families. She added to these ideas the insights she gained in her firsthand observations of the devastation of the war, both to United States immigrants and to the nations caught up in the conflict. She rejected the glorification of war and instead used her annual reports to convey the anguish immigrants felt as they lost touch with or heard of the deaths of family members in Europe. In her report for 1914, for instance, she told the story of a young Polish woman who had scrimped and saved to send money back to her family so they could buy a cow. When the war came, Abbott declared, the young woman appealed to the IPL for help in reaching her family and "inquire[d] again and again whether we think her mother and sister were able to escape and are by some miracle alive and undishonored."[49] This young woman, for Abbott, represented what war really meant: war was not manhood proved on the battlefield but men running amuck, tearing apart families, sexually assaulting women, and sowing sorrow and fear.

Abbott also continued to advocate the idea that the government's first responsibility should be to safeguard its citizens, and she criticized the move to pour resources into military spending. She leveled strong criticism at the government's "laissez faire policy" on immigration, which, she said, led to "a reckless squandering of [the immigrants'] ideals as well as their health and a jeopardizing of their material welfare." She continued to hold up the Immigrants' Protective League as a model for government action, saying that it "is the oldest organization working with all nationalities and all creeds and it is therefore looked to for leadership in this work."[50] By 1916, however, the restriction arguments she had dismissed as mere "race prejudice" had gained power, and she had to confront them with more force. Moreover, her view of a government that safeguarded the most vulnerable came under attack by the forces of "preparedness," and she began to see her vision of a protective, accepting community and government slipping away.

Part of what brought Abbott's political position under suspicion was her unabashed support of pacifism. Like Jane Addams and other women pacifists, Abbott saw a conflict between "government based on military ideals versus government based on social justice."[51] In the spring of 1915, she joined Addams, Alice Hamilton, Emily Greene Balch, Sophonisba Breckinridge, and other members of the Woman's Peace Party to attend a conference, held at The Hague, of representatives of belligerent and neutral nations.[52] After the conference ended, Abbott took a dangerous tour though German-occupied Belgium to see the devastation of the war firsthand, an experience that left her "suddenly very much older and fearfully depressed."[53] And although Abbott wanted to communicate the horror of the war, many in the United States had begun to view pacifists as naïve at best and traitors at worst. Abbott and Addams' former political ally, Theodore Roosevelt, dismissed the conference as "silly and base" and called on the women to cease their "vague and hysterical demands."[54] When Jane Addams returned from Europe and gave a speech criticizing the "old man's war," she faced vicious attacks.[55] Abbott herself, in her advocacy for immigrants, would also feel some of the growing backlash against women activists.

Abbott felt it acutely when she testified before the House Immigration and Naturalization Committee against the literacy test bill in January of 1916. She came at the invitation of Adolph Sabath, a Chicago Democratic congressman and longtime ally of the IPL. As the only woman asked to testify, she at first sought to use her limited time to criticize the unfair impact a literacy test would have on unmarried immigrant women subject to it by pointing out that girls had fewer educational opportunities than boys in southeastern Europe. As she had earlier, Abbott continued to argue that immigrants, and especially immigrant women, were dedicated to family and community, and that their presence strengthened the nation.[56]

Soon into her testimony, however, Abbott faced a sustained attack on her racial views. After she declared that supporters of immigration restriction demonstrated racial and religious prejudice, restrictionist members of the committee pounced, particularly Albert Johnson, Republican representative from the state of Washington. Johnson, a Seattle newspaperman who had become involved in politics by agitating against Japanese immigration, represented one of the aggressive new Western voices in Congress who advocated for restriction. He began hectoring Abbott about how far her racial sympathy went by asking whether she would admit all immigrants, including Asians and Mexicans. Democrat John Raker of

California furthered this point, asking Abbott whether she would she go as far as to say that she wanted "Hindu" immigration. Abbott attempted to divert the question, responding that she had no personal expertise about "the racial difficulties which are charged to the Hindu, the Chinese, or the Japanese immigrant."[57] Later in the testimony, Johnson made his hostility clear, saying he resented the statement "that Members of Congress, or any other broad-minded people, can not discuss the question of the future welfare of the United States and the dangers through the incoming of the hordes from the Mediterranean, principally, without being accused of having racial or religious prejudices."[58] Even as he dismissed southern European immigrants as "hordes," he insisted that his was the more enlightened view because he considered the larger population and the future of the race, not simply the troubles of present-day individuals.

Raker further questioned the whole notion that government should devote resources to aiding immigrants while many native-born Americans struggled in poverty. Abbott remarked that these conditions came about because politicians in the United States failed to do their duties. At this remark, Johnson exploded, and angrily asked, "If too many people come to the United States from any country; if the point where they live offers too low a wage; if they can not themselves see how to take care of themselves or their children; if Americans and others must take care of them, is it not time that we should restrict immigration?" Abbott snapped back, "I was suggesting that the American officials had not done what they were paid to do—to care for all the people in their official capacity." She then said directly to Johnson, "You are paid to legislate in the interests of all the people, not merely those who are native born," to which Johnson replied angrily, "I am doing what I can right at this table, thank God."[59] At this point, Adolph Sabath sought to defuse the situation, apologized for Johnson's outburst, and let Abbott have the final word. She ended by praising the immigrant women with whom she worked, saying that they "are making much more valuable contributions to the life of Chicago than I am going to be able to make," and that they "are a very real and helpful element there. They have succeeded in overcoming difficulties you would think insurmountable."[60]

Even though she got the final word at the hearing, Abbott's arguments would face derision beyond the halls of Congress. The men of the IRL mocked the kinds of sympathetic approaches to immigration that Abbott espoused. For instance, Robert DeCourcy Ward included a section in his *Scientific American Monthly* article titled "The Idealist and Immigration Restriction" in which he caricatured arguments made by reformers like Grace Abbott, sneeringly referring to those who "shudder at the mere thought of a further regulation of immigration" and who "hold fast to the vision of the universal brotherhood of man."[61] Henry Pratt Fairchild shared this dismissive tone in an article that was later published as a pamphlet for the IRL. He sought to debunk arguments made by idealists by saying that they opposed the literacy test for reasons that had "to do with 'natural rights' and 'liberties' and with American traditions and duties, with the inherent obligation of the favored to share their blessings with the less fortunate." Fairchild countered what he considered mis-guided humanitarianism by highlighting "the right of every nation to protect its interest as against the interests of any individual." He also insisted that "we cannot render our highest service to mankind by hastily and inconsiderately yielding to the demands of a specious humanitarianism and dissipating to-day what should be the heritage of future generations."[62] Ward and Fairchild, then, attempted to turn Abbott's arguments about the government's duty to protect the vulnerable back on her by claiming a higher ground. True humanitarianism, they argued, took into account more abstract notions of future progress, which would be assured by the racial strength of future citizens. To achieve that end, they argued, the government needed to institute a restriction policy, preferably the literacy test.

The IPL's purported ally in the literacy test debate, the AAFLN, also challenged the vision of a nurturing, protective government. Grace Abbott's view on the vital place of immigrants in American life sat well enough with the AAFLN, and articles in the *American Leader* had promoted the work of Abbott and the IPL,[63] but the AAFLN sought to define itself as an organization that would not shirk its mili-tary duty by expressing scorn for the pacifist view that the nation should promote peace rather than prepare for war. Around the same time that the *Leader* reprinted an article written by Abbott, it also published articles that she would have found abhorrent, such as "The Foreign Born Ready to Serve Uncle Sam," "American Naval Strength," "Business for Military Training," "Universal Military Service for Americans," and "Compulsory Military Training."[64]

Articles in the *Leader* linked the AAFLN's position on preparedness to broader arguments about an over-regulating nanny state, and this theme became especially prominent in editorials against prohibition. Between 1915 and 1916, the *Leader* pub-lished a series of articles titled "Personal Liberty," which was bylined by Louis Ham-merling but could very well have been written by Percy Andreae, a vice president of the AAFLN and liquor promoter who directed much advertising to foreign language papers.[65] This series linked regulatory moves by the government, particularly prohibi-tion, to a passive and destructive femininity, and argued that the end cause would be the sapping of the masculine strength of the country. One article from 1915 criti-cized the way patriotism was being taught in schools, saying that teachers extol "the moral courage of inaction," and arguing that "where intensities and stimulants were, there are now cautions and restraints." It continued: "It is a feminine ideal. It aims for good by the method of reduction of evils. The masculine complement, the aim for good by the method of increase of good, is lacking."[66] In 1916, Percy Andreae wrote another article in which he admonished the critics of preparedness, saying, "God made us men among men, to strive with each other and contend with each other for what we believe right and for what we consider just. If we refuse to cultivate and use the power [with] which we have been endowed for that very purpose, on the plea that we may abuse it, we shall stand forth stamped as moral cowards in the eyes of both God and man."[67] Masculinity, in Andreae's schema, denoted strength and independence; femininity, weakness and over-regulation.

In the face of hostility from Congress, restrictionists, and antipacifists, Grace Abbott realized that she could no longer count on her achievements and direct experience with immigrants to bolster her arguments against restriction. Unlike the AAFLN, though, she did not shift her arguments to meet the mood of the times, but instead she became more aggressive in her critiques, and tied her point of view to a Progressive, optimistic view of the nation and of human potential, and one that was rooted in the quest for peace. Abbott could no longer ignore or dismiss her opponents' contentions about the racial inferiority of southeastern Europeans and the threat of racial degeneration caused by the "breeding" of immigrants. While she wanted to see these arguments as the narrow-minded grumblings of marginalized reactionaries, she had to face the fact that these views had begun to be adopted by mainstream politicians and academics. In response, she developed a counter-argument about how ethnic diversity strengthened the nation.

In 1916, as militaristic rhetoric came to dominate political discourse, Abbott began to promote the idea of diversity as a positive quality. Inspired by the women's peace conference at The Hague, she organized a Conference of Oppressed and Dependent Nationalities, which took place in December, 1916.[68] The program included spokesmen and women, mostly naturalized citizens, who represented subjugated groups, such as Albanians, Armenians, Syrians, Poles, and Russian Jews.[69] The goal of the conference, according to a report in the *Survey*, was to educate native-born Americans about the "peculiar circumstances" of oppressed peoples in order to gain insights into how different nationalities can live together and thereby find "solutions which will prove permanent and beneficial not only to this or that nation but to the world at large."[70]

Abbott expressed this argument further in a 1916 article for the *Survey* titled "The Democracy of Internationalism, Which We Are Working out in Our Immigrant Neighborhoods in America." She began by attacking restrictionists with greater force than in the past, sarcastically referring to those who promote "fear of the 'inferior peoples' who are coming to 'dilute the old American stock,' and to 'destroy the old American ideals.'" She decried the restrictionists' eugenic reasoning as a "logical fallacy" and criticized them for "concluding that because the civilization of the United States is higher than in some of the more backward communities from which the peasant comes to us, the American aptitude for civilization is also higher."[71] Not only was this belief in error, it was also self-defeating because it divided the nation just when the United States needed to serve as a model for a "democracy not of nationalism but of internationalism." If, Abbott declared, "all the races of the earth can live together," if "we can respect those differences which result from a different social and political environment and see the common interests that unite all people, we will meet the American opportunity." By showing that immigrants from all the warring powers could live together in peace, America had the opportunity not only to promote an expansive democracy at home, but also to "urge that the terms of peace which shall end this war shall make for a lasting settlement."[72]

For Abbott, then, the arguments against immigration restriction and for immigrant integration acquired a new force. She sought to prove that a vigorous defense of immigrants was not mere sentimentality, but in fact had to do with the future power and influence of the nation. Proper immigration policy did not just make stronger communities, or even a stronger nation. The way the nation handled immigration, Abbott insisted, would determine the United States' role as a global leader both during the war and beyond. In this reframing of the stakes of immigration restriction, she argued, an unthinking policy of stigmatizing and restricting immigrants became counterproductive, even reckless. She reiterated these claims in her 1917 magnum opus, *The Immigrant and the Community*. Throughout the book, she culled examples from the IPL's annual reports and from her own articles to reinforce the points she had been making for the past ten years—that immigrants brought with them to the United States a vibrant commitment to family, and the government needed to protect the wage-earning capacity of immigrant men and the virtue of immigrant women in order to allow them to be contributors to the community, rather than burdens on it. The point of her book, she declared, was "to show concretely how the immigrant and indirectly the community have suffered both materially and spiritually from our failure to plan for his protection and his adjustment to American life."[73]

Abbott went further than she had previously done in criticizing restrictionists, specifically by referring to the eugenic arguments made by the Immigration Restriction League. Her concluding chapter, "The Immigrant's Place in a Social Program," directly took on the notion that immigrant breeding and potential interbreeding with Anglo-Saxons would lead to "national deterioration." She mocked the argument that "the declining birth-rate among the native Americans is the result of [immigrants'] coming" and E. A. Ross's contention that "American women must eventually lose their reputation for beauty because of the mingling of what he calls 'mongrel types.'"[74] She also referred to fears about declining manliness due to racial intermixture, saying that there had "been much concern lest the virility of our racial stock be destroyed by the absorption of constantly increasing numbers of those who belong to quite different ethnographical groups."[75] To counter these arguments, she cited Franz Boas, saying that his research showed that fears of "mongrelization" were unfounded. She quoted his argument from *The Mind of Primitive Man* about the "intermixture" happening in the United States, saying that "no evidence is available that would allow us to expect a lower status of the developing new types in America."[76] Abbott was finally forced to acknowledge the concerns about race mixture—which she had all but ignored in the past. But she did so in order to dismiss those fears, insisting instead that "the really important differences, those that separate the desirable from the undesirable citizen or neighbor, are individual rather than racial."[77]

Abbott also used her conclusion to give her final assessment on how to approach immigration legislation. While she criticized knee-jerk restricitonist policies promoted by groups like the IRL, she also made it clear she did not endorse the laissez-faire attitudes like some in the AAFLN endorsed. This approach, she argued, assumed that, since some immigrants had succeeded without aid, there was no role for government protections. She declared, "We cannot measure the success of our immigration policy or lack of policy by the achievements of those possessed of the unusual kind of ability which enables them to overcome all obstacles."[78] Instead, the government needed to study the immigrants' social and economic conditions carefully and then create a program that would "protect those among us whose need of protection is the greatest . . . supplement the immigrants' previous training and experience so he can most successfully meet American conditions," and "make the best that is in him available for community use."[79] She thus painted the IRL's restrictionist solution and the AAFLN's hands-off policy as the two extremes, while her solution—policies which emphasized the protection of immigrant families—served the greater good of the community and nation.

By the time Abbott published her book, however, the debate over immigration restriction had shifted. She said almost nothing about the literacy test because, when the book came out in April of 1917, it was a moot point. In the introduction to the book, Julian Mack said, "The illiterate, irrespective of character, mental or physical condition, are to be excluded," and admitted that "this fundamental controversy is for the present, at least, settled."[80] Congress settled the question in February 1917, when the House and Senate overrode Woodrow Wilson's veto and made the literacy test into law.

The Passage of the Literacy Test

On the eve of the United States' entry into World War I, the literacy test had gained broad support in both houses of Congress. By this point, the issue of immigration restriction transcended party loyalty, with Southern and Western Democrats and Northern and Western Republicans uniting to support a literacy test, while urban

Democrats and Republicans fought it. Politicians from western states also added a provision to keep out Asian immigrants, especially the Japanese and South Asian "Hindus." This measure was eventually enacted through a Senate amendment that set up an "Asiatic Barred Zone" by using lines of longitude and latitude to restrict most migrants from East and South Asia. In the House of Representatives, HR 10384 would pass in March 1916 on a vote of 307 to 87, with solid support coming from congressmen from the West and South. The main opponents of the bill were mostly congressmen representing urban districts with heavily immigrant populations. Many senators were more skittish about passing the literacy test bill when facing an upcoming election, especially those from states with significant immigrant populations. Moreover, Democrats did not want to put Woodrow Wilson in the awkward political position of having to sign or veto a controversial bill in the midst of a Presidential election. So, after a brief debate in August, they postponed passage of the bill until December. At that time, the bill passed the Senate with a vote of 64 to 7, with 25 abstaining.[81]

The contested claims about race, gender, and governmental power made by the IRL, the AAFLN, and the IPL permeated congressional debates over the literacy test bill in 1916 and 1917. As in the congressional debates about the literacy test in the 1890s, congressmen continued either to promote immigration restriction as a way to protect American workers or to criticize it as a detriment to having a strong, vital labor force.[82] The issue of literacy itself became a major point of debate, with restrictionists insisting that a democratic government needed a literate population, and opponents insisting that literacy was a poor indicator of the character of an immigrant.[83] Many congressmen, however, shared the sentiments of Representative William Kent, an Independent from California, who declared that he would "rather have a test of blood and race, and confine our immigration to northern Europe; but failing that, the literacy test."[84] By 1917, a central race question in the literacy test debate was: would immigrant blood mix with American blood?

The shift of Southern Democrats, who had been major opponents of immigration restriction in the 1890s, was most striking. Their strong support of the literacy test demonstrates the success the IRL had in racializing southeastern European immigrants and making immigration restriction about the eugenic preservation of the white race. After declaring that Northern cities would "soon be hardly American," Georgia Democrat Carl Vinson said that "this is the one blessing in disguise the Negro has been to the people of the South, the fact that by his simple presence in the Southland he has kept from our doors a considerable number of the overwhelming tide of ignorant and degenerate immigrants." The presence of "Negroes" in the South, he continued, ultimately prevented undesirable immigrant races from breeding with native-born, white Southerners and "has enabled us to keep our Americanism pure and uncorrupted as it was when first given in charge to us."[85] Other congressmen outside the South echoed these sentiments. Representative John McKenzie, a Republican from Illinois, described the northwestern European immigrants who had predominated in the past as racially desirable, as proven by their physical endowments, achievements, and ability to adjust to American democracy: "With turgid muscles and hopeful hearts they proceeded to make new homes for themselves. It is true they felled the forests and reclaimed the wilderness and quickly adjusted themselves to our form of government." While these immigrants were fit to breed future citizens, McKenzie found, those from southeastern Europe were not. Like the members of the IRL, he invoked "the welfare of unborn generations and its effect upon the perpetuity of the government."[86]

Those who opposed the literacy test used arguments similar to those made by the AAFLN, defending southeastern European immigrant blood as safely white and, in fact, a eugenic benefit to the nation. In criticizing Southern Democrats for their support of the literacy test, Joseph Cannon, a revered Illinois Republican congressman and former Speaker of the House, defended southeastern European immigrants by saying, "I am not afraid of the Caucasian race." Addressing Southerners, he proclaimed that if the South had received even a fraction of the immigrants whom northern states had gotten, they would be "50 years ahead in . . . material development."[87] New York Republican Representative Isaac Siegel stated the case more plainly by defending the eugenic contribution of immigrants. In his extended remarks in support of Wilson's veto, he declared that "the American nation is in fact great because we also are a mixed race," and that when a people "breed in and in," they "go stale, wash out, become decadent." "The old New England Yankee stock," he declared, "can thank God today that a new infusion of immigrant blood is saving it from itself."[88]

The specter of the war also made its way into the debate, and opponents of the literacy test, like members of the AAFLN, argued that the nation would need strong, hardy immigrant men as part of its fighting force. Peter Tague, Democratic Representative from Massachusetts, defended immigrants by claiming that "our generals would prefer good red blood in the rank and file to bulging brows and shrunken limbs, and our statesmen would be wise if in the other contest they would recognize the importance of virile manhood in the enlistment of a virile citizenship to fight the battles of democracy."[89] On the other side of the debate, Carl Vinson, Democrat from Georgia, raised fears about the immigration that would come after the war. "There is not doubt," he declared, "that Europe will dump untold numbers of undesirable aliens on our shores. The better element from the countries now engaged in war will not be permitted to leave or else will not care to abandon their stricken land."[90] The literacy test for him, as for the IRL, would be a safety measure in place for that possibility.

In January of 1917, Woodrow Wilson vetoed the literacy test for the second time. His message contained many arguments against the bill, including an emphasis on the diplomatic harm it could cause to the United States' relationship with Japan. He also made an argument similar to the more humanitarian arguments of the AAFLN and the IPL, saying that the literacy test "constitutes a radical change in policy of the nation which is not justified in principle." He decried the fact that the test would not examine "character, of quality or of personal fitness," but instead would "operate in most cases merely as a penalty for lack of opportunity."[91] For Wilson, then, the literacy test went against the nation's principles of fair play and punished people who were seeking out the opportunities offered by the United States.

Many others in Congress, though, challenged this version of humanitarianism and countered that the best way to uplift the unfortunate would be to ban immigration. David Schall, Republican Congressman of Minnesota, said, "My sympathy begins at home where millions of pitiful, unkempt little children, despondent, despairing American citizens, show us our distressing political conditions, the product of money-maddened industry, the divine right of the dollar kings whose avarice creates this insatiable demand for the spiritless man who does not know his rights, and if he did would not have spirit enough to assert them." Haphazardly taking in these men, Schall argued, would drag down the whole nation. Continuing, he said that the federal government had expanded its power to regulate "the rod in the engine, the brick in the wall . . . cotton and corn, to improve the breed of the cow and the hog," and would then "proceed to overthrow it all by leaving open our ports to the world's mass of illiteracy."[92]

Both Houses of Congress overrode Wilson's veto after a quick debate, with a vote of 287 to 106 in the House and 62 to 19 in the Senate.[93] On February 5, 1917, the literacy test passed into law. A little over a month later, on April 4, 1917, Congress declared war on Germany, and energies in the United States turned toward mobilizing for war. When the literacy test was approved over Wilson's veto, members of the AAFLN and the IPL expressed their disappointment, but their attention quickly turned to other problems, namely the very survival of their organizations. Both would feel pressure as they lost members and financial backers during the war years. More than that, they would see their perspectives about the relationship between race and gender and about the place of immigrants in American society becoming marginalized as Americans privileged militarization and an attitude of "America First."[94]

The Aftermath of the Literacy Test Law

In February of 1917, the *American Leader* gave very little comment on the passage of the literacy test law—only one brief editorial mentioned it.[95] Once the war began in April 1917, the members of the AAFLN faced more serious problems than their disappointment over the literacy test. Their identity as an organization of immigrant newspapers made them automatically suspect in an era when loyalty campaigns were becoming common practice. The leadership of the AAFLN sought to counter suspicion by emphasizing that foreign-language newspapers and the AAFLN were fully behind the United States war effort, and by bragging about the enlistment of its members.[96] Authors for the *American Leader* also kept up their tactic of defending immigrants by praising their manly contribution to the armed services.[97] Soon after the United States declared war, Edward Kemble drew a cartoon with four, square-shouldered soldiers around flags labeled with the dates "1776, 1861, 1898, to-day" (fig. 5.2). The caption read: "To-day, as well as in the past, whenever a great crisis had confronted our nation, the foreign-born have been among the first in offering their services to protect the flag."[98] Another article in the *Leader* held up a regiment of Italian-born troops from Boston, described as "men of fine physical proportions, full of enthusiasm and patriotic fervor," as the ideal. The article then contrasted these muscular, loyal men to the race-proud men like those who ran the Immigration Restriction League. "The men whose ancestors came over in the *Mayflower* and the *Speedwell*," the article argued, "have shown less desire to enlist than they have to write checks."[99] In a January 1918 article about how immigrants were gladly volunteering for the army, the *Leader* mentioned the literacy test, saying, "Surely those who a few years ago were so energetically opposed to immigration and advocated restrictive immigration measures must indeed feel shame-faced at the splendid example of self-sacrifice and loyalty shown by the newer Americans in this critical time of our national welfare."[100]

By 1918, the men of the AAFLN, and Louis Hammerling in particular, were in serious trouble. The Americanization campaign had risen to a fever pitch, and any person or any institution that was not "100 percent American" became suspect. Many foreign language newspapers were forced to fold, or to publish only in English, and the AAFLN ran into financial and political problems. At first, it attempted to defend immigrants who came from nations that were belligerent powers, especially Austria-Hungary.[101] Then, Hammerling was accused of taking money in 1915 to place advertisements for German steamship companies. Hammerling scrambled to defend himself, even offering the Wilson administration a plan to destabilize the Hapsburg monarchy, but he found no political support in the White House.[102] George Creel, the chairman of the Committee on Public Information, told Wilson that "there is no question in my mind that before America entered the war Mr. Louis Hammerling was indirectly an agent of the Imperial Government," but, Creel admitted, no evidence existed that Hammerling had provided financial or editorial support to the enemy.[103] The White House dismissed Hammerling, in any case, as an unsavory but harmless nuisance, and offered him no help.

1776   1861   1898   TO-DAY.
B. KEMBLE.

To-day, as well as in the past, whenever a great crisis has confronted our nation, the foreign-born have been among the first in offering their services to protect the flag.

Figure 5.2. This cartoon appeared soon after the United States declared war on Germany. The cartoonist, Edward B. Kemble, makes the argument that immigrants had always been a vital part of the Untied States armed forces. (Illustration by Edward Kemble. "1776–To-day," *The American Leader* 11 [April 26, 1917]: 468.)

Hammerling himself faced an ignoble end. By August of 1918, the *Leader* had folded, and by early 1919, he was forced to resign from the AAFLN.[104] The Department of Justice had found out that Hammerling had forged his place of birth on his naturalization papers—saying he was born in Hawaii instead of Poland—and they threatened to revoke his citizenship. In 1919, he fled the country and soon after lost his United States citizenship.[105] After spending some time in Poland, and even serving for a short time on the Polish Diet, he managed to reenter the United States in 1924, but could never reestablish himself in any successful way. In 1935, he fell out of his apartment window eighteen stories to his death in what most speculated was suicide.[106]

In 1919, the AAFLN was taken over by Frances Kellor, a Hull House alumna and supporter of women's suffrage.[107] During the war, Kellor broke off from Jane Addams over the issue of pacifism and became an ardent supporter of preparedness and 100 percent Americanism. She advocated for centralized federal government control and aid for immigrants, and argued that the federal government needed to become active in promoting immigrant loyalty and patriotism.[108] After the war, as Americans began to fear Communism as a result of the Russian Revolution and the rise of the Soviet Union, Kellor became a staunch anti-Communist, vowing to make the AAFLN into a bulwark against Bolshevism, to distribute "patriotic articles, admonitions against emigration to Europe, and antiradical propaganda."[109] While in earlier years, the men who ran the AAFLN had ridiculed independent, educated women like Kellor who supported centralized government control, the organization had become, by the 1920s, her vehicle of Americanization.

Grace Abbott, like Hammerling, lost her platform as a spokesperson for immigrants during World War I. By 1917, her attention was beginning to turn away from the IPL, which had been struggling financially. The war made the organization's financial problems more acute, as many of the IPL's reliable donors stopped sending checks.[110] The IPL limped along until 1920, when Ernst Freund, a University of Chicago sociologist and IPL member, convinced the Illinois legislature of the need for more resources to deal with immigrant adjustment. The legislature approved the creation of the Illinois Immigrants' Commission, and made Grace Abbott the Executive Secretary.[111] In that role, she continued monitoring new immigrant arrivals and conducted studies on conditions for immigrants in Illinois.[112] The Commission was shorted lived, however. In 1921, newly elected Democratic Governor Len Small vetoed the Commission's funding when Grace Abbott refused to stock it with partisan appointees.[113] Afterwards, the IPL was an organization on paper only, until it was partially revived in 1925 under the direction of social worker and Hull House resident Adena Miller Rich.[114]

Unlike Hammerling, Abbott was able to find other positions of influence, thanks to her network of educated, middle-class women. She turned her attention to child welfare work, taking a position offered by Julia Lathrop—an old Hull House colleague who ran the Children's Bureau in Washington, DC—to supervise the implementation of the Child Labor Act of 1916.[115] When that Act was ruled unconstitutional in 1918, Abbott turned her attention to international child labor issues and, in the summer of 1919, she went to London to represent the Children's Bureau at the International Labor Organization, a group established by the Treaty of Versailles.[116] After her brief stint with the Illinois Immigrants' Commission, she became the most powerful woman in the federal government when, in 1921, she replaced Lathrop as head of the Children's Bureau.[117]

Abbott came to leadership of the Bureau at a time when women were reaching a peak of political power. During World War I, women activists became divided about whether to prove their value to the nation through supporting the war effort or whether they should maintain a pacifist stance. At the same time, however, women from across the political spectrum continued their agitation for suffrage and, by 1920, the Nineteenth Amendment was ratified.[118] Women were no longer barred from the vote on the basis of sex. Soon after the amendment's passage, politicians, fearing a unified women's vote, passed a good deal of legislation that appealed to Progressive women activists. One piece of legislation that particularly benefited Abbott was the Shepard-Towner Act, which empowered her, as head of the Federal Children's Bureau, to distribute mothers' pensions and fund maternal health clinics.

Another issue that was taken up for debate during this time was the issue of whether women could keep their own citizenship after marriage, instead of being forced to take their husband's citizenship.[119] Abbott engaged with this issue as one of her last acts as head of the Illinois Immigration Bureau in an article titled "After Suffrage, Citizenship." She wrote the article as a defense of the bill, but she also delineated the bill's problems. While feminist supporters of the bill saw it as a way to protect native-born married women, Abbott pointed out the potential disadvantage of this bill for married immigrant women, who would no longer be able to acquire citizenship through their husbands. As in her critique of the literacy test, Abbott pointed out the vulnerable position of immigrant women, who suffered the "social prejudice against the education and independence of women" that permeated communities in eastern Europe.[120] If the citizenship bill passed, she argued, social workers would have to help married immigrant women overcome this stigma and take on the time-consuming and difficult task of learning English and taking citizenship classes.

Yet Abbott saw women's independent citizenship as a crucial political goal. She argued that the bill would have a profound effect on an immigrant woman's "position in the family, the respect she will receive at the hands of her children, her property rights, her status in [the] event of war."[121] Abbott saw that, for immigrant women, the benefits of citizenship extended past their political and economic rights to their power within the family. Moreover, Abbott insisted that the ability of immigrant women to exert more control in their families and communities affected all women in the nation. "Although we establish theoretical equality with reference to citizenship," she declared, "actual equality will come only as one by one all the disadvantages from which women, and particularly immigrant women, have suffered are removed."[122] For Abbott, then, political reforms such as suffrage and women's independent citizenship were but first steps in the process of women's achieving their full potential as equal citizens.

In 1922, Congress passed the Cable Act, which made women's citizenship independent from their husbands'. This law, as Abbott foresaw, ended up having mixed consequences for women. On the one hand, it led to the "recognition and security of women's public value and responsibilities as American citizens."[123] On the other hand, it made it made the situation much more difficult for immigrant women, who had fewer opportunities to attend citizenship classes than men but still had to pass citizenship exams. Even if immigrant husbands became citizens, immigrant wives were no longer guaranteed protections for themselves. Moreover, immigrant women had to be married to men who were racially eligible for citizenship in order to gain their own independent citizenship, a provision that particularly affected women married to Asian men.[124] Proponents of restriction did little to oppose this law, as it provided more hurdles for immigrants, whether women or men, and meant greater restriction overall.[125]

The men of the IRL were all for increasing hurdles to immigration, and after the passage of the literacy test law, they continued to pursue a legislative agenda that would debar immigrants they saw as unfit for United States citizenship. Unlike the AAFLN and the IPL, the IRL was at the apogee of its influence after the literacy test bill passed. After its passage, in 1917, Prescott Hall wrote a celebratory letter to Joseph Lee, saying that that "the League is now all powerful in Washington, with the tide of feeling about foreigners rising. No bill as to immigration can be passed if we object; while any bill we favor has a good chance of passage." He believed that the IRL now had an even graver responsibility as it considered its stances: "Our attitude may conceivably have a profound effect on the future of the United States."[126] As the men of the IRL saw it, their power, and that of white, Anglo-Saxon men had been confirmed, and they wanted to keep it that way.

Even so, IRL members did not remain satisfied with the literacy test as a means of restriction for long. By 1920, Joseph Lee was complaining that "the European crop of learned [immigrants] is bigger than we expected."[127] He and others in the IRL had begun to explore legislative options that would achieve their true objective—racial restriction. Even though Prescott Hall's health had begun to decline and he was confined at home for five months from what he described as a "nervous breakdown," he still kept up his single-minded fight for racial restriction.[128]

In 1919, he wrote an IRL pamphlet titled "Immigration Restriction and World Eugenics." By this point, the IRL's racial arguments were no longer limited by the issue of literacy and, in the pamphlet, Hall insisted that the purpose of immigration restriction should be understood as a means by which "inferior stocks can be prevented from both diluting and supplanting good stocks," a dilution and supplantation which would create future men and citizens who would be "unable to think or act strongly and consistently in any direction."[129]

After the passage of the literacy test law, the IRL sought out legislation that would serve their eugenic ends and set up the most severe restrictions. After the war, they became intrigued by a plan promoted by Dr. Sydney Gullick that would restrict immigrants from any country to a percentage of their nationality already in the United States; this proposition became known as the "quota plan." Gullick, a former missionary from Japan, wanted a "nondiscriminatory" quota that included the Japanese among the nationalities considered for entry.[130] Members of the IRL were drawn to the idea of setting quotas, but balked at the idea of allowing room for Asian immigrants. Hall wrote to Senator Henry Cabot Lodge and said that the IRL wanted "to stand . . . for a white man's country" by promoting a plan that would place stringent limits on European immigration—especially on those from southeastern Europe—and would keep out Asians and other nonwhites completely.[131] By 1924, the members of the IRL saw success again as the Johnson-Reed Act, legislation that they supported, would place prohibitive quotas on immigrants from southeastern Europe and end all immigration from Asia. Moreover, the passage of this Act legitimized the IRL's contention that the United States should be a "white man's country," and others—women and non-Anglo-Saxons—should have no say in the nation's destiny.

The Legacy of the Progressive
Era Literacy Test Debate

When Prescott Hall died in 1921 at the age of fifty-four, Joseph Lee lionized his friend's single-minded drive for literacy test legislation. Hall, Lee maintained, stood at the forefront of the restriction movement from the first, and "the final success of the literacy test in 1917 marked the close of what must have been, I think, the longest legislative fight on record." According to Lee, Hall had noticed "thirty years ago what others began to see during the war, that the most important question for this country was the kind of human material of which its future citizenship should be composed." By forming the Immigration Restriction League (IRL) and tenaciously fighting to keep out southern and eastern Europeans, Hall had prevented the United States from becoming a "breeding ground for the defective and the oppressed—the beaten members of beaten races." What motivated Hall, according to Lee, was "the love of country and the consideration for the future of mankind"[1]

Prescott Hall and his colleagues in the IRL succeeded in seeing the literacy test bill passed, but they did even more than that. They changed the parameters of the debate by framing the consequences of immigration restriction in terms of race, gender, and sex. What kind of men and women, they asked, were racially worthy to become part of the nation's population and breed its future citizens? By the 1920s, this question had become central in American political discourse. Groups that opposed the literacy test, such as the American Association of Foreign Language Newspapers (AAFLN) and the Immigrants' Protective League (IPL), were forced to confront the IRL's question and, in doing so, they offered new possibilities for thinking about American men and women, and white identity. The men of the AAFLN made the case that southern and eastern European immigrants were safely white because of the manly traits they exhibited, such as strong bodies and the ability to fight the nation's wars. These traits, as well as their whiteness, also made these immigrants desirable breeders of the nation's future citizens. The AAFLN imagined a nation where all European nationalities could be collapsed into the category of "white," and all white men, whether industrial laborers or college professors, would be seen as equal citizens, with the freedom to work, live, and marry as they pleased. The participation of Grace Abbott and the IPL in the literacy test debate became part of a larger argument for a more inclusive nation, one to which women and men of all races could contribute as interdependent citizens. Abbott and others in the IPL sought to reframe the problems posed by immigration from questions of race suicide and miscegenation to issues of economically exploited men and sexually exploited women, and, in the process, they made the case that the role of government was not to restrict immigrants, but to protect them.

In 1924, immigration restriction again emerged as a potent political issue as Congress began debating a bill that set severe quotas on immigrants, especially those from southern and eastern Europe. This bill did everything the IRL wanted but, by this point, Prescott Hall was dead and the IRL was a shadow of its former self.[2] Grace Abbott had become ensconced in her position as director of the Children's Bureau, and she made no public pronouncements during the debate. Louis Hammerling had fled the country in disgrace, and the AAFLN was under the control of reformer Frances Kellor. Yet even as the three groups were on the wane or defunct, the arguments their members had made about gender, race, and immigration reverberated into the decade of the 1920s and continued to shape the debate over immigration restriction. As in the literacy test debate, both proponents and opponents of the quota bill, known as the Johnson-Reed Act, employed images of ideal masculinity and femininity and debated whether immigrant races could live up to those ideals.

Gender, Race, and the Johnson-Reed Act

After World War I and the Communist Revolution in Russia, Americans' fears of Bolshevism and radicalism had increased their suspicions of immigrants and reignited campaigns for 100 percent Americanism. The Ku Klux Klan rose in popularity as it expanded its racial critique to include southeastern European immigrants as well as African Americans. Moreover, eugenics had become the basis for public policy on the state and national levels, including laws to sterilize prisoners and "feeble-minded" persons.[3] While many politicians in the 1920s, especially Republicans, had turned against the Progressive idea of government regulation of businesses or working conditions, they insisted that government had the right to regulate undesirable immigration. Restrictionists were also heartened that Republican President Warren G. Harding, who was elected in 1920, believed in immigration restriction.[4]

By the early 1920s, Albert Johnson, a Republican Representative from Washington state, had become the voice for immigration restriction in Congress. His legislative push began in the 67th Congress when Johnson and several other congressmen quickly pushed through a law they called the Emergency Quota Act of 1921. This Act first established the quota principle by limiting immigration from any nationality not from the Western Hemisphere to 3 percent of that nationality's number of immigrants listed in the 1910 United States Census.[5] While some in Congress made racial arguments, most justified this bill by invoking the threat immigration posed to the economy, and they saw the Act only as a temporary measure.[6]

In 1924, Johnson made the move to make the quotas more stringent and permanent. The bill he introduced in the 68th Congress, HR 7995, changed the quota formula in two ways. First, Johnson proposed that the numbers of immigrants from European countries be reduced to 2 percent of each nationality's number as counted by the United States Census. Even more significantly, he changed which census would be used—the 1890 census rather than the one from 1910—thereby greatly reducing the quota allotment of Italians, Poles, Russians, Greeks, and other southeastern European nationalities who had not migrated in great numbers until after that time. Republican Senator David Reed of Pennsylvania, the cosponsor of the bill, pushed for a national origins clause, which stipulated that, after two years, immigration would be limited to 150,000 persons per year, distributed by the national origin composition of all inhabitants of the United States, based on the 1920 census.[7] The final bill also excluded any immigrants who could not become naturalized citizens, that is, immigrants from Africa and Asia. The bill did not, however, limit immigration from the Western Hemisphere, at the behest of congressmen from the Southwest who wanted a free flow of Mexican laborers.[8]

The IRL's eugenic argument that white, Anglo-Saxon men needed to protect the nation from physical and sexual encroachment by lesser races dominated the debate in Congress.[9] Albert Johnson was unequivocal about his motives for his quota formulation: he wanted to keep out immigrants who he thought would make a poor eugenic contribution to the nation. During the committee hearings over his bill, HR 7995, he exerted an iron fist and limited the witness list almost exclusively to eugenicists who believed that immigration posed a threat to the nation's racial stock. Johnson's most prominent witness at the hearings over the bill was Harry Laughlin, the superintendent of the Eugenics Records Office at Cold Spring Harbor, New York. Laughlin epitomized the change in attitude about immigration restriction, testifying that "the economic policy . . . is giving way in the United States to the biological, which weighs primarily the future basic or family stock welfare of the whole nation."[10] In other words, the threat immigrants posed as breeders superseded concerns about the impact they had on wages, over-crowded housing, crime, or other social conditions.

In the debate over the bill in Congress, many emphasized the possibility of intermarriage, interbreeding, and "mongrelization." These threats, according to restrictionists, intensified the immigration problem because they imperiled the very heart of the nation—the potential, the capabilities, and the very bodies of its citizens, and particularly male citizens.[11] Republican Robert L. Bacon of New York insisted that the nation could not risk crossing a race of men "ready to lick the world and do it in a hurry" with southeastern European immigrants or it would risk losing "that element of independence of character, that individuality and initiative engendered in us by those who in earlier days left the physical comforts of Europe to brave the physical hardships and thus to find free play for mental self-reliance and expression in the new world."[12] While Bacon saw a threat to the manly qualities of American citizens, Republican Thomas D. Schall of Minnesota saw a threat to manly bodies. As he claimed, "We are working toward a distinct American type, with well-made bodies, fine features, quick intelligence. If we take in more heterogeneous material than we can assimilate . . . we shall lose all we have gained and be reduced to unlike masses and hopeless disunion."[13]

As in the past, congressmen from districts with high immigrant populations opposed restriction, and these congressmen increasingly were first- and second-generation immigrants from southern and eastern Europe. Democrat Adolph Sabath of Illinois continued to lead in defending immigrants, and he was joined by congressmen like Republican Fiorello LaGuardia and Democrats Emanuel Celler and Samuel Dickstein of New York. Often they found themselves on the defensive. Restrictionist congressmen dismissed the foreign-born opponents of restriction as inherently racially biased, with some even suggesting they should have no part in the debate. Democrat S. P. McReynolds of Tennessee charged that "some able gentlemen from New York City speaking on behalf of Jews and Italians" could not possibly be "impartial judges; they are clinging to the nationalities from which they sprung, and while we have respect for them we can not see their viewpoint."[14] Republican Representative William P. Holaday of Illinois garnered applause in the chamber when he insisted that "there is no prejudice in this country against any particular race unless there is a fear that that race is becoming strong enough to influence legislation in the American Congress."[15] The racial identity of Congressmen of southern and eastern European descent—especially Jewish Congressmen—became a cudgel that could be used against them and their arguments opposing immigration restriction. Thus, like the foreign-born men of the AAFLN before them, these antirestrictionist congressmen's attempts to demonstrate that southeastern European immigrants were racially safe for the nation devolved into a debate about their own status.

To defend themselves, these congressmen used some of the strategies employed by the men of the AAFLN and reiterated their arguments about manly bodies and the virility of immigrants. Adolph Sabath pointed out that nearly half a million immigrants had served in the armed services during the First World War, even though many could have claimed exemption. He then criticized the restrictionists' arguments about the noble racial traits of pioneers of the Anglo-Saxon race, saying, "Did not [immigrants'] service, heroism, devotion and loyalty equal that of the most loyal descendants of the *Mayflower*? I am sure their record more favorably compares with that of the so-called Nordic stocks."[16] Many antirestrictionist congressmen took Sabath's argument further, contending that the mixing of races was not dangerous, but desirable for the development of the nation and its future citizens. James A. Gallivan, a Democrat from Massachusetts, used this sort of logic in his argument:

> The race has ever been on the move. Movement, eternal movement, the ceaseless marching of the peoples, the constant waste and restoration that eliminated the weak and made the strong, that selected the brawn and developed the brain, that gave us the splendid thing we call civilization, that plowed and cultivated the fields from whose soil have sprung religion and culture, law and letters, trade and commerce, and the freedom, peace, happiness and order that are ours today. . . . In my judgement, that constant addition of new energy and new blood to the Republic is as necessary for the health and refreshment, the expansion and continuance of civilization and all it means today.[17]

W. Frank James, Republican, of Michigan, made a similar point by referring to the service of Croat constituents during the war and asking, "How can anyone claim that men like these will not mix with our blood and are not as good Americans as any of us?"[18]

At the same time, restriction opponents set clear boundaries in defining those they considered white. Much like the men of AAFLN, they sought to prove the white racial identity of southeastern European immigrants by contrasting them with those they saw as racially inferior—Japanese and Mexican immigrants. They expressed no opposition to the provision of the bill that called for the total exclusion of the Japanese, and indeed went out of their way to show their support for it.[19] Further, the opponents of restriction criticized the bill because it did not restrict immigration from the Western Hemisphere. In their critique, they pointed out that southeastern European immigrants had proven their qualities of race and manhood much more than Mexican immigrants. Democrat Patrick B. O'Sullivan of Connecticut complained that no quota was set for Mexico and asserted, "The average Italian is as much superior to the average Mexican as a full-blooded Airdale is to a mongrel."[20] Fiorello LaGuardia delineated the fine qualities of southeastern Europeans, and disparaged the restrictionists for "permitting Mexican peons to come by the thousands, knowing they will be exploited in the factories, on the farms, and wherever they will be employed."[21] Just as the restrictionists had done to southeastern European immigrants, antirestrictionists painted Mexican laborers as passive, racially inferior men who harmed the nation.[22]

Overall, the antirestrictionist members of Congress continued the project of the AAFLN. They participated in what Matthew Frye Jacobson has called a shift from "Anglo-Saxon exclusivity" to a "pattern of Caucasian unity."[23]

In other words, when antirestrictionists argued against establishing stringent quotas for European immigrants while encouraging the exclusion of Asian and Mexican immigrants, they made the case that racial acceptability extended beyond Anglo-Saxons, Nordics, Teutons—that is, northwestern European races—to all who came from within Europe's borders. As historian Mae Ngai has argued, even though the 1924 Johnson-Reed Act distinguished between northwestern and southeastern European immigrants, it also "constructed a white American race, in which persons of European descent shared a common whiteness distinct from those deemed to be not white."[24] Ironically, then, even though the antirestrictionists lost the battle about whether and how to establish quotas, their larger goal was on the way to being achieved.

Grace Abbott made no public comment about the Johnson-Reed bill or the advisability of quotas since her political energies were taken up by work at the Children's Bureau. The few antirestrictionist women who did participate in the debate, though, faced increasing problems as women's political capital *as women* began to falter. In 1920, fewer women voted than expected, and by 1924 male politicians had noticed that women were not voting as a bloc but instead voted the same way as the men in their lives. The movement that had brought together women of diverse perspectives to fight for suffrage had begun to break apart, particularly over the proposed Equal Rights Amendment.[25] Moreover, women activists who had achieved prestige during the Progressive Era, like Grace Abbott, began to be derided as busy-body, frustrated spinsters who wanted to create a nanny state. In the 1921 debate over whether to pass the Sheppard-Towner Act, Democratic Senator James Reed of Missouri named all the unmarried women on staff at the Children's Bureau, including Grace Abbott, and ridiculed the idea that single, childless women should be in charge of a government bureau that gave advice and help to mothers. "Better," he said, to "reverse the proposition and provide for a committee of mothers to take charge of the old maids and teach them how to acquire a husband and have babies of their own."[26] Reed's rhetoric reflected a growing critique of unmarried, educated women from the earlier Progressive activist tradition. By the 1920s, women who took up political causes were more frequently dismissed by their opponents as strident, frustrated women who could not get husbands and were quite possibly lesbians.[27]

The remaining members of the IRL also used this rhetoric to ridicule female opponents of immigration restriction and cast any liberalization of the quotas as feminine weakness. Even before the bill came to the floor of Congress, James Patten, the IRL's representative in Washington, complained about the "confound[ed] temperamental sentimentality" and the "sob stuff" in congressional hearings about restriction, and he warned his colleagues that "one of the investigators to appear is a woman."[28] Members of the IRL showed particular animus toward Frances Kellor, who had absorbed the American Association of Foreign Language Newspapers into her group, the Interracial Council. While Kellor believed strongly in 100 percent Americanism, she also wanted more lenient quotas with more exceptions for family members of immigrants.[29] Patten, in remarking that Kellor was on Capitol Hill lobbying for family inclusion, questioned her femininity by mocking her fashion sense: "Miss Frances Kellor is here on the job—a symphony in *brown*: shoes, dress, picture hat and even brief case."[30] Madison Grant warned Albert Johnson to be on his guard about Kellor, saying that "she seems to be able to fool a great many people." He also displayed his anti-Semitism, arguing that "Jewish banking interests" backed her research and that "her mother's name was Sprau."[31]

At the same time, Grace Abbott's key argument about the central role of family became a central tenet of the 1924 law. U.S. citizens' wives and children who were under the age of eighteen were exempt from the quota, and 50 percent of each nationality's quota was allotted to parents and older children of U.S. citizens. Some in Congress introduced amendments to liberalize the quotas to include more family members. Victor Berger of Wisconsin, a German-born immigrant and the lone Socialist in Congress, proposed an amendment to expand nonquota status to family members of immigrants who declared their intention to become citizens. This amendment, Berger stated, was "simply to protect the family."[32] Like Grace Abbott, the supporters of the amendment argued that supporting families benefited the whole nation. Unlike Abbott, though, they kept their focus solely on how a family helped *men* be better citizens. Republican Representative Hays B. White of Kansas declared that fair-minded people should support a man "who, by his industry and frugality, has accomplished that worthy achievement—the establishment of a home." This man, White declared, "is entitled to and should be permitted to have admitted his wife and minor children to share in the enjoyment of that home."[33] Berger further maintained that "you will most assuredly build up a better citizen if you encourage the immigrant to send for his wife, his children or his parents."[34] Overall, Berger and other supporters of the amendment made the argument that Congress needed to bolster the citizenship potential of immigrant men by insuring that they could both support and be supported by a family.

In the end, though, Berger's amendment went nowhere. Most in Congress insisted that the racial stock, not individual families, needed to be protected. The supporters of restriction used the IRL's logic about the danger of bowing to sentimentality when the future of the race was at stake. R. E. L. Allen of West Virginia stated the case bluntly. "The primary reason for the restriction of the alien stream," he insisted, "is the necessity for purifying and keeping pure the blood of America. The danger line has been reached, if not passed." Allen strongly argued against those who employed sentimental stories about separated families, and maintained, "It is to our descendants that we owe our first obligations. No misguided sympathy for the unfortunate inhabitants of other countries should ever permit us to jeopardize the welfare of our future population."[35] The American stock must remain Anglo-Saxon, he insisted, "if we are to insure the predominance of our race, the sanctity of the American home, the survival of Christian thought, and the preservation of our political institutions."[36] The restrictionists insisted that, to keep the nation strong, hard-headed masculine reasoning, and not sentimental feminine feelings, must rule the day. As Democrat Thomas D. McKeown of Oklahoma put it, "A country that is so weak and impotent that it cannot protect itself deserves to fall."[37]

The perspective Grace Abbott offered to the literacy test debates, then, was both incorporated into the Johnson-Reed Act and marginalized by it. The structure of the quotas privileged the family relationship, and congressmen held up the notion that men were better citizens when they fulfilled their roles in a family.[38] Through the remainder of the 1920s, the major changes and reforms to the law concerned shifting quota allotments to allow more family members into the U.S.[39] At the same time, women's second-class citizenship was enshrined in immigration laws. While the 1924 Act granted to wives of U.S. citizens nonquota status, husbands of U.S. citizens did not get this designation until 1928, and it only counted for those married on or before that year.[40] While the arguments of women reformers that appealed to real-life tragedies, like the separation of families, could be dismissed as overly sentimental "sob stuff," emotional arguments made in favor of restriction, like those that implied a possibility of a "weak and impotent" nation, were generally viewed as the stuff of sound, scientific reasoning.

In 1924, restrictionists' fear for the nation's racial future won the day. Republican President Calvin Coolidge, like his predecessors, was reluctant to sign the bill. He was facing an election that year and did not want to alienate the immigrant vote. Nor did he want to insult the Japanese, who were rising as a military power. Moreover, Coolidge felt uncomfortable with the way the bill set up restriction based on race. Restrictionist congressmen and cabinet members, however, made Coolidge see the political writing on the wall—the majority of Americans supported restriction based on race and, if he vetoed the bill, he would be humiliated by a quick overturning of his veto. On May 26, 1924, Coolidge signed the bill into law.[41]

The Legacy of Early-Twentieth-Century Immigration Restriction Debates

The Johnson-Reed Act is one of the most significant pieces of legislation in the nation's history, and the consequences of it shaped the United States through the rest of the twentieth century. It excluded all immigrants who could not become citizens, which meant the exclusion of all those who were not the "free white persons" designated by the Naturalization Act of 1890. The passage of the law meant that all Asian immigration ceased until 1952, when naturalization was opened to all, regardless of race. Americans of Asian decent remained second-class citizens, with the most dramatic illustration of their inferior status being the internment of 120,000 Japanese and Japanese Americans during World War II. The quota's basis in the 1890 census and the later adoption of the national origins clause also led to drastic changes in European immigration: the percentage of immigrants from southeastern Europe fell dramatically. The sharp decrease in all immigration led to the division of families, possibly never to be reunited. When Jewish refugees from eastern Europe attempted to flee Nazi persecution in the 1920s, the quotas stood firmly in place, dooming most of them to death in the concentration camps. The quotas affected foreign policy, particularly during the Cold War, when the United States was attempting to win over the alliance of Asia and Africa even as it refused entry to their citizens. By setting up quotas, the act also created the category of "illegal alien," a person who had no legal claim to the rights of citizenship in the State.[42]

The Immigration Act of 1965, known as the Hart-Cellar Act, seemed to signal a sea change in United States immigration policy. This law opened up quotas to migrants from Asia and Africa, thus ending the total restriction of those groups. At the same time, stringent quotas were established for nations in the Western Hemisphere for the first time, initially limiting the total hemispheric quota to 120,000 migrants. This limitation particularly affected Mexican migrants, whose total quota was set at twenty thousand per year—a 40 percent reduction from the pre-1965 levels of migration.[43] While this number increased in subsequent years, the establishment of the quota reinforced and expanded the category of illegal immigration, and the debate over undocumented workers became central to debates about immigration in the United States. Since 1965, the border between the United States and Mexico has become militarized, with the U.S. border patrol expanding by over 400 percent and occasionally violent citizen militias patrolling the border.

In the late twentieth and early twenty-first centuries, immigration restriction has again become a hot-button political issue. While the issues and contours of immigration debates have changed, those who participate in them continue to make appeals based on race and gender. In 1994, the citizens of California voted on Proposition 187, a ballot initiative that, among other things, banned undocumented immigrants from social services like public education. Supporters of Proposition 187 were labeled by the media as "angry white men," a label that many of the supporters embraced. The assumption behind the media's claim was that white men saw their birthright as Americans—that is, their jobs and their status in the nation—being taken away by immigrants who worked for less money and gobbled up social resources.[44] As in economic critiques of immigration a century earlier, critics in the 1990s invoked the idea that immigrants imperiled the ability of white men to make their living and support their families in the proper American way. Moreover, undocumented immigrant women also became the focus in the debate over Proposition 187. Critics accused pregnant Mexican women of coming to the United States in order to give birth to children who would be American citizens. One opponent of Mexican immigration complained that Mexican immigrant women come to the nation and "breed like rabbits." He tied their childbearing to a loss of white political power, saying that "eventually the whole legislature's gonna be Latino."[45] In the end, over 59 percent of Californians voted in favor of Proposition 187, and while the California Supreme Court overturned its most draconian provisions, the Proposition's electoral success illustrates the anger many native-born Americans felt about the changing nature of American society.

Debates about immigration and the position of undocumented immigrants in American society flared again in the twenty-first century. President George W. Bush engaged with the immigration issue during his second term, and he proposed a bill that would raise the numbers of guards at the borders, institute temporary work permits for immigrants, and provide undocumented immigrants already in the United States a path to citizenship. Opposition to these reforms became intense, as members of the President's own political party decried the measures as encouraging criminal behavior. At the same time, immigrants and their supporters took to the streets in unprecedented numbers in March of that year, defending their place in the nation. In the end, Bush backed off from his proposals and never achieved immigration reform during his Presidency.

While early-twenty-first-century critics of immigration no longer use the early-twentieth-century language of eugenics, some of them invoke the idea that immigrants will overwhelm the white population and lead the nation into decline. For instance, journalist and political commentator Patrick Buchanan, in a populist manifesto titled "America in 2050: Another Country," echoed this idea. In his article, he discussed, in dire tones, a census report that predicts that Americans of European descent will no longer be a majority by the year 2050. Like the IRL, Buchanan imagined an ideal past—in this case going back to 1960—when the nation was homogeneous and there was only a "smattering" of Latinos and Asians in the United States. He then warned that the immigration of Latinos was about to overwhelm the population of true Americans—that is, Euro-Americans—who are on the verge of losing their country. He blamed the "treason of elites" in business and academia for encouraging the immigration that would change the United States into "a nation unrecognizable to our parents, a giant Brazil of the North."[46]

On the other side of the debate, contemporary defenders of immigrants continue to use family imagery, especially that of mothers and children, as a way to criticize policies they see as too draconian. In a report to Congress in 2008, Janet Murguía, president and CEO of the National Council of La Raza, condemned recent workplace raids conducted by United States Immigration and Customs Enforcement officials to detain and deport undocumented workers. To illustrate her argument about the cruelty of these practices, Murguía emphasized the separation of families. She particularly stressed the forcible weaning of infants when breast-feeding mothers were held in detention and denied contact with their children.[47] *New York Times* columnist David Brooks also invoked mothers and children to demonstrate the exemplary family values of Mexican immigrants. In a column arguing that social conservatives should embrace a pro-immigrant position, he explained that "women who have recently arrived from Mexico have bigger, healthier babies than more affluent non-Hispanic white natives. That's because strong family and social networks support these pregnant women, reminding them what to eat and do."[48] Like Grace Abbott before him, Brooks made the case that immigrant women could show their native-born counterparts how to live up to the American value of dedication to family.

In both the present and the past, debates about immigration restriction have exposed as much about how Americans see themselves as they do about how Americans see outsiders. As we debate who can get into the country and who can stay, we make a larger case about what it takes to belong in the nation and have a say in its future. Almost a century ago, Grace Abbott, Louis Hammerling, and Prescott Hall used the literacy test debate to offer a broader vision about the limits and possibilities of the United States. Today, we continue that project, and in the process of debating the sort of men and women we want, we also reveal the sort of men and women we strive to be.

Notes

Introduction

1. As Roger Daniels points out, the signifiers of "old" and "new" for immigrants, while popular at the turn of the century and while congruent with some historical aspects of immigration, are misleading because they do not help historians understand "that there are similarities and differences over time both between groups and within groups." He suggests that a more useful description of difference between migration experiences would be to distinguish between migrants who mostly settled in rural areas (like those from Japan and Scandinavia) and those who settled in urban areas (like those from Ireland and Italy). Roger Daniels, *Coming to America: A History of Immigration and Ethnicity in American Life* (New York: Harper Perennial, 1990), 124, 122. For a broader view of Atlantic migrations in the late nineteenth and early twentieth centuries, see Walter Nugent, *Crossings: The Great Transatlantic Migrations, 1870–1914* (Bloomington: Indiana University Press, 1992).

2. It is not totally clear what the authors of the Naturalization Act of 1790 meant by "white," but historians suggest that it was meant to exclude Africans and those wholly or partially of African descent. This designation of whiteness carried over from state constitutions, like that of Virginia, which sought to ensure that free Northern blacks could not claim citizenship in their states. Noah Pickus, *True Faith and Allegiance: Immigration and American Civic Nationalism* (Princeton, NJ: Princeton University Press, 2005), 53–56.

3. "Statement of the Immigration Restriction League," in *Reports of the Immigration Commission: Statements and Recommendations Submitted by Societies and Organizations Interested in the Subject of Immigration* (Washington, DC: Government Printing Office, 1911), 107.

4. Ibid., 106–7.

5. Ibid., 107.

6. Ibid., 106–7.

7. Louis Hammerling, "Literacy and Character," *American Leader* 9 (April 13, 1916): 390.

8. Henry Mann, "Common Sense and Immigration," *American Leader* 4 (July 10, 1913): 37–38.

9. "Statement of the Immigrants' Protective League," in *Reports of the Immigration Commission*, 58.

10. This quote came from a speech Abbott gave at the National Conference for Good City Government in 1910. Grace Abbott, "The Education of Foreigners in American Citizenship," in *Proceedings of the National Conference for Good City Government* (Philadelphia: The League, 1910), 381.

11. E. P. Hutchinson, *Legislative History of American Immigration Policy, 1798–1965* (Philadelphia: University of Pennsylvania Press, 1981), 465–68.

12. Ibid., 63–109.

13. Quoted in Erika Lee, *At America's Gates: The Exclusion Era, 1882–1943* (Chapel Hill: University of North Carolina Press, 2003), 27.

14. Roger Daniels, *Guarding the Golden Door: American Immigration Policy and Immigrants since 1882* (New York: Hill and Wang, 2004), 3. For more on how the Chinese Exclusion Act shaped restriction against southeastern European immigrants, see Erika Lee, "The Chinese Exclusion Example: Race, Immigration, and American Gatekeeping, 1882–1924," *Journal of American Ethnic History* 21 (Spring 2002): 36–62; Lucy E. Salyer, *Laws Harsh as Tigers: Chinese Immigrants and the Shaping of Modern Immigration Law* (Chapel Hill: University of North Carolina Press, 1995).

15. David R. Roediger, *Working toward Whiteness: How America's Immigrants Became White* (New York: Basic Books, 2005), 50–54. For discussion on the racial construction of southeastern European immigrants during this time, see Nancy Foner, *In a New Land: A Comparative View of Immigration* (New York: New York University Press, 2005), 11–18; Stephen Cornell and Douglas Hartmann, "Conceptual Confusions and Divides: Race, Ethnicity, and the Study of Immigration," in *Not Just Black and White: Historical and Contemporary Perspectives on Immigration, Race, and Ethnicity in the United States*, ed. Nancy Foner and George M. Frederickson (New York: Russell Sage Foundation, 2004), 23–41.

16. *Congressional Record*, 54th Cong., 1st sess., 1896, vol. 28, pt. 3:2817.

17. *Congressional Record*, 54th Cong., 2nd sess., 1897, vol. 29, pt. 3:2667–68.

18. There has been much historiographical debate about the periodization and common attributes of the Progressive Era. In her essay "Men Are from the Gilded Age and Women Are from the Progressive Era," Elisabeth Israels Perry argues for a flexible periodization of the era as a way to be more inclusive of the political and social experiences of women. I agree that the movements for reform, especially those spearheaded by women, ranged from the late part of the nineteenth century through the New Deal Era, but since I am focusing on a policy debate, I am using the periodization of the Progressive Era that is more favored among political historians, between about 1900 and 1920. It was during this period that the greatest *legislative* response occurred to the changes caused by industrialization. See Perry, "Men Are from the Gilded Age and Women Are from the Progressive Era," *Journal of the Gilded Age and Progressive Era* 1 (October 2002): 25–48; Maureen A. Flanagan, *America Reformed: Progressives and Progressivisms, 1890s–1920s* (New York: Oxford University Press, 2007); Steven J. Diner, *A Very Different Age: Americans of the Progressive Era* (New York: Hill and Wang, 1998); Lewis L. Gould, *America in the Progressive Era, 1890–1914*, Seminar Series in History (New York: Pearson Education, 2001); John Whiteclay Chambers, II, *The Tyranny of Change: America in the Progressive Era, 1890–1920*, 2nd ed. (New Brunswick, NJ: Rutgers University Press, 2000); Alan Dawley, *Struggles for Justice: Social Responsibility and the Liberal States, 1877–1919* (Cambridge, MA: Belknap, 1991); John Milton Cooper, Jr., *The Pivotal Decades: The United States, 1900–1920* (New York: Norton, 1990); Richard McCormick, *The Party Period and Public Policy: American Politics from the Age of Jackson to the Progressive Era* (New York: Norton, 1970). For more analysis of the scholarship on the era, see Robert D. Johnson,

"Re-Democratizing the Progressive Era: The Politics of Progressive Era Political Historiography," *Journal of the Gilded Age and Progressive Era* I (January 2002): 68–92.

19. Congress passed two Immigration Acts during the first decade of the twentieth century, in 1903 and 1907. The Naturalization Act was passed in 1906. Hutchinson, *Legislative History*, 128–33, 138–42. For analysis of the relationship between physical disability and immigration law, see Douglas C. Bayton, "Defectives in the Land: Disability and American Immigration Policy, 1882–1924," *Journal of American Ethnic History* 24 (Spring 2005): 31–44.

20. For more on Roosevelt's views on immigration and the machinations around the 1907 Immigration Act, see Hans P. Vought, *The Bully Pulpit and the Melting Pot: American Presidents and the Immigrant, 1897–1933* (Macon, GA: Mercer University Press, 2004), 27–60; Robert F. Zeidel, *Immigrants, Progressives and Exclusion Politics* (DeKalb: Northern Illinois University Press, 2004), 21–36.

21. Zeidel, *Immigrants, Progressives and Exclusion Politics*, 114.

22. Ibid., 103–11.

23. Hutchinson, *Legislative History*, 149–68.

24. Daniels, *Guarding the Golden Door*, 34. For more on Taft's veto, see Zeidel, *Immigrants, Progressives and Exclusion Politics*, 123–25.

25. Quoted in Daniels, *Guarding the Golden Door*, 34. See also Zeidel, *Immigrants, Progressives and Exclusion Politics*, 126–28.

26. In the 1913–14 fiscal year, some 1.2 million people immigrated to the United States. In the 1915–16 fiscal year, that number was down to 300,000. Furthermore, an additional 125,000 immigrants migrated back to their homelands that year, so the net gain was just over 150,000. Roger Daniels, *Not Like Us: Immigrants and Minorities in America, 1890–1924*, The American Ways Series (Chicago: Ivan R. Dee, 1997), 80.

27. Nell Irvin Painter, *Standing at Armageddon: The United States, 1877–1919* (New York: Norton, 1987), 110–40.

28. Daniels, *Coming to America*, 122–24. As Walter Nugent points out, there was a great deal of return migration during this era, and so, while over 10 million arrived, the net gain to the American population was about 6.3 million. Nugent, *Crossings*, 150.

29. John Higham, *Strangers in the Land: Patterns of American Nativism, 1860–1925*, 2nd ed. (1955; repr., New Brunswick, NJ: Rutgers University Press, 1988), 70–72, 115. For more on how class ideologies shaped progressive reform, see Shelton Stromquist, *Re-Inventing "The People": The Progressive Movement, the Class Problem and the Origins of Modern Liberalism* (Urbana: University of Illinois Press, 2006).

30. Diner, *A Very Different Age*, 201.

31. See, for instance, Linda Gordon, "Putting Children First: Women, Maternalism, and Welfare in the Early Twentieth Century," in *U.S. History as Women's History: New Feminist Essays*, ed. Linda Kerber, Alice Kessler-Harris, and Kathryn Kish Sklar (Chapel Hill: University of North Carolina Press 1995), 63–86; Kathryn Kish Sklar, *Florence Kelley and the Nation's Work* (New Haven, CT: Yale University Press, 1995); Robyn Muncy, *Creating a Female Dominion in American Reform, 1890–1935* (New York: Oxford University Press, 1991); Gwendolyn Mink, *The Wages of Motherhood: Inequality in the Female State, 1917–1942* (Ithaca, NY: Cornell

University Press, 1995); Theda Skocpol, *Protecting Soldiers and Mothers: The Political Origins of Social Policy in the United States* (Cambridge, MA: Belknap, 1992); Noralee Frankel and Nancy S. Dye, eds., *Gender, Class, Race, and Reform in the Progressive Era* (Lexington, KY: University Press of Kentucky, 1991).

32. The number of children who attended high school increased 160 percent in the first decade of the twentieth century. Michael McGerr, *A Fierce Discontent: The Rise and Fall of the Progressive Movement in America* (New York: Free Press, 2003), 109–10. For more on the focus on education during this period, see Julie A. Reuben, "Beyond Politics: Community Civics and the Re-Definition of Citizenship in the Progressive Era," *History of Education Quarterly* 37 (Winter 1997): 399–420; Ronald K. Goodenow and Arthur White, eds., *Education and the Rise of the New South* (Boston: Hall, 1981).

33. Stromquist, *Re-Inventing "The People,"* 136; Pickus, *True Faith and Allegiance,* 96–100.

34. Kevin Gaines, *Uplifting the Race: Black Leadership, Politics, and Culture in the Twentieth Century* (Chapel Hill: University of North Carolina Press, 1996), 32–41; Neil R. McMillen, *Dark Journey: Black Mississippians in the Age of Jim Crow* (Urbana: University of Illinois Press, 1990), 72–108.

35. Maureen Flanagan, *Seeing with their Hearts: Chicago Women and the Vision of a Good City* (Princeton, NJ: Princeton University Press, 2002), 45–46.

36. In 1890, Mississippi became the first state to pass a literacy test as a means to disenfranchise African Americans and some poor whites. See McMillan, *Dark Journey,* 38–48, and Edward L. Ayers, *The Promise of the New South: Life after Reconstruction* (New York: Oxford University Press, 1992), 145–49. By 1908, seven Southern states (Mississippi, South Carolina, Louisiana, North Carolina, Alabama, Virginia, and Georgia) had a literacy provision for suffrage. J. Morgan Kousser, *The Shaping of Southern Politics: Suffrage Restriction and the Establishment of the One-Party South, 1880–1910* (New Haven, CT: Yale University Press, 1974), 239.

37. Bruce Baum, *The Rise and Fall of the Caucasian Race: A Political History of Racial Identity* (New York: New York University Press, 2006), 118–62; Roediger, *Working toward Whiteness,* 35–44.

38. Eric L. Goldstein, *The Price of Whiteness: Jews, Race and American Identity* (Princeton, NJ: Princeton University Press, 2006), 1–4.

39. Pickus, *True Faith and Allegiance,* 77–83.

40. For an examination of Franz Boas' impact, see Elazar Barkan, *The Retreat of Scientific Racism: Changing Concepts of Race in Britain and the United States between the World Wars* (Cambridge: Cambridge University Press, 1993), 66–132.

41. For work on the eugenics movement in the United States, see Daniel J. Kevles, *In the Name of Eugenics: Genetics and the Uses of Human Heredity* (Cambridge, MA: Harvard University Press, 1995); Edwin Black, *War against the Weak: Eugenics and America's Campaign to Create a Master Race* (New York: Thunder's Mouth, 2003).

42. Gary Gerstle, *American Crucible: Race and Nation in the Twentieth Century* (Princeton, NJ: Princeton University Press, 2001), 3–11. See also Rogers M. Smith, *Civic Ideals: Conflicting Visions of Citizenship in United States History* (New Haven, CT: Yale University Press, 1997), 448.

43. For an analysis of how civic nationalism was part of the literacy test debate, see Zeidel, *Immigrants, Progressives and Exclusion Politics,* 3–5.

44. Higham, *Strangers in the Land*, 3–11, 131–57, 191–93, 202–3. See also Daniels, *Guarding the Golden Door*, 31–35. For historians who developed the idea of racial nativism, see Barbara Miller Solomon, *Ancestors and Immigrants: A Changing New England Tradition* (Cambridge, MA: Harvard University Press, 1956); Thomas F. Gossett, *Race: The History of an Idea in America* (Dallas: Southern Methodist University Press, 1963); John S. Haller, Jr., *Outcasts from Evolution: Scientific Attitudes of Racial Inferiority, 1859–1900* (Urbana: University of Illinois, 1971); Philip Gleason, "American Identity and Americanization," in *Harvard Encyclopedia of American Ethnic Groups* (Cambridge, MA: Belknap, 1980), 41.

45. Matthew Frye Jacobson, *Whiteness of a Different Color: European Immigrants and the Alchemy of Race* (Cambridge, MA: Harvard University Press, 1998), 75. For more on the contingent nature of Euro-Americans' white identities in relation to immigration law, see Roediger, *Working toward Whiteness*, 133–56. For other literature dealing with the formation of white identities, particularly in the nineteenth century, see David R. Roediger, *The Wages of Whiteness: Race and the Making of the American Working Class* (New York: Verso, 1991); Neil Foley, *The White Scourge: Mexicans, Blacks and Poor Whites in Texas Cotton Culture* (Berkeley: University of California Press, 1997). See also Vron Ware, *Out of Whiteness: Color, Politics and Culture* (Chicago: University of Chicago Press, 2002); Matthew Pratt Guterl, *The Color of Race in America, 1900–1940* (Cambridge, MA: Harvard University Press, 2001); Alexander Saxton, *The Rise and Fall of the White Republic: Class Politics and Mass Culture in Nineteenth Century America* (New York: Verso, 1990); Theodore W. Allen, *The Invention of the White Race, Volume One: Racial Oppression and Social Control* (New York: Verso, 1994); Noel Ignatiev, *How the Irish Became White* (New York: Routledge, 1995); Russell A. Kazal, "Revisiting Assimilation: The Rise, Fall, and Reappraisal of a Concept in American Ethnic History," *American Historical Review* 100 (April 1995): 462.

46. Thomas Guglielmo, *White on Arrival: Italians, Race, Color and Power in Chicago, 1890–1945* (Oxford: Oxford University Press, 2003), 59–75.

47. Mae M. Ngai, *Impossible Subjects: Illegal Aliens and the Making of Modern America* (Princeton, NJ: Princeton University Press, 2004), 7.

48. Desmond King, *Making Americans: Immigration, Race and the Origins of the Diverse Democracy* (Cambridge, MA: Harvard University Press, 2000), 3. See also, Smith, *Civic Ideals*, 448.

49. Some historians of immigration restriction have looked at how gendered rhetoric was part of the racial construction of immigrants and native-born Americans, but this subject has not been a central part of their analysis of race. See Gerstle, *American Crucible*, 54–59.

50. Alice Kessler-Harris, *In Pursuit of Equity: Women, Men, and the Quest for Economic Citizenship in Twentieth Century America* (New York: Oxford University Press, 2001), 6.

51. There are many examples of scholarship that examine the ways Americans deployed gender ideologies in Progressive Era political debates. For a general analysis, see Perry, "Men Are from the Gilded Age," 25–48. For examples of specific ways these ideologies worked, see Kathryn Kish Sklar, "Two Political Cultures in the Progressive Era: The National Consumer's League and the American Association of Labor Legislation," in Kerber, Kessler-Harris, and Sklar, *U.S. History as Women's History*, 36–62; Glenda Elizabeth Gilmore, *Gender and Jim Crow: Women and the Politics of White Supremacy in North Carolina, 1896–1920* (Chapel Hill: University of North Carolina Press, 1996); Kristin Hoganson, *Fighting for American Manhood: How Gender Politics Provoked the Spanish-American and Philippine-American Wars* (New Haven,

CT: Yale University Press, 1998); Richard Slotkin, *Gunfighter Nation: The Myth of the Frontier in the Twentieth Century* (New York: Atheneum, 1992); Arnoldo Testi, "Gender and Reform Politics: Theodore Roosevelt and the Culture of Masculinity," *Journal of American History* 81 (March 1995): 1509–33; Susan Zeiger, "She Didn't Raise Her Boy to Be a Slacker: Motherhood, Conscription, and the Culture of the First World War," *Feminist Studies* 22 (Spring 1996): 9–12.

52. Evelyn Nakano Glenn, *Unequal Freedom: How Race and Gender Shaped American Citizenship and Labor* (Cambridge, MA: Harvard University Press, 2002), 13. Historians of African American women were some of the first scholars to analyze the interconnected construction of race and gender. See, for example, Deborah Grey White, *Aren't I a Woman: Female Slaves in the Plantation South* (New York: Norton, 1985); Hazel Carby, *Reconstructing Womanhood: The Emergence of the Afro-American Woman Novelist* (Oxford: Oxford University Press, 1987); Elsa Barkley Brown, "Womanist Consciousness: Maggie Lena Walker and the Independent Order of Saint Luke," *Signs* 14 (March 1989): 610–33. By the 1990s, historians were arguing that serious analysis of women's and gender history could not be done without analysis of race. See Evelyn Brooks Higginbotham, "African American Women's History and the Metalanguage of Race," *Signs* 17 (Winter 1992): 251–74; Iris Berger, Elsa Barkley Brown, and Nancy Hewitt, "Symposium—Intersections and Collision Courses: Women, Blacks and Workers Confront Gender, Race and Class," *Feminist Studies* 18 (Summer 1992): 283–326.

53. For example, see Jacquelyn Dowd Hall, *Revolt Against Chivalry: Jessie Daniel Ames and the Women's Campaign against Lynching* (New York: Columbia University Press, 1979); Kathleen Blee, *Women of the Klan: Racism and Gender in the 1920's* (Berkeley: University of California Press, 1991); Kristin Hoganson, "Garrisonian Abolitionists and the Rhetoric of Gender, 1850–1860," *American Quarterly* 45 (December 1993): 558–95; Nancy MacLean, *Behind the Mask of Chivalry: The Making of the Second Ku Klux Klan* (New York: Oxford University Press, 1994); Gail Bederman, *Manliness and Civilization: A Cultural History of Gender and Race in the United States, 1880–1917* (Chicago: University of Chicago Press, 1995); Gilmore, *Gender and Jim Crow*; Martha Hodes, *White Women, Black Men: Illicit Sex in the Nineteenth Century South* (New Haven, CT: Yale University Press, 1999).

54. Moreover, this act changed the 1802 National Act, which stated that if a "parent" was a citizen, then so was the child, and decreed that only the father of a child had to be a citizen to make the child a citizen. Candice Lewis Bredbenner, *A Nationality of Her Own: Women, Marriage and the Law of Citizenship* (Berkeley: University of California Press, 1998), 18–21.

55. Eithne Luibhéid, *Entry Denied: Controlling Sexuality at the Border* (Minneapolis: University of Minnesota Press, 2002), 41–42. This law was especially aimed at Chinese women. See also Lee, *At America's Gates*, 77–109; Martha Gardner, *The Qualities of a Citizen: Women, Immigration, and Citizenship, 1870–1965* (Princeton, NJ: Princeton University Press, 2005).

56. Nancy F. Cott, *Public Vows: A History of Marriage and the Nation* (Cambridge, MA: Harvard University Press, 2000), 136–37; Gardner, *Qualities of a Citizen*, 50–60.

57. For work on race, nineteenth-century women, and political activism, see Alisse Portnoy, *Their Right to Speak: Women's Activism in the Indian and Slave Debates* (Cambridge, MA: Harvard University Press, 2005); Lori Ginzberg, *Women and the Work of Benevolence: Morality, Politics, and*

Class in the Nineteenth Century United States (New Haven, CT: Yale University Press, 1990); Nancy Isenberg, *Sex and Citizenship in Antebellum America* (Chapel Hill: University of North Carolina Press, 1998); Susan Zaeske, *Signatures of Citizenship: Petitioning, Anti-Slavery, and Women's Political Identity* (Chapel Hill: University of North Carolina Press, 2003); Louise Michele Newman, *White Women's Rights: The Racial Origins of Feminism in the United States* (New York: Oxford University Press, 1999). For work on how white, middle-class women articulated political and economic places for themselves at the turn of the century, see Muncy, *Creating a Female Dominion*, 1–37; Seth Koven and Sonya Michel, eds., *Mothers of a New World: Maternalist Politics and the Origins of Welfare States* (New York: Routledge, 1993).

58. This relationship between citizenship and belonging became a highly gendered point of contestation in immigration policy debates. See Gardner, *Qualities of a Citizen*, 8–9. For works that break down binary views of gender in order to explore the relationship between gender and citizenship, see Barbara Hobson and Ruth Lister, "Citizenship," in *Contested Concepts in Gender and Social Politics*, ed. Barbara Hobson, Jane Lewis, and Birte Siim (Cheltenham, UK: Edward Elgar, 2002), 23–48; Birte Siim, *Gender and Citizenship: Politics and Agency in France, Britain and Denmark* (Cambridge: Cambridge University Press, 2000); Peggy Pascoe, "Miscegenation Law, Court Cases, and Ideologies of 'Race' in Twentieth-Century America," *Journal of American History* 83 (June 1996): 44–69; Nancy Fraser and Linda Gordon, "A Genealogy of Dependency: Tracing a Keyword of the U.S. Welfare State," *Signs* 19 (December 1994): 323–42.

59. Testi, "Gender and Reform Politics," 1512.

60. For work on how men and women used competing ideologies of masculinity and femininity in policy debates, see Sklar, "Two Political Cultures," 36–62.

Chapter One

1. Walter Nugent points out that the number of German and English migrants continued to grow, but only by about 25–30 percent, while the number from Poland grew by 300 percent and those from Italy and Russia grew by over 400 percent. While English, Irish, and German migrants still made up the majority, southeastern European immigrants had become a much bigger share of the total by 1890. Nugent, *Crossings*, 151.

2. "Publications of the Immigration Restriction League, no. 1: The Present Aspect of the Immigration Problem," 1894, Papers of the Immigration Restriction League, vol. 1, Boston Public Library, p. 14. (Collection hereafter cited as IRL Papers, BPL.)

3. Daniels, *Guarding the Golden Door*, 31. Lodge publicly advocated for restriction in 1891 in a series of articles: "The Restriction of Immigration," *The North American Review* 152 (January 1891): 27–36; and "Lynch Law and Unrestricted Immigration," *The North American Review* 152 (May 1891): 602–12. A record of the strong connection between Lodge and the Immigration Restriction League can be found in a scrapbook titled "Records of the Executive Committee of the Immigration Restriction League and the Meetings of the League, May 1894–December 1902, Volume 1," Records of the Immigration Restriction League, Box 2, Houghton Library, Harvard University. (Collection hereafter cited as IRL Records, HL.) See also Charles Warren, "Immigration Restriction League Annual Report

of the Executive Committee for 1895," submitted January 13, 1896, IRL Records, Box 7, HL. See also Solomon, *Ancestors and Immigrants*, 116–19.

4. Lodge declared in a letter that the bill he would introduce in the Senate, S. 2147, "was drawn by the Immigration Restriction League of Boston." Henry Cabot Lodge to Lawrence Cummings, Esq., 18 December 1895, Henry Cabot Lodge Letterbooks, vol. 31, pt. 1, Massachusetts Historical Society, Boston, MA. (Collection hereafter cited as Lodge Letterbooks, MHS.)

5. *Congressional Record*, 54th Cong., 1st sess., 1896, vol. 28, pt. 3:2817. The idea of a literacy test was first introduced by economist Edward Bemis, and he saw as its purpose restricting southeastern European immigrants. Edward W. Bemis, "Restriction of Immigration," *Andover Review* 9 (March 1888): 263. See also John Higham, "Origins of Immigration Restriction, 1882–1897: A Social Analysis," *Mississippi Valley Historical Review* 39 (June 1952): 81.

6. *Congressional Record*, 54th Cong., 1st sess., 1896, vol. 28, pt. 3:2820. Here Lodge was quoting the observation of M. Paul Bourget, a French novelist.

7. Ibid., 3:2819–20. Lodge was quoting Gustave LeBon when describing the qualities of Anglo-Saxons. Often these definitions contrasted men with women, who did not possess these qualities. See Cynthia Eagle Russett, *Sexual Science: The Victorian Construction of Womanhood* (Cambridge, MA: Harvard University Press, 1989), 81, 91; Bederman, *Manliness and Civilization*, 16–31. See also E. Anthony Rotundo, "Learning about Manhood: Gender Ideals and the Middle-Class Family in Nineteenth Century America," in *Manliness and Morality: Middle-Class Masculinity in Britain and America, 1800–1940*, ed. J. A. Mangan and James Walvin (New York: St. Martin's, 1987), 35–51.

8. *Congressional Record*, 54th Cong., 1st sess., 1896, vol. 28, pt. 3:2819–20.

9. Ibid., 3:2819. Daniels, *Guarding the Golden Door*, 31.

10. *Congressional Record*, 54th Cong., 1st sess., 1896, vol. 28, pt. 3:2820.

11. Jacobson, *Whiteness of a Different Color*, 77–78.

12. For more on the development of ideas about Social Darwinism and eugenics in the nineteenth century, and the distinction between different branches, see Kevles, *In the Name of Eugenics*, 3–21; Mike Hawkins, *Social Darwinism in European and American Thought, 1860–1945: Nature as Model and Nature as Threat* (Cambridge: Cambridge University Press, 1997), 61–68, 104–22, 186–91; Black, *War against the Weak*, 12–16; Alexandra Mina Stern, *Eugenic Nation: Faults and Frontiers of Better Breeding in Modern America* (Berkeley: University of California Press, 2005), 14–15.

13. *Congressional Record*, 54th Cong., 1st sess., 1896, vol. 28, pt. 3:2820.

14. A third founder, Charles Warren, was to become an eminent Constitutional historian and fell away from the IRL soon after its founding.

15. Solomon, *Ancestors and Immigrants*, 89–102.

16. Bluford Adams, "World Conquest or a Dying People? Racial Theory, Regional Anxiety, and the Brahmin Anglo-Saxonists," *Journal of the Gilded Age and Progressive Era* 8 (April 2009): 192.

17. Solomon, *Ancestors and Immigrants*, 1–2; Gossett, *Race*, 304.

18. Painter, *Standing at Armageddon*, 110–40.

19. For work on nineteenth-century women and political activism, see Ginzberg, *Women and the Work of Benevolence*, and Isenberg, *Sex and Citizenship*.

20. Jennings L. Wagoner, Jr., "Charles W. Eliot, Immigrants, and the Decline of American Idealism," *Biography* 8, no. I (1984): 27.

21. Solomon, *Ancestors and Immigrants*, 100.

22. Ibid., 101.

23. Higham, *Strangers in the Land*, 3–11.

24. For a discussion of the Chinese Exclusion Act, see Lee, *At America's Gates*, 19–74; Ronald Takaki, *Strangers from a Different Shore: A History of Asian Americans* (Boston: Little, Brown, 1989), 197–212.

25. Higham, *Strangers in the Land*, 68–87.

26. As both Barbara Solomon and John Higham have argued, the IRL clearly approached the immigration issue from an educated, patrician point of view, and class privilege suffused their work. Higham, *Strangers in the Land*, 102, Solomon, *Ancestors and Immigrants*, 99–102.

27. Daniels, *Guarding the Golden Door*, 31.

28. Records of the Executive Committee of the Immigration Restriction League, vol. I, May 1894–December 1902, 17 August 1894 meeting, IRL Records, Box 2, HL.

29. The figurehead president of the IRL was John Fiske. The vice presidents listed in 1896 were Samuel B. Capen, Hon. James R. Dunbar, Hon. George F. Evans, George Hale, Henry Lee, Richmond Mayo Smith, Robert Treat Paine, Hon. Henry Parkman, Thomas Ring, and Nathaniel Shaler. Records of the Executive Committee of the Immigration Restriction League, vol. I, May 1894–December 1902, IRL Records, Box 2, HL. The majority of the membership was from New England, particularly Massachusetts, but in their first annual report they emphasized the need to expand membership beyond that region. Immigration Restriction League Annual Report of the Executive Committee, 14 January 1895, IRL Papers, vol. I, BPL.

30. According to their annual report, by January of 1895, the IRL had 531 members and had created 5 documents, of which they circulated a total of thirty-eight thousand copies. Immigration Restriction League Annual Report of the Executive Committee, 14 January 1895, IRL Papers, vol. I, BPL.

31. Right from the beginning, they advocated a three-pronged approach to immigration restriction: imposing a head tax of ten dollars per person; having consular officials exclude undesirables before they got on the boats; and requiring immigrants to pass a literacy test. See "Publication of the Immigration Restriction League, no. I: The Present Aspect of Our Immigration Problem," IRL Papers, vol. I, BPL. By the late 1890s, however, the literacy test had become the focus of their attention.

32. "Publications of the Immigration Restriction League, no. 6: The Educational Test as a Means of Further Restricting Immigration," IRL Papers, vol. 2, BPL. For other examples, see "Publications of the Immigration Restriction League, no. 2: Study These Figures and Draw Your Own Conclusions," 1895; "Publications of the Immigration Restriction League, no. 7: Latest Statistics about Immigration to April 1895"; "Publications of the Immigration Restriction League, no. 10: Distribution of Illiterate Immigrants"; "Publications of the Immigration Restriction League, no. 15: Immigration Figures for 1896";

"Publications of the Immigration Restriction League, no. 19: Immigration Figures for 1897"; "Publications of the Immigration Restriction League, no. 20: Endorsements of the Illiteracy Test," Joseph Lee Papers, Box 7, Massachusetts Historical Society, Boston, MA. (Collection hereafter cited as Joseph Lee Papers, MHS.) These pamphlets were distributed to both individuals and newspapers.

33. For the way the Chinese Exclusion Act shaped immigration restriction of Europeans, as well as the administrative and judicial approaches to immigration, see Lee, "The Chinese Exclusion Example," 36–62; Salyer, *Laws Harsh as Tigers*. For information on the class-based arguments against Chinese immigrants, see Peter Kwong, *Forbidden Workers: Illegal Chinese Immigrants and American Labor* (New York: The New Press, 1997), 145–51.

34. For an example of how Americans connected issues of manliness to white supremacy, see Bederman, *Manliness and Civilization*, 16–31. For other works on the construction of manhood during this time, see Kim Townsend, *Manhood at Harvard: William James and Others* (New York: Norton, 1996); Mark Carnes, *Meanings for Manhood: Constructions of Masculinity in Victorian America* (Chicago: University of Chicago Press, 1990); E. Anthony Rotundo, *American Manhood: Transformations in Masculinity from the Revolution to the Modern Era* (New York: Basic Books, 1993); Ava Baron, "An 'Other' Side of Gender Antagonism at Work: Men, Boys, and the Remasculinization of Printers' Work, 1830–1920," in *Work Engendered: Toward a New History of American Labor*, ed. Ava Baron (Ithaca, NY: Cornell University Press, 1991), 47–69.

35. Nayan Shah, *Contagious Divides: Epidemics and Race in San Francisco's Chinatown* (Berkeley: University of California Press, 2001), 77. For work on the gender ratio of Chinese immigrants and the migration of Chinese women, see Karen J. Leong, "'A Distant and Antagonistic Race': Constructions of Chinese Manhood in the Exclusionist Debates, 1869–1878," in *Across the Great Divide: Cultures of Manhood in the American West*, ed. Matthew Basso, Laura McCall, and Dee Garceau (New York: Routledge, 2000), 131–48. Nineteenth-century California doctors also linked Chinese immigration to the opium trade, which they argued threatened white domesticity by degenerating bodies and increasing the sexual appetites of women. Diana L. Ahmad, "Opium Smoking, Anti-Chinese Attitudes, and the American Medical Community," *American Nineteenth Century History* 1 (Summer 2000): 59.

36. "Publications of the Immigration Restriction League, no. 4: Twenty Reasons Why Immigration Should be Further Restricted Now," 1896, Joseph Lee Papers, Box 7, MHS.

37. "Publications of the Immigration Restriction League, no. 1: The Present Aspect of the Immigration Problem," 7.

38. Mayo Smith's book *Emigration and Immigration*, published in 1890, was the first academic tome that used scientific criteria to support immigration restriction. Richmond Mayo Smith, *Emigration and Immigration: A Study in Social Science* (New York: Charles Scribner's Sons, 1890). For Mayo Smith's views on race, see Solomon, *Ancestors and Immigrants*, 128–29.

39. Richmond Mayo Smith, "The Assimilation of Nationalities II," *Political Science Quarterly* 9 (December 1894): 670.

40. Prescott Hall to the Editor of the *Boston Herald*, 25 June 1894, IRL Papers, vol. I, BPL.

41. A. M. Craig to the Editor of the *Boston Herald*, 3 July 1894, IRL Papers, vol. I, BPL.

42. Prescott Hall to the Editor of the *Boston Herald*, 5 July 1894, IRL Papers, vol. I, BPL.

43. For analysis of eugenics as a form of control, see Christina Cogdell, *Eugenic Design: Streamlining America in the 1930s* (Philadelphia: University of Pennsylvania Press, 2004), 4–5.

44. Hawkins, *Social Darwinism*, 201–3.

45. See, for example, speeches in the House of Representatives by Republican Representatives Richard Bartholdt, Robert Tracewell, John Corliss, and Elijah Morse. *Congressional Record*, 54th Cong., 1st sess., 1896, vol. 28, pt. 6:5417–34.

46. Ibid., 6:5417. Also, congressmen added many other provisions to this bill, including one that excluded so-called birds of passage, that is, migrant laborers who went back and forth from the United States to their homelands.

47. Painter, *Standing at Armageddon*, ix–xiii; Higham, *Strangers in the Land*, 107–9. For work on the changing conditions of working-class men, see David Montgomery, "Workers' Control of Machine Production in the Nineteenth Century," *Labor History* 17 (Fall 1976): 485–509, and David Halle, *America's Working Man: Work, Home, and Politics among Blue Collar Property Owners* (Chicago: University of Chicago Press, 1984). For work on the implications of these changes on gender ideologies, see Thomas Winter, *Making Men, Making Class: The YMCA and Workingmen, 1877–1920* (Chicago: University of Chicago Press, 2002), and Baron, "An 'Other' Side."

48. Jeanne Petit, "Breeders, Workers and Mothers: Gender and the Congressional Literacy Test Debates, 1896–97," *Journal of the Gilded Age and Progressive Era* 3 (January 2004): 48–52.

49. Cott, *Public Vows*, 142.

50. *Congressional Record*, 54th Cong., 1st sess., 1896, vol. 28, pt. 6:5417.

51. For works on the relationship between work and middle-class manhood and womanhood in the nineteenth century, see Mary P. Ryan, *Cradle of the Middle Class: The Family in Oneida County, New York, 1790–1865* (Cambridge: Cambridge University Press, 1981); Jeanne Boydston, *Home and Work: Housework, Wages, and the Ideology of Labor in the Early Republic* (New York: Oxford University Press, 1990); Paula Baker, "The Domestication of Politics: Women and American Political Society, 1780–1920," *American Historical Review* 89 (June 1984): 625–27. See also Nancy F. Cott, "Marriage and Women's Citizenship in the United States, 1830–1934," *American Historical Review* 103 (December 1998): 1440–74. For the role of immigrant women in manufacturing work, see Alice Kessler-Harris, *Out to Work: A History of Wage-Earning Women in the United States* (Oxford: Oxford University Press, 1982), 123–28. See also Donna Gabaccia, *From the Other Side: Women, Gender and Immigrant Life in the United States, 1820–1990* (Bloomington: Indiana University Press, 1994); Susan Glenn, *Daughters of the Shtetl: Life and Labor in the Immigrant Generation* (Ithaca, NY: Cornell University Press, 1990); Elizabeth Ewen, *Immigrant Women in the Land of Dollars: Life and Culture in the Lower East Side, 1890–1925* (New York: Monthly Review, 1985).

52. *Congressional Record*, 54th Cong., 1st sess., 1896, vol. 28, pt. 6:5418. Some of the illiteracy rates of immigrants from specific nations listed on the chart were: Italy, 52.93%; Poland, 39.82%; Russia, 36.42%; England, 3.5%; The Netherlands, 3.38%; Germany, 2.49%; Sweden, 0.74%.

53. *Congressional Record*, 54th Cong., 1st sess., 1896, vol. 28, pt. 6:5423.

54. *Congressional Record*, 54th Cong., 2nd sess., 1897, vol. 29, pt. 2:1677.

55. Ibid., 2:1230.

56. Cott, *Public Vows*, 135–36. For work on how gender ideologies shaped the ways Americans understood Chinese immigrants, see Leong, "'A Distant and Antagonistic Race,'" 131–48; Shah, *Contagious Divides*, 77; George Anthony Peffer, *If They Don't Bring Their Women Here: Chinese Female Immigration before Exclusion* (Urbana: University of Illinois Press, 1999).

57. Hutchinson, *Legislative History*, 120.

58. *Congressional Record*, 54th Cong., 2nd sess., 1897, vol. 29, pt. 2:1219.

59. Ibid., 2:1227.

60. Ibid., 2:1222.

61. Many accused Lodge and other supporters of the bill as using it to limit the power of Democrats in Congress, which was no doubt partly true, but the supporters of election reform also wanted to help enfranchise African Americans. Richard E. Welch, Jr., "The Federal Elections Bill of 1890: Postscripts and Prelude," *Journal of American History* 52 (December 1965): 511–26.

62. See McMillen, *Dark Journey*, 38–48, and Ayers, *Promise of the New South*, 145–49. By 1908, seven Southern states (Mississippi, South Carolina, Louisiana, North Carolina, Alabama, Virginia, and Georgia) had a literacy provision for suffrage. Kousser, *Shaping of Southern Politics*, 239.

63. Higham, *Strangers in the Land*, 113. See also Rowland T. Berthoff, "Southern Attitudes toward Immigration, 1865–1914," *Journal of Southern History* 17 (August 1951): 328–60.

64. *Congressional Record*, 54th Cong., 1st sess., 1896, vol. 28, pt. 6:5436. Louisiana had a high percentage of Italian immigrants and Italian-Americans in its population, particularly in New Orleans, so it would make sense that Louisiana congressmen would stand up and defend Italian migration. Daniels, *Coming to America*, 192–93. By the 1890s, however, Italians in Louisiana were facing more hostility. See George E. Cunningham, "The Italian, a Hindrance to White Solidarity in Louisiana, 1890–1898," *Journal of Negro History* 50 (January 1965): 22–36.

65. *Congressional Record*, 54th Cong., 2nd sess., 1897, vol. 29, pt. 2:1926. Caffery was quoting an Italian official when he made this point.

66. *Congressional Record*, 54th Cong., 1st sess., 1896, vol. 28, pt. 6:5481.

67. *Congressional Record*, 54th Cong., 2nd sess., 1897, vol. 29, pt. 2:1425.

68. Cott, *Public Vows*, 11–12.

69. For work on nineteenth-century women and political activism, see Portnoy, *Their Right to Speak*; Zaeske, *Signatures of Citizenship*. The link between white supremacy and women's political activism is made most explicitly in Newman, *White Women's Rights*. For work on how white, middle-class women articulated political and economic places for themselves at the turn of the century, see Muncy, *Creating a Female Dominion*, 1–37; Koven and Michel, *Mothers of a New World*.

70. *Congressional Record*, 54th Cong., 2nd sess., 1896, vol. 29, pt. 1:72. Vest was responding to an earlier bill of Lodge's, one that he had presented to the Senate before the conference committee even met.

71. Lodge's contention that immigrant women posed a racial threat by their breeding foreshadowed eugenic arguments against immigrant women in the early twentieth century. See Katrina Irving, *Immigrant Mothers: Narratives of Race and Maternity, 1890–1925* (Urbana: University of Illinois Press, 2000), and Ann Marie Nicolosi, "'We Do Not Want Our Girls to Marry Foreigners': Gender, Race and American Citizenship," *NWSA Journal* 13 (Fall 2003): 1–21.

72. *Congressional Record*, 54th Cong., 2nd sess., 1896, vol. 29, pt. 1:72.

73. *Congressional Record*, 54th Cong., 2nd sess., 1897, vol. 29, pt. 2:1222–23.

74. Linda Kerber argues that, during the time of the Early Republic, women had begun to make a case for citizenship by arguing that their roles as mothers had national significance. See Linda Kerber, *Women of the Republic: Intellect and Ideology in Revolutionary America* (New York: Norton, 1986).

75. *Congressional Record*, 54th Cong., 2nd sess., 1896, vol. 29, pt. 1:73–74.

76. *Congressional Record*, 54th Cong., 2nd sess., 1897, vol. 29, pt. 2:1921. Cott, *Public Vows*, 141–42. For analysis of how marital status affected the legal status of immigrant women, see Gardner, *Qualities of a Citizen*, 13–49; Bredbenner, *A Nationality of Her Own*, 15–44.

77. Hutchinson, *Legislative History*, 121.

78. Of the 217 affirmative votes for the bill in the House, 178 came from Republicans, 36 came from Democrats, and 3 came from Populists. *Congressional Record*, 54th Cong., 2nd sess., 1896, vol. 29, pt. 2:1677, 1937–38.

79. Of the 36 votes against the final literacy test bill in the House, 25 came from Democrats from former slave states, and 2 came from Republicans from former slave states (7 other Republicans also voted against it). In the Senate, 25 of the 31 votes against the bill came from Democrats, and 16 of those were Democrats from former slave states. Four Republicans and a member of the Silver Party (Stewart of Nevada) also voted against the bill.

80. Vought, *Bully Pulpit*, 11–12, 19–20.

81. *Congressional Record*, 54th Cong., 2nd sess., 1897, vol. 29, pt. 3:2667–68.

82. Prescott Hall, "Annual Report of the Executive Committee for 1896," submitted 11 January 1897, IRL Records, Box 7, HL.

83. Prescott Hall to Members of the IRL, 4 March 1897, IRL Records, Box 7, HL.

84. Daniels, *Guarding the Golden Door*, 33.

85. Higham, *Strangers in the Land*, 106–7.

86. Notes from the Saturday, April 1, 1899 Meeting, Records of the Executive Committee of the Immigration Restriction League, May 1894–December 1902, IRL Records, Box 2, HL.

Chapter Two

1. Daniels, *Coming to America*, 122–24. As Walter Nugent points out, there was a great deal of return migration during this era, and so while over 10 million immigrants arrived, the net gain to the American population was only about 6.3 million. Nugent, *Crossings*, 150.

2. Robert DeCourcy Ward, "National Eugenics in Relation to Immigration," *North American Review* 192 (July 1910): 59.

3. Abbott, "Education of Foreigners," 377, 382.

4. Ibid., 384.

5. Ward, "National Eugenics," 63.

6. Higham, *Strangers in the Land*, 106–30. See also Rivka Shpak Lissak, "The National Liberal Immigration League and Immigration Restriction, 1906–1917," *The American Jewish Archives* 47, no. 2 (1994): 197–246; Robert C. Parmet, *Labor and Immigration in Industrial America* (Boston: Twayne, 1981), 152.

7. Parmet, *Labor and Immigration*, 152; Higham, *Strangers in the Land*, 128–29.

8. Higham, *Strangers in the Land*, 164.

9. Quoted in Hutchinson, *Legislative History*, 127–28.

10. Ibid., 128–33.

11. In March of 1903 Lodge wrote to Prescott Hall, "As it was the short session and we were blocked with the statehood bill, the determined opposition of one or two men would have been sufficient to defeat the bill. For this reason we took out the educational test in order to save the rest which was of very great value indeed in its administrative features and especially so after the Senate added what were known as the 'Anarchist clauses.'" Henry Cabot Lodge to Prescott Hall, 20 March 1903, IRL Records, Box 5, HL.

12. For analysis on the relationship between physical disability and immigration law, see Bayton, "Defectives in the Land," 31–44.

13. Hutchinson, *Legislative History*, 138–42.

14. For more on Roosevelt's views on immigration and the machinations around the 1907 Immigration Act, see Vought, *Bully Pulpit*, 27–60; Zeidel, *Immigrants, Progressives and Exclusion Politics*, 21–36.

15. Lissak, "National Liberal Immigration League," 215, 223.

16. Zeidel, *Immigrants, Progressives and Exclusion Politics*, 27–36.

17. The IRL kept files of the literature of opposition groups, including the Society for the Protection of Italian Immigrants, the United Hebrew Charities, and the National Americanization Committee. Hall also struck up a fairly congenial correspondence with the head of the National Liberal Immigration League, with whom he traded literature and debated points. IRL Records, Box 5, HL.

18. Prescott Hall to C. H. Parkhurst, 24 January 1907, IRL Records, Box 5, HL. Hall also pointed out that Jews were the managers of the North German Lloyd and Hamburg American shipping lines that transported many of the immigrants from Europe, and that Jewish bankers were close to transportation interests.

19. Solomon, *Ancestors and Immigrants*, 123–26, 136–40. In a letter years later, Joseph Lee described Patten's work in detail in order to counter the charge that the IRL was a "purely academic" organization. Patten, he wrote, attended numerous conventions and pushed to have restriction amendments added to various groups' platforms. In Lee's words, Patten was "on the most intimate terms with a great many members of Congress," and "conducted hearings, drafted amendments, and sat up nights with them devising plans of campaign." Joseph Lee to Mrs. Moors, 9 August 1917, Joseph Lee Papers, Box 2, File 18, MHS.

20. In the first year after their reorganization, for instance, they issued seven pamphlets—with titles like "Census Figures for 1900," "Immigration Figures for 1901," and "Digest of Immigration Statistics"—that continued to show what they saw as an alarming increase of southeastern European immigrants. Other pamphlets, such as "Reasons for the Education Test" and "Effects of the Educational Test on Germans," clearly demonstrated, in the minds of the IRL, that a literacy test would target southeastern Europeans over desirable northwestern European immigrants, like Germans. Immigration Restriction League Annual Report of the Executive Committee for the Period from May 16, 1901, to June 30, 1902, Submitted by the Secretary, Prescott Hall, 30 June 1902, IRL Records, Box 7, HL.

21. William Ripley, *The Races of Europe: A Sociological Study* (New York: D. Appleton, 1899). See also Higham, *Strangers in the Land*, 154–56, and Guterl, *Color of Race in America*, 16–22.

22. Roediger, *Working toward Whiteness*, 11.

23. "Publications of the Immigration Restriction League no. 48: General Immigration Statistics—Effects of Immigration upon the United States and Reasons for Further Restriction," 1904, IRL Records, Box 7, HL.

24. Mendel had originally published his theories in 1866, but at the time they remained ignored. It was not until around 1900 that German, Dutch, British, and American scientists rediscovered his writings. Kevles, *In the Name of Eugenics*, 41–43; Black, *War against the Weak*, 25–27.

25. For background on Charles Davenport and positive and negative eugenics, see Black, *War against the Weak*, 18–19, 33–41; Kevles, *In the Name of Eugenics*, 41–56; Garland Allan, "The Misuse of Biological Hierarchies: The American Eugenics Movement, 1900–1940," *History and Philosophy of the Life Sciences* 5, no. 2 (1983): 110–12; Stern, *Eugenic Nation*, 9.

26. Diane Paul, *Controlling Human Heredity: 1865–Present* (Atlantic Highlands, NJ: Humanities Press, 1995), 76–77.

27. Wendy Kline, *Building a Better Race: Gender, Sexuality, and Eugenics from the Turn of the Century to the Baby Boom* (Berkeley: University of California Press, 2001), 5. For other work on gender ideologies and eugenics, see Nancy Leys Stepan, *The Hour of Eugenics: Race, Gender and Nation in Latin America* (Ithaca, NY: Cornell University Press, 1991).

28. For more on John Commons' scholarship and approach to immigration, see Roger Horne, "John R. Commons and the Progressive Context," *Midwest Quarterly* 22 (Spring 1991): 336–37.

29. John R. Commons, *Races and Immigrants in America*, 2nd ed. (New York: Macmillan, 1920), 7.

30. "Publications of the Immigration Restriction League no. 48."

31. Edward A. Ross, "The Causes of Racial Superiority," *Annals of the American Academy of Political and Social Science* 18 (July 1901): 88. See Gail Bederman's discussion of E. A. Ross and race suicide in *Manliness and Civilization*, 200–206.

32. John D'Emilio and Estelle B. Freedman, *Intimate Matters: A History of Sexuality in America* (New York: Harper and Row, 1988), 86.

33. Books that deal with the relationship between race and sexual power include: Hall, *Revolt Against Chivalry*; Blee, *Women of the Klan*; MacLean, *Behind the Mask of Chivalry*; Gilmore, *Gender and Jim Crow*; Grace Elizabeth Hale, *Making Whiteness: The Culture of Segregation in the South,*

1890–1940 (New York: Vintage, 1998). See also Gail Bederman, "'Civilization,' the Decline of Middle-Class Manliness, and Ida B. Wells's Anti-Lynching Campaign (1892–94)," *Radical History Review* 52 (Winter 1992): 5–30.

34. Hale, *Making Whiteness*, 46; Bederman, *Manliness and Civilization*, 46–53. For an examination of the formation of Jim Crow Laws, see McMillen, *Dark Journey*. For an examination of scientific racism at this time, see Haller, Jr., *Outcasts from Evolution*.

35. For work on the desire of white Southern farmers for immigrant labor, see Berthoff, "Southern Attitudes," 328–60.

36. Robert DeCourcy Ward, "Immigration and the South," *Atlantic Monthly* 96 (November 1905): 612.

37. The first question asked respondents to list the order of "classes of persons . . . which are desired," and it listed "native born; persons from northern Europe; skilled persons; families with some money, intending to settle in the country; British; Scandinavians; Germans." The next question asked the reader to list which persons were not desired, and under this heading it listed "foreign born; southern and eastern Europeans; Asiatics; illiterates; those settling in the city and adverse to country life; immigrants distributed from eastern cities." Survey written by Prescott Hall, 22 July 1905, IRL Records, Box 5, HL.

38. Prescott Hall to Henry Cabot Lodge, 23 January 1906, IRL Records, Box 5, HL.

39. Robert DeCourcy Ward, "Alien Immigration and the Need of Farm Labor," *Official Proceedings of the 25th Annual Convention of the Farmers' National Congress of the United States* (Indianapolis: Farmers' National Congress, 1905), 105–9.

40. Prescott Hall, *Immigration and Its Effects upon the United States* (New York: Henry Holt, 1908), 305.

41. Prescott Hall, "Eugenics, Ethics and Immigration," Joseph Lee Papers, Box 7, MHS, p. 10. This idea was first suggested in a 1903 IRL pamphlet, "Demand of American Labor for Restriction of Immigration and an Illiteracy Test for Immigrants," which was, in part, a reprint of a letter by Samuel Gompers of the American Federation of Labor. In his letter, Gompers made an economic, rather than racial, argument about survival of the fittest: "The fittest survive; that is, those that fit the conditions best. But it is the economically weak, not the economically strong, that fit the conditions of the labor market. They fit because they can be got to work cheapest . . . the Chinaman and others drive out the American, the German and the Irishman." IRL Records, Box 7, HL.

42. Prescott Hall, "Eugenics, Ethics and Immigration," 7.

43. Ward "National Eugenics," 61–62.

44. Ibid., 63.

45. This quote comes from a statement by Addams presented in the IPL's statement to the Dillingham Commission. "Statement of the Immigrants' Protective League," 61.

46. Faith Rogow, *Gone to Another Meeting: The National Council of Jewish Women, 1893–1993* (Tuscaloosa: University of Alabama Press, 1993), 136–42. For more on the work of the NCJW and the connections between the NCJW and the WTUL and the creation of the IPL, see Suronda Gonzalez, "Immigrants in Our Midst: Grace Abbott, The Immigrants' Protective League of Chicago, and the New American Citizenship, 1908–1924" (PhD diss., State University of New York, 2004), 49–59. For a history of the IPL, see Lela

B. Costin, *Two Sisters for Social Justice: A Biography of Grace and Edith Abbott* (Urbana: University of Illinois Press, 1983), 68–99; Seth Korelitz, "'A Magnificent Piece of Americanization Work': The Americanization Work of the National Council of Jewish Women," *American Jewish History* 83, no. 2 (1995): 177–204.

47. Costin, *Two Sisters for Social Justice*, 69.

48. Edith Abbott focused particular attention on working and housing conditions of working-class immigrants. Ibid., 118.

49. For information on the women social workers affiliated with the University of Chicago, see Ellen Fitzpatrick, *Endless Crusade: Women Social Scientists and Progressive Reform* (New York: Oxford University Press, 1990).

50. Grace and Edith Abbott Papers, Box 8, Folder 9, Addenda, Regenstein Special Collections, University of Chicago. (Collection hereafter cited as Grace and Edith Abbott Papers, UC.)

51. She also became an advocate for African Americans. In an unpublished biography, Edith Abbott, Grace's sister, described an incident in which Jane Addams wanted to hire an African American cook for Hull House, but also wanted the cook to belong to a union. The different Chicago unions flatly refused to accept the man for membership. Edith tells the story: "When Grace finally got back and after she had had a conference with the union, she came home with a new and, as usual, very practical solution. The Negro Cook was to join a Negro local in St. Louis, Hull House would still have a union restaurant and everything moved along happily again." Edith Abbott, unpublished biography of Grace Abbott, Grace and Edith Abbott Papers, Box 8, Folder 9, Addenda, UC.

52. For work on the connections between white women's feminism and race in the late nineteenth and early twentieth centuries, see Newman, *White Women's Rights*.

53. For work on maternalism, see Mink, *Wages of Motherhood*; Muncy, *Creating a Female Dominion*; Linda Gordon, *Pitied but Not Entitled: Single Mothers and the History of Welfare* (New York: Free Press, 1994); Molly Ladd-Taylor, *Mother-Work: Women, Child Welfare, and the State, 1890–1930* (Urbana: University of Illinois Press, 1994); and Koven and Michel, *Mothers of a New World*.

54. Koven and Michel, *Mothers of a New World*, 2. (Emphasis in original.)

55. Gordon, *Pitied but Not Entitled*, 55.

56. Mink, *Wages of Motherhood*, 5.

57. Suronda Gonzalez, "Complicating Citizenship: Grace Abbott and the Immigrants' Protective League, 1908–1921," *Michigan Historical Review* 24 (Fall 1998): 56–75.

58. Grace Abbott, "The Chicago Employment Agency and the Immigrant Worker," *American Journal of Sociology* 14 (November 1908): 289–305.

59. Historians have shown that sometimes reformers overreacted to the problems posed by these institutions and that, in fact, they were an integral part of immigrant community networks. See Rivka Shpak Lissak, *Pluralism and Progressives: Hull House and the New Immigrants, 1890–1919* (Chicago: University of Chicago Press, 1989), and John Bodnar, *The Transplanted: A History of Immigrants in Urban America* (Bloomington: Indiana University Press, 1985), 68–70.

60. Regina Kunzel, *Fallen Women, Problem Girls: Unmarried Mothers and the Professionalization of Social Work* (New Haven, CT: Yale University Press, 1993), 21. See also Joanne Meyerowitz, *Women Adrift: Independent Wage Earners in Chicago, 1880–1930* (Chicago: University of Chicago Press, 1988), 43–68; Carolyn Strange, *Toronto's Girl Problem: The Perils and Pleasures of the City, 1880–1930* (Toronto: University of Toronto Press, 1995).

61. Grace Abbott, "The Chicago Employment Agency and the Immigrant Worker," 291.

62. Ibid., 291.

63. Ibid., 292.

64. Ibid., 289.

65. Ibid., 305.

66. Here Abbott was quoting Ivan Doseff, a worker among Bulgarian immigrants. Grace Abbott, "The Bulgarians of Chicago," *Charities and the Commons: A Weekly Journal of Philanthropy and Social Advance* 21 (January 9, 1909): 657.

67. Grace Abbott "A Study of Greeks in Chicago," *American Journal of Sociology* 15 (October 1909): 381.

68. Abbott, "The Bulgarians of Chicago," 655–56.

69. Abbott, "A Study of Greeks in Chicago," 385.

70. Ibid., 381.

71. Overall Greek migration to the United States in the late nineteenth and early twentieth centuries was 87 percent male. Daniels, *Coming to America*, 202.

72. George Chauncy has examined sexual relationships between men in immigrant communities in which the migration was dominated by men, particularly the Italians in New York. See George Chauncy, *Gay New York: Gender, Urban Culture and the Makings of the Gay Male World, 1890–1940* (New York: Basic Books, 1994), 75–86. For more on the policing of male sexual behavior, see Angus McLaren, *The Trials of Masculinity: Policing Sexual Boundaries, 1870–1930* (Chicago: University of Chicago Press, 1997).

73. Abbott, "A Study of Greeks in Chicago," 384–85.

74. Ibid., 387–88.

75. Theodore Roosevelt appointed two academics, Jeremiah Jenks and Charles P. Neill, and California businessman William Wheeler. The House appointees were Representatives John Burnett, a Democrat from Alabama; William Bennet, Republican from New York; and Benjamin F. Howell, New Jersey Republican. The Senate appointed Republicans William Dillingham of Vermont and Henry Cabot Lodge of Massachusetts. The third Democratic Senate appointee shifted, owing to the death of two appointees, Asbury Latimer of South Carolina and Anselm McLaurin of Mississippi. LeRoy Percy of Mississippi became the final Senate Democrat appointed in February 1910. For more background on these men, see Zeidel, *Immigrants, Progressives and Exclusion Politics*, 37–47.

76. Ibid., 51–68.

77. Ibid., 89.

78. These reports are contained in volume 41 of *Reports of the Immigration Commission*.

79. Zeidel, *Immigrants, Progressives and Exclusion Politics*, 110.

80. Joseph Lee to Lawrence Lowell, 4 August 1910, Joseph Lee Papers, Box 1, File 10, MHS.

81. Joseph Lee to Prescott Hall, 12 March 1910, Joseph Lee Papers, Box 1, Folder 6, MHS.

82. Hall wrote the general letter to the men in *Who's Who in America* on March 21, 1910. "Statement of the Immigration Restriction League," 111.

83. W. Z. Ripley to Prescott Hall, 16 February 1909, IRL Records, Box 7, HL.

84. "Statement of the Immigration Restriction League," 106–7.

85. Ibid., 106–9.

86. Ibid., 107. Hall was quoting George William Curtis, the nineteenth-century editor of *Harper's Weekly*.

87. Ibid., 106.

88. Hall proudly bragged that favorable replies came from "the presidents of 2 colleges and universities, 38 lawyers, 126 educators, 55 authors, 48 doctors, 29 clergymen, 21 army and navy officers, 12 engineers, 11 jurists, 11 businessmen, 1 chemist, 1 inventor, 1 criminologist, 1 police commissioner." "Statement of the Immigration Restriction League," 110–11.

89. Ibid., 112–39.

90. David Starr Jordan to Prescott Hall, 28 February 1910, IRL Records, Box 1, HL.

91. "Statement of the Immigration Restriction League," 124.

92. Ibid., 121.

93. Ibid., 124.

94. Ibid., 135.

95. Luther Burbank to Prescott Hall, 7 March 1910, IRL Records, Box 1, HL. "Statement of the Immigration Restriction League," 118.

96. "Statement of the Immigrants' Protective League," 58.

97. Ibid., 56.

98. Ibid., 58.

99. Ibid., 59.

100. Ibid., 60–61.

101. Ibid., 61.

102. Ibid., 62.

103. Ibid., 66.

104. For Grace Abbott's report, see "Statement of the Immigrants' Protective League," 65–77. There were a few smaller sections, including statements about publications, future plans, and cooperation with other societies.

105. Ibid., 67.

106. Ibid.

107. Ibid.

108. Ibid., 70.

109. Ibid., 72.

110. Kathy Lee Peiss, *Cheap Amusements: Working Women and Leisure in Turn-of-the-Century New York* (Philadelphia: Temple University Press, 1986), 98, 178–84.

111. "Statement of the Immigrants' Protective League," 70–71.

112. Ibid., 71.

113. Ibid., 73.

114. Ibid., 73–74.

115. Ibid., 73.

116. Ibid., 74.

117. Ibid., 73.

118. Zeidel, *Immigrants, Progressives and Exclusion Politics*, 114.

119. Ibid., 103–11.

120. Franz Boas, *Reports of the Immigration Commission, Volume 38: Changes in Bodily Form of Descendants of Immigrants* (Washington, DC: Government Printing Office, 1911). See also Zeidel, *Immigrants, Progressives and Exclusion Politics*, 86–100; King, *Making Americans*, 65–70.

121. He vowed that the IRL would "make good" to Lodge and help him in his reelection in 1910. Joseph Lee to Lawrence Lowell, 13 December 1910, Joseph Lee Papers, Box I, File II, MHS.

122. Joseph Lee to Lawrence Lowell, 25 March 1911, Joseph Lee Papers, Box I, File 12, MHS.

123. Richards M. Bradley to Joseph Lee, 16 March 1911, Joseph Lee Papers, Box I, File 12, MHS.

124. Joseph Lee, "The Restriction Recommendations," *Survey* 25 (January 7, 1911): 525.

125. Ibid., 526.

126. Grace Abbott, "Adjustment—Not Restriction," *Survey* 25 (January 7, 1911): 527–28.

127. Ibid., 529.

Chapter Three

1. "Statement of Mr. Louis N. Hammerling, President American Association of Foreign Language Newspapers, New York," in *Relative to the Further Restriction of Immigration: Hearings, 1912, United States, 62nd Congress, Second Session, House Committee on Immigration and Naturalization* (Washington, DC: Government Printing Office, 1912), 3.

2. Ibid., 3, 17.

3. "Statement of Rev. C. L. Orbach, President Slovak v. Amerike, Slovak Semiweekly, New York City," in *Relative to the Further Restriction of Immigration*, 23.

4. Gerstle, *American Crucible*, 6.

5. For explanations of ways of conceptualizing American citizenship, see Rogers M. Smith, "The 'American Creed' and American Identity: The Limits of Liberal Citizenship in the United States," *Western Political Quarterly* 41 (June 1988): 228–40.

6. Vought, *Bully Pulpit*, 86–87; Higham, *Strangers in the Land*, 165–75.

7. For an analysis of how the Burnett Bill was a reaction to the Dillingham Commission Report, see Zeidel, *Immigrants, Progressives and Exclusion Politics*, 120–23.

8. For more on Sabath, see Burton A. Boxerman, "Adolph Joachim Sabath in Congress: The Early Years, 1907–1932," *Journal of the Illinois State Historical Society* 66 (Fall 1973): 327–40.

9. Hutchinson, *Legislative History*, 150–54.

10. Daniels, *Guarding the Golden Door*, 34. For more on Taft's veto and Nagel's influence on it, see Zeidel, *Immigrants, Progressives and Exclusion Politics*, 123–25.

11. The vote in the Senate was 72 to 18 to override, and the vote in the House was 213 to 14. Hutchinson, *Legislative History*, 154.

12. Ibid., 160–63.

13. Quoted in Zeidel, *Immigrants, Progressives and Exclusion Politics*, 126.

14. Lissak, "The National Liberal Immigration League," 215; Zeidel, *Immigrants, Progressives and Exclusion Politics*, 126.

15. Quoted in Daniels, *Guarding the Golden Door*, 34. See also Zeidel, *Immigrants, Progressives and Exclusion Politics*, 126–28.

16. Hutchinson, *Legislative History*, 163.

17. Higham, *Strangers in the Land*, 186–93.

18. Zeidel, *Immigrants, Progressives and Exclusion Politics*, 124. For an example of one of the circular letters, see Prescott Hall to Francis H. Atkins, 15 April 1912, IRL Records, HL. Writing after the House passed the bill and anticipating passage in the Senate, Hall said, "Will you not write a personal letter to Hon. Charles D. Hilles, Secretary to the President, urging that this measure ought to become law, and telling him that it will help and not hurt him [the President] with the great mass of voters?"

19. One pamphlet declared, "Mr. Taft has allowed Secretary Nagel to veto the most thorough and comprehensive immigration restriction bill which has ever been drafted. Because of the literacy test which it contains, which is drawn so as to deny admission only to adults unable to read or write in their own language, the President has permitted the active antagonism of the Secretary of Commerce to set aside a bill which had 246 votes in the House and which passed the Senate by a vote of 58–59." Pamphlet quoted in the *Boston Journal*, 15 February 1913, IRL Records, Box 2, HL.

20. Robert DeCourcy Ward to Joseph Lee, 27 February 1913, Joseph Lee Papers, Box 2, File 2, MHS.

21. The leadership of the IRL believed that men of prestige were essential to their political efforts. For instance, in 1915, as they were gearing up to get the Burnett Bill passed in the 63rd Congress, Prescott Hall wrote a letter to the membership, saying, "A most effective method of exerting pressure upon Congress is in the form of personal letters to congressmen and senators. The League desires at this time to enlarge its 'influence list' composed of persons in sympathy with its objections who can be asked to write their congressmen and senators at critical times when bills are pending." Prescott Hall to membership of the IRL, 13 April 1915, IRL Records, Box 5, HL.

22. For background on Charles Davenport, see Black, *War against the Weak*, 33–41; Kevles, *In the Name of Eugenics*, 41–56; Allan, "Misuse of Biological Hierarchies," 110–12. The ABA was founded through the Department of Agriculture by plant and animal breeders who were interested in keeping up with advancements in genetic science. But in 1907, led by Harvard PhD Charles Benedict Davenport, the organization embraced eugenics as a focus, and it later became the American Eugenics Society. Black, *War against the Weak*, 38–40, 57–61; Higham, *Strangers in the Land*, 151.

23. After the Dillingham Report was released, Jenks, along with his partner W. Jett Lauck, published a book promoting the findings of the Commission and stressing the need for a literacy test. See Jeremiah W. Jenks and W. Jett Lauck, *The Immigration Problem* (New York: Funk and Wagnalls, 1912).

24. For instance, in 1914 John R. Commons wrote to Prescott Hall and told him to remind Wilson that he favored the restriction bill. John R. Commons to Prescott Hall, 6 October 1914, IRL Records, Box 1, HL. By 1916, social scientists were also working with the IRL to gain support for the literacy test from Wilson's Republican opponent, Charles Hughes. Joseph Lee took Ross and Henry Pratt Fairchild, whom he called "two of the best men in the country on the subject [of immigration]" to seek Charles Hughes' support of restriction in 1916. Joseph Lee to Mr. Crane, 2 August 1916, Joseph Lee Papers, Box 2, File 14, MHS. By 1915, Jeremiah Jenks had started writing numerous pamphlets for the IRL, including "Immigration Issue to be Revived," "Save that Bill!," "Immigration as a National Issue," "The Watchful West," and "3,000,000,000 Lost by Uncle Sam in Ten Years." IRL Records, Box 5, HL. For more on the relationship between social science and immigration restriction, see Dorothy Ross, *The Origins of American Social Science* (Cambridge: Cambridge University Press, 1991), 219–56; Ronald M. Pavalko, "Racism and the New Immigration: A Reinterpretation of the Assimilation of White Ethnics in American Society," *Sociology and Social Research* 65, no. 1 (1980): 57–59.

25. Julius Weinberg, "E. A. Ross: The Progressive as Nativist," *Wisconsin Magazine of History* 50, no. 3 (Spring 1967): 244.

26. See Gail Bederman's discussion of E. A. Ross and race suicide in *Manliness and Civilization*, 200–206.

27. E. A. Ross, "Western Civilization and the Birth-Rate," *The American Journal of Sociology* 12 (March 1907): 612–14.

28. Quoted in Guterl, *Color of Race in America*, 39; see also 27–31, 43. For more on Madison Grant's life and attitudes, see Jonathan Peter Spiro, *Defending the Master Race: Conservation, Eugenics and the Legacy of Madison Grant* (Burlington: University of Vermont Press, 2009), and Charles C. Grant, "Prophet of American Racism: Madison Grant and the Nordic Myth," *Phylon* 23 (Spring 1962): 173–74. For more on Grant's work in zoology, see Helen L. Horowitz, "Animal and Man in the New York Zoological Park," *New York History* 56, no. 4 (1975): 426–55.

29. E. A. Ross suggested to Hall that he tell Wilson that he favored restriction, and that he also send the President his articles from the *Century Magazine*. These articles, he stated, compare "old" and "new" immigration and "make clear the broad differences between the two types." E. A. Ross to Prescott Hall, 12 March 1914, IRL Records, HL. Madison Grant also made an appeal to former President Roosevelt in 1915, and was happy to find that Roosevelt supported restriction. Grant wrote that Roosevelt's "opinion of the Jews is all that could be desired, and his only objection to the literacy test was that it didn't keep them out." Madison Grant to Prescott Hall, 18 November 1915, IRL Records, HL.

30. Gossett, *Race*, 169.

31. Guterl, *Color of Race in America*, 32.

32. For work on how the writings of Jean-Baptiste Lamarck (1744–1829) influenced American thought, see George W. Stocking, Jr., "Lamarckianism in American Social Science:

1890–1915," *Journal of the History of Ideas* 23 (April–June 1962): 239–56. See also Hawkins, *Social Darwinism*, 39–44; Haller, Jr., *Outcasts from Evolution*, 154.

33. Black, *War against the Weak*, 25–27; Kevles, *In the Name of Eugenics*, 70–71. For more on the relationship between Larmarckianism and Mendelianism, see Cogdell, *Eugenic Design*, 16–23.

34. Prescott Hall to Francis H. Atkins, 15 April 1912, IRL Records, Box 1, HL.

35. Victor R. Greene, *The Slavic Community on Strike: Immigrant Labor in Pennsylvania Anthracite* (Notre Dame, IN: University of Notre Dame Press, 1968), 182. See also Herbert Parson to Charles D. Norton, 27 July 1910, William Howard Taft Papers, Library of Congress (collection hereafter cited as Taft Papers, LC); see also "The Servian Club's Dinner," *American Leader* 5 (February 26, 1914): 270.

36. "The American Association of Foreign Language Newspapers," *American Leader* 1 (February 29, 1912): 58. The languages said to be represented were "Armenian, Austrian, Bohemian, Bulgarian, Chinese, Croatian, Finnish, French, Greek, Hollandish, Hungarian, Italian, Japanese, Yiddish, Lettish, Lithuanian, Norwegian-Danish, Polish, Portuguese, Romanian, Russian, Ruthenian, Servian, Slovak, Slovenik, Spanish, Swedish, Swiss and Syrian."

37. Lissak, "The National Liberal Immigration League," 221.

38. "The Association's Eighth Year," *American Leader* 10 (October 12, 1916): 506–8. In 1912, Hammerling claimed that the AAFLN reached eighteen million when 508 newspapers belonged to the organization. In 1918, when membership dropped to 753 from 813, Hammerling still claimed to have reached thirty-two million. He did not, however, have accurate numbers about the number of immigrants reached, so he used the 1910 census to determine the numbers of each nationality in the United States whose language was represented by a newspaper in the AAFLN. In other words, his numbers were quite unreliable.

39. For a study of the cultural meanings of advertising, see T. Jackson Lears, *Fables of Abundance: A Cultural History of Advertising in America* (New York: Basic Books, 1994).

40. Alan C. Reiley, "Advertising and the Melting Pot," *American Leader* 9 (April 27, 1916): 474.

41. "The Educational Value of Reading Ad Pages," *American Leader* 5 (February 12, 1914): 159.

42. See, for example, letters critical of Hammerling in the Taft Papers, LC: Herbert Parsons, Congressman from New York, to Charles D. Norton, Secretary to the President, 27 July 1910; and Arthur Koppell of the United Publishers Association of New York to William Howard Taft, 19 January 1912.

43. See, for example, the list of guests at the 1913 Banquet, which included the heads of the postal savings organization and the corn products organization, as well as others who had had articles sympathetic to their cause in the *Leader*. "Our Banquet," *American Leader* 3 (February 13, 1913): 131–33.

44. Nagel had shown strong support for immigrants in general, and in his tenure helped many circumvent immigration restriction laws. He did, however, express some trepidation about potential "colonization" of immigrants in the United States and the power of the immigrant press. He said that he was happy the *Leader* was going to reprint translated articles "because we may, in that way, get some inkling of what is going on." Charles Nagel to Charles Hilles, Secretary to the President, 6 April 1912, Taft Papers, LC.

45. This pamphlet was reprinted in the *Leader*. Louis N. Hammerling, "From Lincoln to Taft: 1854–1912, The Republican Party: A Record of Nearly Sixty Years," *American Leader* 2 (July 25, 1912): 81–111.

46. See, for instance, Horace L. Brand, "Shall We Mark Time?" (translated), *American Leader* 2 (August 8, 1912): 165–69; "William H. Taft," *American Leader* 1 (June 27, 1912): 20–21; "President Taft to the Italians," *American Leader* 2 (October 24, 1912): 471–73; Ira E. Bennett, "The Proposed Revision of the Immigration Laws," *American Leader* 1 (February 29, 1912): 48–51.

47. For instance, one article criticized "another party's candidate"—meaning Roosevelt—for actively campaigning before the nomination. See Louis N. Hammerling, "A Plea for Dignity," *American Leader* 2 (July 11, 1912): 8–9. Another article criticized Roosevelt for seeking more than two terms, thus breaking the tradition of George Washington. See Ira E. Bennett, "The Tenure of the Presidency," *American Leader* 8 (June 13, 1912): 10–14.

Hammerling once sent Taft a copy of a speech by Wilson that had been printed in the *Jewish Daily Warheit*. Hammerling had marked the part he saw as "the weak part of the letter, which shows that he is really an anti-immigrationist instead of favoring immigration." Louis N. Hammerling to William Howard Taft, 28 August 1912, Taft Papers, LC.

48. See, for instance, "The Association and Friends Visit President Wilson," *American Leader* 3 (May 22, 1913): 598–600; "The Association's Testimonial to President Wilson," *American Leader* 7 (February 25, 1915): 198–99.

49. M. A. Mokarzel, "Is the United States to Be the Upholder of Freedom?" *American Leader* 1 (May 9, 1912): 43.

50. "A Banquet to Our Editor," *American Leader* 1 (June 13, 1912): 23–24. For other articles that lavished praise on Hammerling, see J. George Frederick, "The American Leader: Why It Has Come to Stay and What It Means to Accomplish," *American Leader* 1 (February 29, 1912): 19–20; "Mr. Louis N. Hammerling Honored," *American Leader* 3 (June 12, 1913): 665–66.

51. Louis N. Hammerling, "Address of Welcome," *American Leader* 5 (February 12, 1914): 168.

52. See Edwin Bird Wilson, "A Native American's Impressions of the Foreign Editor's Annual Meeting," *American Leader* 1 (June 13, 1912): 43–46; Louis N. Hammerling, "The Influence of the Foreign-Language Press in America," *American Leader* 1 (June 27, 1912): 32–36; Alexander McCormick, "Who Are Americans?" *American Leader* 2 (August 22, 1912): 218–24; "The Loyalty of the Foreign Press," *American Leader* 9 (February 24, 1916): 197–98.

53. "Unity in America," *American Leader* 2 (September 12, 1912): 272.

54. Joseph Lee to George H. Ellis, 11 November 1911, Joseph Lee Papers, Box 1, File 15, MHS. See also Higham, *Strangers in the Land*, 102, Solomon, *Ancestors and Immigrants*, 99–102.

55. See, for instance, Jacob Sphirstein, "The Department of Labor" (translated), *American Leader* 2 (August 8, 1912): 171; "Morrison on Immigration," *American Leader* 4 (November 27, 1913): 585. See also "A Friend of Immigration," *American Leader* 2 (September 12, 1912): 267.

56. For more on how Americans linked manliness with pioneers and western expansion, see Gail Bederman's discussion about Theodore Roosevelt in *Manliness and Civilization*, 170–215; and Slotkin, *Gunfighter Nation*, 51–62.

57. E. A. Ross, *The Old World in the New: The Significance of Past and Present Immigration to the American People* (New York: Century, 1914), 290.

58. Madison Grant, *The Passing of the Great Race, or the Racial Basis of European History*, 4th ed. (1916; repr., New York: Charles Scribner's Sons, 1922), 90. This quote, which represents Grant's views about the "Nordic" colonists, was not in the original 1916 version of his book, but it did appear in later versions. The rest of the Madison Grant quotes in this chapter appear in the 1916 edition. For more on the different editions of *The Passing of the Great Race*, see Spiro, *Defending the Master Race*, 161–66.

59. Ross, *Old World in the New*, 285.

60. Ibid. (Emphasis in original.)

61. Grant, *Passing of the Great Race*, 139, 147.

62. Ibid., 92

63. Ross, *Old World in the New*, 300.

64. Ibid., picture facing page 249.

65. Ibid., 304.

66. For work on representations of manhood and labor, see Winter, *Making Men*; Mark Seltzer, *Bodies and Machines* (London: Routledge, 1992); Donald Reid, *Paris Sewers and Sewermen: Realities and Representations* (Cambridge, MA: Harvard University Press, 1991).

67. William S. Bennet, "America a Haven of Justice for Those Who Seek to Escape the Tyrannous Oppression of Certain Monarchial [*sic*] Countries," *American Leader* 1 (June 13, 1912): 29.

68. William S. Bennet, "Faith in the Foreign-Born," *American Leader* 2 (September 12, 1912): 289.

69. J. George Frederick, "Discovering Our Brother American," *American Leader* 1 (March 14, 1912): 12–14.

70. Peter S. Lambros, "The New Immigration," *American Leader* 2 (December 12, 1912): 686.

71. N. L. Piotrowski, "Against the Burnett Bill," *American Leader* 3 (February 27, 1913): 229–30.

72. Armour Caldwell, "The Educational Test: A Defense of Illiterate Immigrant Labor," *American Leader* 1 (April 25, 1912): 31–32.

73. Ira E. Bennett, "The Educational Test," *American Leader* 1 (April 11, 1912): 18.

74. Ralph H. Wallace, who worked for the Erie Railroad, was a strong proponent of immigrant redistribution to the countryside. See Ralph H. Wallace, "How to Help the Immigrant," *American Leader* 2 (July 11, 1912): 42. Another frequent *Leader* author, Henry Green, worked for the American Immigration Distribution League, and argued that the government needed to finance the transportation of immigrants to the countryside. See Henry Green, "The Immigrant: What He Owes America and What America Owes Him," *American Leader* 2 (July 11, 1912): 22–27; Henry Green, "Congestion and Distribution," *American Leader* 1 (May 23, 1912). For work on the promotion of westward settlement by

railroad, see Robert F. Zeidel, "Peopling the Empire: The Great Northern Railroad and the Recruitment of Immigrant Settlers to North Dakota," *North Dakota History* 60 (Spring 1993): 14–23.

75. See, for instance, Frank Misuraca, "The Italian Exodus Begins," *American Leader* 2 (October 24, 1912): 465; and "Jewish Farmers Meet," *American Leader* 6 (December 10, 1914): 731.

76. Edward Kemble, "The Problem of Distribution," *American Leader* 9 (September 10, 1914): 281.

77. See Bennet, "The Proposed Revision of the Immigration Laws," 49–51; Ira E. Bennett, "The Situation in Washington," *American Leader* 1 (March 28, 1912): 9–10.

78. Around 720,000 Mexicans migrated to the United States in the years after the Revolution began. Daniels, *Coming to America*, 307.

79. "Some Illuminating Facts," *American Leader* 3 (March 13, 1913): 275. Interestingly, in the same article, the author pointed out that Rhode Island had a high rate of illiteracy, and that its immigration was mostly Irish and French Canadian. But instead of condemning those immigrants (who were nonsoutheastern Europeans) he said that "they are universally admitted to be highly acceptable settlers" (276).

80. "Immigration in 1913," *American Leader* 4 (October 9, 1913): 413.

81. Prescott Hall to the Editor of the *Hartford Post*, 5 April 1915, IRL Records, Box 5, HL.

82. Madison Grant to Prescott Hall, 3 March 1913, IRL Records, Box 1, HL.

83. For work on the racialization of Jews in the United States, see Karen Brodkin, *How Jews Became White Folks and What That Says about Race in America* (New Brunswick, NJ: Rutgers University Press, 1998); Eric L. Goldstein, "'Different Blood Flows in Our Veins': Race and Jewish Self-Definition in Late Nineteenth Century America," *American Jewish History* 85 (March 1997): 29–55.

84. See, for instance, Joseph Patten to Joseph Lee, 1 June 1911, Joseph Lee Papers, Box 1, File 13, MHS; Congressman William Kent (First District, CA) to Prescott Hall, 27 March 1913, IRL Records, Box 5, HL. Overall, the men of the IRL saw Jewish leaders as behind most of the opposition to the literacy test legislation. The IRL complained of steamship companies which they emphasized were owned by Jews and were "thoroughly organized and . . . working on an elaborate scale, with plenty of funds." IRL fundraising letter, 15 June 1911, Joseph Lee Papers, Box 1, File 13, MHS. E. A. Ross explained in his book that Jews in New York created a powerful congressional block opposed to restriction legislation, and stated that "the systematic campaign in newspapers and magazines to break down all arguments for restriction and to calm nativist fears is waged by and for one race," the race he called "Hebrew." Ross, *Old World in the New*, 144.

85. Hall wrote to Boas that, since it was impossible for the widely separated committee to get together for meetings, "Prof. Ward and myself took it upon ourselves to prepare this report with the idea of informing the members of the ABA more fully on the subject and arousing interest in the work of the committee." Prescott Hall to Franz Boas, 19 July 1912, IRL Records, Box 1, HL.

86. "First Report of the Immigration Committee of the Eugenics Section, American Breeders Association," IRL Records, Box 1, HL.

87. Ibid.

88. Prescott Hall reported this quote in a letter to committee member James Field. Prescott Hall to James Field, 28 August 1912, IRL Records, HL.

89. Prescott Hall to James Field, 28 August 1912, IRL Records, Box 1, HL.

90. Boas, *Changes in Bodily Form of Descendants of Immigrants* (Washington, DC: Government Printing Office, 1911).

91. For more on Boas' criticism of Grant, see Spiro, *Defending the Master Race*, 160–61.

92. Madison Grant to Senator F. W. Simmons, 5 April 1912, IRL Records, Box 2, HL.

93. For work on miscegenation fears, see Pascoe, "Miscegenation Law," 44–69; Hall, *Revolt Against Chivalry*; Blee, *Women of the Klan*.

94. Ross, *Old World in the New*, 150; Grant, *Passing of the Great Race*, 91.

95. Ross, *Old World in the New*, 289–90.

96. Grant, *Passing of the Great Race*, 18.

97. Prescott Hall, "The Future of American Ideals," *North American Review* 195 (January 1912): 95.

98. Ibid., 99.

99. See Charles Davenport to Prescott Hall, 25 April 1913, and Hall to Davenport, 13 May 1913, IRL Records, Box 1, HL. Madison Grant held a particularly strong animosity for Boas, who severely panned *The Passing of the Great Race* in *The New Republic* (Franz Boas, "Inventing a Great Race," *The New Republic* 9 [January 13, 1917]: 305–7). Grant requested that Hall contact a friend at Columbia University and "bring his attention to the continuance of the employment of Prof. Boas," and to encourage the firing of Boas. Madison Grant to Prescott Hall, 23 September 1918, IRL Records, Box 1, HL.

100. "Second Report of the Committee on Immigration of the Eugenic Section of the American Genetics Association," 1914, IRL Records, Box 3, HL.

101. George W. Stocking, Jr., *Race, Culture and Evolution: Essays in the History of Anthropology* (New York: Free Press, 1968), 305.

102. Gerstle, *American Crucible*, 45; Daylanne English, *Unnatural Selections: Eugenics in American Modernism and the Harlem Renaissance* (Chapel Hill: University of North Carolina Press, 2004), 17.

103. Mann, "Common Sense and Immigration," 37–38.

104. Rossiter Johnson, "The Causes of Unrest," *American Leader* 1 (June 27, 1912): 5–6.

105. Charles Nagel, "Immigration: Legislation and Administration," *American Leader* 4 (December 24, 1913): 717.

106. "Literacy and Character," *American Leader* 9 (April 13, 1916): 390.

107. Armour Caldwell, "On Purity of Race," *American Leader* 7 (May 27, 1915): 624.

108. For Olson's relationship to the eugenic movement, see Michael Willrich, "The Two Percent Solution: Eugenic Jurisprudence and the Socialization of American Law, 1900–1930," *Law and Labor History Review* 16 (Spring 1998): 63–111.

109. Harry Olson, "Against the Burnett Bill," *American Leader* 3 (March 13, 1913): 299.

110. George L. Dyer, "What Is an American?" *American Leader* 10 (October 12, 1916): 490–91.

111. Jacobson, *Whiteness of a Different Color*, 203–22. For more on manhood and empire, see Jonathan Rutherford, *Forever England: Reflections on Race, Masculinity and Empire* (London: Lawrence and Wishart, 1997); Ruth Roach Pierson and Nupur Chaudhuri, eds., *Nation, Empire, Colony: Historicizing Gender and Race* (Bloomington: Indiana University Press, 1998); Liam Kennedy, "Alien Nation: White Male Paranoia and Imperial Culture in the United States," *Journal of American Studies* 30 (April 1996): 87–100.

112. To see how Britain and the United States relied on a common racial identity as they built an alliance before World War I, see Stuart Anderson, *Race and Rapprochement: Anglo-Saxonism and Anglo-American Relations, 1895–1904* (Cranbury, NJ: Associated University Press, 1980).

113. Louis N. Hammerling, "The Centenary of Peace: The Attitude of the Foreign-born Population of the United States Towards It," *American Leader* 3 (May 22, 1913): 604–5.

114. Louis N. Hammerling, "Personal Liberty," *American Leader* 5 (April 23, 1914): 510–11.

115. "Illiteracy and Sex," *American Leader* 7 (January 28, 1915): 116–17.

116. Joseph Lee to the Hon. Charles D. Hilles, 26 March 1912, Joseph Lee Papers, Box I, File 16, MHS; Madison Grant to Senator Elihu Root, IRL Records, Box 1, HL.

117. Rossiter Johnson, "Some Interesting Questions," *American Leader* 3 (January 23, 1913): 74–76.

118. "The Association Gathers in New York," *American Leader* 7 (March 25, 1915): 335.

119. Grant, *Passing of the Great Race*, 82.

120. Ibid., 71.

121. Ross, *Old World in the New*, 219.

122. "An American Ideal in Danger," *American Leader* 4 (August 14, 1913): 134–35.

123. Ross, *Old World in the New*, 285–88.

124. Armour Caldwell, "The Typical American Girl," *American Leader* 4 (November 27, 1913): 622–23.

Chapter Four

1. Hayes' particular focus was on excluding all Asians, and he introduced numerous amendments in Congress on that issue. See Hutchinson, *Legislative History*, 143–63.

2. "Statement of Miss Grace Abbott of Chicago," in *Relative to the Further Restriction of Immigration*, 53.

3. Jane Addams and Grace Abbott to Oscar Underwood, 23 January 1911, Jane Addams Papers, Jane Addams Memorial Collection, Richard M. Daley Library, University of Illinois at Chicago. (Collection hereafter cited as Jane Addams Papers, UIC.) While Jane Addams was not as vocal as Grace Abbott in the literacy test debate, both women agreed that literacy

provided a poor test for whether someone should be allowed to enter the United States since it did not take into account the lack of opportunity many immigrants had. See Jane Addams, "Pen and Book as Test of Character," *Survey* 29 (January 26, 1913): 419–20.

4. "Fifth Annual Report of the Immigrants' Protective League for the Year Ending January 1, 1914," Papers of the Immigrants' Protective League, Folder 59A, Box Four, Supplement II, p. 17, Jane Addams Memorial Collection, Department of Special Collections, University of Illinois at Chicago Library. (Papers of the Immigrants' Protective League hereafter cited as IPL Papers, UIC. All IPL annual reports cited are from this collection.)

5. Jane Addams to Ada James, 29 January 1913, Jane Addams Papers, 1860–1960, UIC.

6. Marshall E. Dimock, "The Inner Substance of a Progressive: An Address," in "A Meeting in Honor of, and in Memory of Grace Abbott, November 17, 1878–June 19, 1939, Held at the University of Chicago, October Eighteenth, 1939," Grace and Edith Abbott Papers, Folder 33, Box 1, UC.

7. "Report of the Immigrants' Protective League for 1911–1912," 21.

8. Costin, *Two Sisters for Social Justice*, 81–84. See also Grace Abbott's diary of the trip in the Grace and Edith Abbott Papers, UC.

9. Robert L. Buroker, "From Voluntary Association to Welfare State: The Illinois Immigrants' Protective League, 1908–1926," *Journal of American History* 58 (December 1971): 655.

10. Costin, *Two Sisters for Social Justice*, 258.

11. While white, middle-class women formed the majority of the women who participated in the Progressive movement, women from other race and class backgrounds also found opportunities to find political voices. They were, however, often actively marginalized in the Progressive movement. See, for example, Flanagan, *America Reformed*, 37; Nancy Hewitt, *Southern Discomfort: Women's Activism in Tampa, Florida, 1880s–1920s* (Urbana: University of Illinois Press, 2001), 234–37; Gilmore, *Gender and Jim Crow*, 147–50. See also Nancy S. Dye, *Equal as Sisters: Feminism, the Labor Movement and the Women's Trade Union League of New York* (Columbia: University of Missouri Press, 1980); Frankel and Dye, *Gender, Class, Race, and Reform*.

12. For insight into the political influence during this era of white, middle-class women, and Jane Addams in particular, see Flanagan, *Seeing with Their Hearts*, 85–120; Victoria Bissell Brown, "Jane Addams, Progressivism, and Woman Suffrage: An Introduction to 'Why Women Should Vote,'" in *One Woman, One Vote: Rediscovering the Woman Suffrage Movement*, ed. Marjorie Spruill Wheeler (Troutdale, OR: New Sage, 1995), 179–95.

13. For more on the founding of the Children's Bureau, see Gordon, *Pitied but Not Entitled*, 88–91; Muncy, *Creating a Female Dominion*, 38–65.

14. Diner, *A Very Different Age*, 218–23.

15. For more on the scope of the development of suffrage during this era, including class, regional, and racial fissures in the movement, see Sara Hunter Graham, *Woman Suffrage and the New Democracy* (New Haven, CT: Yale University Press, 1996); Ellen Carol Dubois, *Harriot Stanton Blatch and the Winning of Woman Suffrage* (New Haven, CT: Yale University Press, 1997); Suzanne M. Marilley, *Woman Suffrage and the Origins of Liberal Feminism in the United States,*

1820–1920 (Cambridge, MA: Harvard University Press, 1996); Beverly Beeton, *Women Vote in the West: The Woman Suffrage Movement, 1869–1896* (New York: Garland, 1986); Ellen Carol Dubois, *Feminism and Suffrage: The Emergence of an Independent Women's Movement in America, 1848–1869* (Ithaca, NY: Cornell University Press, 1978).

16. For more on the political activism of Grace Abbott, see Gonzalez, "Immigrants in Our Midst," 278–95.

17. Edith Abbott, "Grace Abbott and Hull House, 1908–1921, Part II," *Social Service Review* 24 (December 1950), 500–501.

18. Quoted in Dubois, *Harriot Stanton Blatch,* 144.

19. Costin, *Two Sisters for Social Justice,* 46–47. For a description of the Hull House connection to the 1912 convention, see Allen F. Davis, *Spearheads for Reform: The Social Settlements and the Progressive Movement, 1890–1914* (New York: Oxford University Press, 1967), 194–201. For more on Roosevelt's view of women's suffrage, see Testi, "Gender and Reform Politics," 1524.

20. Abbott, "Grace Abbott and Hull House," 502.

21. Vought, *Bully Pulpit,* 86–87.

22. Davis, *Spearheads for Reform,* 207.

23. Abbott, "Grace Abbott and Hull House," 493.

24. In arguing for protections, Abbott was partaking in a larger project launched by Progressive women reformers. See Eileen Boris, "Reconstructing the 'Family': Women, Progressive Reform, and the Problem of Social Control," in Frankel and Dye, *Gender, Class, Race and Reform,* 81–82.

25. "Statement of Miss Grace Abbott of Chicago," 55, 60.

26. Ibid.

27. Ibid., 54.

28. Ibid., 59.

29. "Report for the Year Ending January 1, 1916," 15.

30. "Report for the Year Ending January 1, 1914," 13.

31. "Report for the Year Ending January 1, 1916," 10.

32. "Report for the Year Ending January 1, 1914," 13.

33. "Statement of Miss Grace Abbott of Chicago," 58.

34. "Report for the Year Ending January 1, 1915," 8.

35. "Statement of Mr. Alexander McCormick," in *Hearings before the Committee on Immigration and Naturalization, House of Representatives, 63rd Congress, Second Session on HR 6060* (Washington, DC: Government Printing Office, 1913), 79, 86–89.

36. Abbott did tell stories of the economic exploitation of women. See, for instance, "Report for the Year Ending January 1, 1913," 13–15. Most of these kinds of stories, however, revolved around men.

37. "Report for the Year Ending January 1, 1914," 14.

38. "Report for the Year Ending January 1, 1915," 10.

39. Ibid., 11.

40. "Report for the Year Ending January 1, 1913," 13.

41. "Report for the Year Ending January 1, 1914," 11.

42. "Report for the Year Ending January I, 1913," 21.

43. Ibid., 10.

44. "Report for the Year Ending January I, 1915," 17.

45. See "Report for the Year Ending January I, 1913," 10; "Report for the Year Ending January I, 1915," 17.

46. "Report for the Year Ending January I, 1916," 13.

47. "Statement of Miss Grace Abbott of Chicago," 53.

48. Ibid., 53–54.

49. "Report for the Year Ending January I, 1914," 17.

50. Abbott's call for immigrant tolerance but female equality mirrors distinctions between the "Woman Question" and the "Jewish Question" in late-nineteenth-century Europe. As Historian Wendy Brown writes, "Practices of tolerance are tacit acknowledgements that the other remains politically outside the norm of citizenship, that the other remains politically other, and that it has not been fully incorporated by the liberal discourse of equality and cannot be managed through a division of labor suffused with the terms of its subordination." See Wendy Brown, "Tolerance and Equality: 'The Jewish Question' and 'the Woman Question,'" in *Going Public: Feminism and the Shifting Boundaries of the Private Sphere*, ed. Joan Scott and Debra Keates (Urbana: University of Illinois Press, 2004), 15–42.

51. "Report for the Year Ending January I, 1915," 23.

52. "Report for the Year Ending January I, 1916," 5.

53. Ibid., 27.

54. "Report for the Year Ending January I, 1914," 14.

55. Ibid., 11, 13.

56. "Report for the Year 1911–1912," 6.

57. "Report for the Year Ending January I, 1913," 21.

58. Ibid., 13.

59. "Report for the Year Ending January I, 1914," 7–9.

60. "Report for the Year 1911–1912," 8.

61. "Report for the Year Ending January I, 1916," 11.

62. Ibid., 15–16.

63. Ibid., 20.

64. Ibid., 23.

65. Ibid., 20–21.

66. Ibid., 21.

Chapter Five

1. There were some new amendments to this bill, such as restrictions against chronic alcoholics, those with tuberculosis, and those with "constitutional psychopathic inferiority." The bill also proposed an "Asiatic Barred Zone," which is discussed below. Hutchinson, *Legislative History*, 166.

2. "Statement of Mr. J. H. Kimble," in *Restriction of Immigration: Hearings before the Committee on Immigration and Naturalization, House of Representatives, Sixty-Fourth Congress, First Session on HR 558* (Washington, DC: Government Printing Office, 1916), 38. James H. Patten, who represented IRL interests in Congress, also worked with the Farmer's National Congress, the organization Kimble represented. Patten had Kimble include briefs by the Immigration Restriction League in the record of the committee.

3. "Statement of Mr. Louis Hammerling," in *Restriction of Immigration*, 4.

4. "Statement of Miss Grace Abbott," in *Restriction of Immigration*, 8.

5. Ibid., 4.

6. In the 1913–14 fiscal year, some 1.2 million people immigrated to the United States. In the 1915–16 fiscal year, that number was down to 300,000. Furthermore, an additional 125,000 immigrants migrated back to their homelands that year, so the net gain was just over 150,000. Daniels, *Not Like Us*, 80.

7. Robert H. Zieger, *America's Great War: World War I and the American Experience* (Lanham, MD: Rowman and Littlefield, 2000), 7.

8. Higham, *Strangers in the Land*, 193, 196–97; King, *Making Americans*, 90–91.

9. Hans P. Vought, "Division and Reunion: Woodrow Wilson, Immigration, and the Myth of American Unity," *Journal of American Ethnic History* 13, no. 3 (Spring 1994): 25–26. For more on the hyphen issue in United States politics, see Higham, *Strangers in the Land*, 198–99.

10. Higham, *Strangers in the Land*, 198. See also Gerstle, *American Crucible*, 56–57.

11. King, *Making Americans*, 94–95; Diner, *A Very Different Age*, 253.

12. Alan Dawley, *Changing the World: American Progressives in War and Revolution* (Princeton, NJ: Princeton University Press, 2003), 113; Diner, *A Very Different Age*, 255–56.

13. McGerr, *A Fierce Discontent*, 281. See also Diner, *A Very Different Age*, 259–60; Muncy, *Creating A Female Dominion*, 90; Ellis W. Hawley, *The Great War and the Search for Modern Order: A History of the American People and Their Institutions* (New York: St. Martin's, 1979), 1–30.

14. For an overview of the splits in Progressivism and the debate about "preparedness," see Zieger, *America's Great War*, 33–40; David M. Kennedy, *Over Here: The First World War and American Society*, Twenty-Fifth Anniversary Edition (1980; repr., New York: Oxford University Press, 2004), 32.

15. Flanagan, *America Reformed*, 223–23; Dawley, *Changing the World*, 95.

16. Higham, *Strangers in the Land*, 199–200.

17. Kennedy, *Over Here*, 32; Zieger, *America's Great War*, 40–46.

18. Flanagan, *America Reformed*, 244–46.

19. Barbara Steinson, *American Women's Activism in World War I* (New York: Garland, 1982), 48–60; Costin, *Two Sisters for Social Justice*, 54–56.

20. Kathleen Kennedy, *Disloyal Mothers and Scurrilous Citizens: Women and Subversion during World War I* (Bloomington: Indiana University Press, 1999), 5–11.

21. Gerstle, *American Crucible*, 83–84; Dawley, *Changing the World*, 110–11.

22. Dawley, *Changing the World*, 111. For more on the gendered language used to describe pacifism and preparedness, see Zeiger, "She Didn't Raise Her Boy to Be a Slacker," 9–12; Kennedy, *Over Here*, 30–31.

23. Madison Grant to Prescott Hall, 15 November 1915, IRL Records, Box I, HL.

24. For the problems that racial nativists faced during World War I, see Higham, *Strangers in the Land*, 210.

25. See in particular the news release of Jeremiah Jenks and E. A. Ross, "The Illiterate Immigrant and Our Posterity," IRL Records, Box 5, HL. Other press releases that Jenks sent out under IRL auspices include "Immigration Issue to be Revived," "Save that Bill!," "Immigration as a National Issue," "The Watchful West," and "3,000,000,000 Lost by Uncle Sam in Ten Years." IRL Records, Box 5, HL.

26. "Statement of Mr. J. H. Kimble," 26, 28. These statements were an addendum to Kimble's testimony. Ross' and Fairchild's statements were originally made at a White House meeting in January of 1915.

27. "Publications of the Immigration Restriction League, no. 66: The Case for the Literacy Test," Joseph Lee Papers, p. 9, Box 7, MHS. This pamphlet was a reprint of an article from the January–March issue of the *Unpopular Review*.

28. Grant, *Passing of the Great Race*, 184. All the quotes used here also appeared in the 1916 edition.

29. Ibid., 191.

30. Ibid., 184.

31. Peter S. Lambros, "The Mission of the Foreign-Language Newspaper in the United States," *American Leader* 7 (May 9, 1915): 536.

32. "The Honorable Hyphen," *American Leader* 10 (July 13, 1916): 9.

33. "Compulsory Citizenship," *American Leader* 9 (June 8, 1916): 649.

34. Percy Andreae, "On Preparedness," *American Leader* 10 (July 13, 1916): 23.

35. T. W. Gregory, "A Race of Races," *American Leader* 10 (October 12, 1916): 406.

36. Rabbi Abram Hirschberg, "Preparedness: A Jewish View," *American Leader* 9 (April 13, 1916): 420.

37. Ibid.

38. As Graham Dawson has argued, "the soldier-hero has proved to be one of the most durable and powerful forms of idealized masculinity within Western cultural tradition since the ancient Greeks. Military virtues such as aggression, strength, courage and endurance have repeatedly been defined as the natural and inherent qualities of manhood." Graham Dawson, *Soldier Heroes: British Adventure, Empires and the Imagining of Masculinities* (London: Routledge, 1994), 1.

39. Edward B. Kemble, "Americans—All," *American Leader* 5 (May 14, 1914): 597.

40. Ira E. Bennett, "Immigrants and the Flag," *American Leader* 5 (May 14, 1914): 588–89.

41. Louis N. Hammerling, "If We Went to War: A Letter to the New York Times with a Reply," *American Leader* 7 (January 14, 1915): 29–30.

42. "The Literacy Test in New York," *American Leader* 11 (February 8, 1917): 161. This article was dealing with a specific law in New York, which had made literacy a requirement for voting.

43. For an analysis of how Grant connected race and gender to World War I, see Guterl, *Color of Race in America*, 35–41.

44. Madison Grant to Prescott Hall, 15 November 1915, IRL Records, Box 1, HL.

45. Grant, *Passing of the Great Race*, 74.

46. Robert DeCourcy Ward, "Immigration and the War," *Scientific American Monthly* 2 (May 1916): 438.

47. Ibid., 443.

48. Ibid., 449.

49. "Sixth Annual Report of the Immigrants' Protective League for the Year Ending January 1, 1915," 22.

50. "Eighth Annual Report of the Immigrants' Protective League," 22.

51. Kathryn Kish Sklar, "'Some of Us Who Deal with the Social Fabric': Jane Addams Blends Peace with Social Justice, 1907–1919," *Journal of the Gilded Age and Progressive Era* 2 (January 2003): 83.

52. The nations that sent representatives included Britain, Germany, Belgium, and the Netherlands, but not France or Russia.

53. Quoted in Costin, *Two Sisters for Social Justice*, 56.

54. Ibid., 54.

55. Steinson, *American Women's Activism in World War I*, 66–67.

56. "Statement of Miss Grace Abbott of Hull House, Chicago," 3–4.

57. Ibid., 5–6.

58. Ibid., 9.

59. Ibid., 8–9.

60. Ibid., 9–10.

61. Robert DeCourcy Ward, "Immigration and the War," 444–45.

62. "The Case for the Literacy Test," 20.

63. One article in the *American Leader* reported on the work of the IPL. Also: Alexander McCormick, who became a president of the IPL, spoke at a banquet for Louis Hammerling in 1913. See "The Immigrants' Protective League," *American Leader* 3 (May 8, 1913): 571–72; McCormick, "Who Are Americans?" 218–24.

64. Grace Abbott, "The Democracy of Internationalism," *American Leader* 10 (September 28, 1916): 364–70. This article was reprinted from an article in the *Survey* and is discussed below. The other articles mentioned appeared in volume 10 of *American Leader* between July and December 1916.

65. Percy Andreae authored most of the other articles against prohibition in the AAFLN, and the style of Hammerling's "Personal Liberty" articles is very close to that of Andreae's.

66. Louis Hammerling, "Personal Liberty," *American Leader* 7 (April 22, 1915): 464.

67. Andreae, "On Preparedness," 24.

68. Bruno Lasker, "Spokesmen of Submerged Peoples: The Conference of Oppressed and Dependent Nationalities," *Survey* 36 (December 16, 1916): 293. Lasker describes the goals and content of the conference in this article. For more on the conference, see Gonzalez, "Immigrants in Our Midst," 347–51; Costin, *Two Sisters for Social Justice*, 57–58.

69. The program for the conference can be found in the IPL Papers, File 53a, Box 5, UIC.

70. Lasker, "Spokesmen of Submerged Peoples," 295.

71. Abbott, "Democracy of Internationalism," 479–80.

72. Ibid., 480.

73. Grace Abbott, *The Immigrant and the Community* (New York: Century, 1917), vii.

74. Ibid., 283.

75. Ibid., 289.

76. Ibid., 289.

77. Ibid., 290–91.

78. Ibid., 291–92.

79. Ibid., 297.

80. Ibid., vi.

81. Hutchinson, *Legislative History*, 165–67.

82. See, for instance, speeches by Alabama Democrat John Burnett and California Republican Julius Kahn. *Congressional Record*, 64th Cong., 1st sess., 1916, vol. 53, pt. 5:4773, 4792.

83. See, for instance, speeches by Illinois Republican John McKenzie, Georgia Democrat Carl Vinson, and Pennsylvania Republican Joseph Moore. Ibid., 5:4777, 4786, 4844.

84. Ibid., 5:4782.

85. Ibid., 5:4786

86. Ibid., 5:4776.

87. Ibid., 5:4778, 4781.

88. *Congressional Record*, 64th Cong., 2nd sess., 1917, vol. 53, pt. 3:2449.

89. *Congressional Record*, 64th Cong., 1st sess., 1916, vol. 53, pt. 5:4815.

90. Ibid., 5:4786.

91. *Congressional Record*, 64th Cong., 2nd sess., 1917, vol. 54, pt. 3:2443.

92. *Congressional Record*, 64th Cong., 1st sess., 1916, vol. 53, pt. 5:4798.

93. Hutchinson, *Legislative History*, 167.

94. Zieger, *America's Great War*, 77–84.

95. "The Literacy Test Becomes Law," *American Leader* 11 (February 22, 1917): 197.

96. "The Association Sends Another Man to the Front," *American Leader* 13 (March 14, 1918): 205.

97. See, for example, "900 Greeks Ready to Fight for U.S.," *American Leader* 11 (April 26, 1917): 455–56; "The Italians of America Organizing," *American Leader* 11 (April 26, 1917): 457; "Poles off for War Camp," *American Leader* 12 (December 13, 1917): 656; "Tribute to Jews in the Army," *American Leader* 12 (November 22, 1917): 591–92.

98. Edward Kemble, "Cartoon," *American Leader* 11 (April 26, 1917): 468.

99. "Patriotism of the Foreign-born," *American Leader* 12 (July 12, 1917): 8.

100. "America's New Sons Volunteer Gladly," *American Leader* 13 (January 24, 1918): 71–72.

101. See, for example, "Alien Austro-Hungarians," *American Leader* 12 (December 27, 1917): 734; Jareslav Cisar, "The Czechoslovaks in America," *American Leader* 13 (May 9, 1918): 528.

102. For information on Hammerling's attempts to defend himself, see Louis Hammerling to Joseph P. Tumulty, 21 October 1917, Woodrow Wilson Papers, Library of Congress,

Washington, DC (collection hereafter cited as Wilson Papers, LC); *New York Times*, "Admits Campaign to Stop Munitions," December 4, 1918. For information on Hammerling's plan, see Louis Hammerling, "Memorandum," 22 July 1918, Wilson Papers, LC. He said his object was "the overthrow of the Austro-Hungarian Empire from within" by "creating a rebellious spirit among the subject races now under its domination susceptible to that end by reason of their own national aspirations, superinduced by personal suffering caused by the war. These races comprise the various Slavonic nationalities, Italian Irridentists and Roumanians, within the Dual Monarchy." Wilson dismissed this plan because it "too nearly resembles German methods." Woodrow Wilson to Joseph P. Tumulty, 30 July 1918, Wilson Papers, LC.

103. Memorandum for the President by George Creel, Wilson Papers, LC.

104. *New York Times*, "Hammerling Resigns," March 5, 1919.

105. Frank Zotti to Joseph P. Tumulty, 20 October 1919, Wilson Papers, LC. Zotti, an enemy of Hammerling's, wrote to complain about Hammerling's obtaining a passport.

106. *New York Times*, "18 Story Fall Kills Hammerling," April 28, 1935. Greene, *Slavic Community on Strike*, 247.

107. The AAFLN did not have much of a relationship with Kellor before this, although they did publish an article by her in 1912. See Frances Kellor, "Guarding the Immigrant," *American Leader* 2 (September 12, 1912): 285–87.

108. Fitzpatrick, *Endless Crusade*, 162–64. For more on Kellor's Americanization campaigns, see Higham, *Strangers in the Land*, 239–50.

109. *New York Times*, "Will Combat Bolshevism," May 26, 1919; Higham, *Strangers in the Land*, 258.

110. Gonzalez, "Immigrants in Our Midst," 325–26, 359.

111. Henry Leonard, "The Immigrants' Protective League of Chicago," *Journal of the Illinois State Historical Society* 66, no.3 (1973): 282.

112. These studies continued to press the themes Abbott had developed in the IPL: the importance of immigrants to the whole community, the special needs and contributions of immigrant women, and the need for the federal government to set up institutions to improve the condition of immigrants. Grace Abbott, *Bulletin of the Immigrants' Commission No. 1: The Educational Needs of Immigrants in Illinois* (Springfield: State of Illinois Department of Registration and Education, 1920).

113. Leonard, "The Immigrants Protective League of Chicago," 282; Costin, *Two Sisters for Social Justice*, 120; Gonzalez, "Immigrants in Our Midst," 371–72.

114. After the Illinois Immigration Commission was shut down, private organizations, such as the Chicago Community Trust and the Young Women's Christian Association, haphazardly supported an Immigrants' Protective League, and those involved in immigration protection activities hoped that more money would be appropriated. When they finally despaired of these hopes, they decided on a formal reorganization of the IPL. For a short time, Iris Wood was director of the IPL, but the board, which included Jane Addams, Sophonisba Breckinridge, and Edith Abbott, was not satisfied with her performance. General Abel D. Davis, the president of the IPL, explained that, although Wood was "honest of purpose" and had a "charming personality," he did not feel that she had "sufficient

executive ability" to lead the organization. Edith Abbott replied that she had approached Mrs. Adena Miller Rich, who had served as the assistant director under Grace Abbott, and Edith believed she would make an ideal director. See "Immigrants' Protective League Reorganizes," offprint, IPL Papers, Box 5, Folder 62; IPL Papers, Box 6, UIC.

115. Costin, *Two Sisters for Social Justice*, 97.

116. Gonzalez, "Immigrants in Our Midst," 360–63.

117. Costin, *Two Sisters for Social Justice*, 121–24.

118. For divisions within the suffrage movement caused by the war, see Graham, *Woman Suffrage*, 100–110.

119. For work on women's independent citizenship, see Gardner, *Qualities of a Citizen*; Bredbenner, *A Nationality of Her Own*, 80–112; Wendy Sarvasy, "Beyond the Difference versus Equality Policy Debate: Postsuffrage Feminism, Citizenship, and the Quest for a Feminist Welfare State," *Signs* 17 (Winter 1992): 351–55; Virginia Sapiro, "Women, Citizenship and Nationality: Immigration and Naturalization Policies in the United States," *Politics and Society* 13, no. 1 (1984): 1–26.

120. Grace Abbott, "After Suffrage—Citizenship," *Survey* 44 (September 1, 1920): 656.

121. Ibid., 656.

122. Ibid., 657.

123. Bredbenner, *A Nationality of Her Own*, 12.

124. Gardner, *Qualities of a Citizen*, 139.

125. Bredbenner, *A Nationality of Her Own*, 111.

126. Prescott Hall to Joseph Lee, 11 March 1917, Joseph Lee Papers, Box 2, File 16, MHS.

127. Joseph Lee to Dr. Sleght, 25 October 1920, Joseph Lee Papers, Box 3, Folder 5, MHS. Lee wrote in a letter to Cameron Forbes in 1921 that "the literacy test has not accomplished what we thought it would." Joseph Lee to Cameron Forbes, 18 February 1921, Joseph Lee Papers, Box 3, Folder 8, MHS.

128. Prescott Hall to Joseph Lee, 31 December 1917, Joseph Lee Papers, Box 2, File 18, MHS.

129. Prescott Hall, "Publications of the Immigration Restriction League no. 71: Immigration Restriction and World Eugenics," Joseph Lee Papers, Box 7, MHS.

130. Higham, *Strangers in the Land*, 302. For more on Gullick's plan, see Zeidel, *Immigrants, Progressives and Exclusion Politics*, 133–35.

131. Prescott Hall to Henry Cabot Lodge, 15 May 1919, IRL Records, Box 2, HL.

Chapter Six

1. Joseph Lee to the Editors of the *Springfield Republican* and the *Boston Herald*, 1 June 1921, IRL Records, Box 4, HL.

2. Higham, *Strangers in the Land*, 313. For the ways in which the men of the IRL were involved in the new debate, see Kenneth M. Ludmerer, "Genetics, Eugenics and the Immi-

gration Restriction Act of 1924," *Bulletin of the History of Medicine* 46, no. 1 (1972): 74; Guterl, *Color of Race in America*, 47.

3. Kevles, *In the Name of Eugenics*, 96–112.

4. For Harding's view on restriction, see Vought, *Bully Pulpit*, 155–80. For more on the political and cultural context of the 1920s, see Lynn Dumenil, *The Modern Temper: American Culture and Society in the 1920s* (New York: Hill and Wang, 1995).

5. The quota was applied from April 1, 1921, to June 30, 1922. In 1922, Congress voted to extend the quota for two more years. See Hutchinson, *Legislative History*, 469.

6. Daniels, *Guarding the Golden Door*, 48.

7. Reed had wanted to continue basing quotas on the 1910 census for fear of offending urban immigrant constituencies. When his attempts to work with Johnson to change the bill failed, he offered a compromise, as an attempt to give more of an appearance of fairness. When the national origins provision was to go into effect, however, a snag developed. The select committee, made up of Calvin Coolidge's Secretaries of State, Commerce, and Labor, complained of the enormity of their task and sought to solve difficulties with the quota by "taking the percentage of each group in the United States in 1890 and then tracing the additions to that number by subsequent immigration." The end result was that English immigrants made up most of the quota numbers—almost 50 percent of the total 150,000—since the committee selected by the President determined that, based on the names listed in the census, 50 percent of Americans could trace their origins to England. In the end, the national origins quota did not go into effect until 1929. Robert A. Divine, *American Immigration Policy, 1924–1952* (New Haven, CT: Yale University Press, 1957), 28.

8. For an overview of the provisions of the Johnson-Reed Act, see Hutchinson, *Legislative History*, 185–94; Higham, *Strangers in the Land*, 316–24. For other works on the racial implications of the law, see Ngai, *Impossible Subjects*, esp. ch. 1, "The Johnson-Reed Act of 1924 and the Reconstruction of Race in Immigration Law," pp. 19–55; Daniels, *Guarding the Golden Door*, 49–58; King, *Making Americans*, 208–9; Gerstle, *American Crucible*, 107–8; Foley, *White Scourge*, 45–46.

9. Arguments about immigration as a threat to working-class manhood were still present in the 1924 debate. See, for example, the speech by David Kincheloe of Kentucky. *Congressional Record*, 68th Cong., 1st sess., 1924, vol. 65, pt. 6:6236. But these arguments were muted in favor of eugenic and racial arguments.

10. Ludmerer, "Genetics, Eugenics and the Immigration Restriction Act of 1924," 68. For more on the influence of Laughlin's eugenic beliefs, see Jacobson, *Whiteness of a Different Color*, 84–85; and Garland E. Allen, "The Eugenics Record Office at Cold Spring Harbor, 1910–1940," *Osiris*, 2nd ser., 2 (1986): 245–50. Only one critic of Laughlin was brought in at the last minute—Herbert Spencer Jennings. Even he did not question the idea that characteristics were innate and biological, but he blamed the Irish, not southeastern Europeans, for the "immigrant problem." Elazar Barkan, "Reevaluating Progressive Eugenics: Herbert Spencer Jennings and the 1924 Immigration Legislation," *Journal of the History of Biology* 24, no. 1 (1991): 102–3.

11. Gerstle, *American Crucible*, 107–8.

12. *Congressional Record*, 68th Cong., 1st sess., 1924, vol. 65, pt. 6:5902, 5904.

13. Ibid., 6:5695.

14. Ibid., 6:5857.

15. Ibid., 6:6255.

16. Ibid., 6:5651.

17. Ibid., 6:5849.

18. Ibid., 6:5669.

19. At another point, when a congressman made an attack on Japanese immigrants, Adolph Sabath, who served on the House Immigration and Naturalization Committee, interrupted to say, "I may say that all the committee are in favor of exclusion of the Japanese." Ibid., 6:5681.

20. Ibid., 6:5900.

21. Ibid., 6:5657.

22. Of course, many restrictionists wanted to exclude Mexicans totally, particularly Representative John C. Box of Texas. For more on the racialization of Mexican immigrants in the 1920s, see Foley, *White Scourge*, 40–44.

23. Jacobson, *Whiteness of a Different Color*, 94. See also Roediger, *Working toward Whiteness*, 139–56; Arnold R. Hirsch, "E Pluribus Duo? Thoughts on 'Whiteness' and Chicago's 'New' Immigration as a Transient Third Tier," *Journal of American Ethnic History* 23 (Summer 2004): 7–44.

24. Ngai, *Impossible Subjects*, 24–25. Court cases dealing with naturalization also show, in the words of historian Ian F. Haney Lopez, "the imprecisions and contradictions inherent in the establishment of racial lines between Whites and non-Whites." Ian F. Haney Lopez, *White by Law: The Legal Construction of Race* (New York: New York University Press, 1996), 2. See also Ngai, *Impossible Subjects*, 37–50; Pascoe "Miscegenation Law," 44–69.

25. For historians who have examined the tensions between equality and difference in the 1920s, see Nancy F. Cott, *The Grounding of Modern Feminism* (New Haven, CT: Yale University Press, 1987); Estelle B. Freedman, "Separatism as Strategy: Female Institution Building and American Feminism, 1870–1930," *Feminist Studies* 5, no. 3 (1979): 512–29.

26. Costin, *Two Sisters for Social Justice*, 141–42. See also Muncy, *Creating a Female Dominion*, 132.

27. For more on changing perceptions of women during this time, see Cott, *Grounding of Modern Feminism*, 143–74.

28. James Patten to Richards M. Bradley, 9 December 1923, Joseph Lee Papers, Box 4, File 10, MHS; James Patten to Madison Grant, 18 November 1921, Joseph Lee Papers, Box 4, File 10, MHS. Patten, in general, tended to show especial hostility to women who supported immigrants. See James Patten to Richards M. Bradley, 15 December 1921, Joseph Lee Papers, Box 4, File 10, MHS.

29. Fitzpatrick, *Endless Crusade*, 206–7.

30. James Patten to the Executive Committee of the IRL, 13 December 1923, Joseph Lee Papers, Box 4, File 10, MHS. (Emphasis in original.)

31. Madison Grant to Albert Johnson, 22 June 1921, Joseph Lee Papers, Box 3, File 13, MHS.

32. *Congressional Record*, 68th Cong, 1st sess., 1924, vol. 65, pt. 6:6135. Victor Berger had a dramatic career in Congress. In 1919, the House of Representatives refused to seat him because he had opposed the United States' entry into World War I and because he had been convicted under the Espionage Act. He successfully appealed the conviction and won the 1922 election. Kennedy, *Over Here*, 290.

33. *Congressional Record*, 68th Cong, 1st sess., 1924, vol. 65, pt. 6:5897.

34. Ibid., 6:6135.

35. Ibid., 6:5693.

36. Ibid., 6:5694.

37. Ibid., 6:6115.

38. Gardner, *Qualities of a Citizen*, 131–32; Cott, *Public Vows*, 154–55.

39. Hutchinson, *Legislative History*, 196–210. Adena Miller Rich, who became director of the Immigrants' Protective League after 1925, became a strong advocate for letting family members of landed aliens have nonquota status. See her reports in IPL Papers, Box 5, UIC.

40. Daniels, *Guarding the Golden Door*, 54.

41. For more on the bill and Coolidge's reservations about it, see Vought, *Bully Pulpit*, 181–85; Higham, *Strangers in the Land*, 324, King, *Making Americans*, 199–206; David Goldberg, *Discontented America: The United States in the 1920s* (Baltimore: The Johns Hopkins University Press, 1999), 160–63; Cheryl Shanks, *Immigration and the Politics of American Sovereignty, 1890–1990* (Ann Arbor: University of Michigan Press, 2001).

42. For the long-term consequences of the Johnson-Reed Act, see Ngai, *Impossible Subjects*; Daniels, *Guarding the Golden Door*; Gerstle, *American Crucible*; King, *Making Americans*; George Sanchez, *Becoming Mexican American: Ethnicity, Culture and Identity in Chicano Los Angeles, 1900–1945* (New York: Oxford University Press, 1993); Roediger, *Working toward Whiteness*.

43. Ngai, *Impossible Subjects*, 261.

44. For more on the critique that immigrants did not fulfill American economic citizenship, see Robin Dale, *The New Nativism: Proposition 187 and the Debate over Immigration* (Minneapolis: University of Minnesota Press, 2008), 66–88.

45. Ibid., 122–23.

46. Patrick Buchanan, "America in 2050: Another Country" (http://buchanan.org/blog/pjb-america-in-2050-another-country-588).

47. Janet Murguía, "The Implications of Immigration Enforcement on America's Children, Presented At: Hearing on ICE Workplace Raids: Their Impact on U.S. Children, Families, and Communities," Publications of the National Council of La Raza, May 20, 2008 (http://www.nclr.org/content/publications/detail/52035/).

48. David Brooks, "Immigrants to Be Proud of," *New York Times*, March 30, 2006.

Bibliography

Manuscript Collections

Adena Miller Rich Papers. Jane Addams Memorial Collection. Department of Special Collections. University of Illinois at Chicago Library.

Grace and Edith Abbott Papers. Regenstein Special Collections. University of Chicago.

Papers of the Immigrants' Protective League. Jane Addams Memorial Collection. Department of Special Collections. University of Illinois at Chicago Library.

Joseph Lee Papers. Massachusetts Historical Society. Boston, MA.

Records of the Immigration Restriction League. Houghton Library. Harvard University.

Manuscript Collections on Microfilm

Henry Cabot Lodge Letterbooks. Massachusetts Historical Society. Boston, MA.

Jane Addams Papers. Jane Addams Memorial Collection. Richard M. Daley Library. University of Illinois at Chicago.

Papers of the Immigration Restriction League. Boston Public Library. Boston, MA.

William Howard Taft Papers. Library of Congress. Washington, DC.

Woodrow Wilson Papers. Library of Congress. Washington, DC.

Government Documents

Boas, Franz. *Reports of the Immigration Commission, Volume 38: Changes in Bodily Form of Descendants of Immigrants.* Washington, DC: Government Printing Office, 1911.

Bulletin of the Immigrants' Commission No. 1: The Educational Needs of Immigrants in Illinois. Springfield: State of Illinois Department of Registration and Education, 1920.

Congressional Record. 54th Cong., 1st sess., 1896. Vol. 28, pt. 3.

Congressional Record. 54th Cong., 1st sess., 1896. Vol. 28, pt. 6.

Congressional Record. 54th Cong., 2nd sess., 1896. Vol. 29, pt. I.

Congressional Record. 54th Cong., 2nd sess., 1897. Vol. 29, pt. 2.

Congressional Record. 54th Cong., 2nd sess., 1897. Vol. 29, pt. 3.

Congressional Record. 64th Cong., 1st sess., 1916. Vol. 53, pt. 5.

Congressional Record. 64th Cong., 2nd sess., 1917. Vol. 53, pt. 3.

Congressional Record. 68th Cong, 1st sess., 1924. Vol. 65, pt. 6.

Hearings before the Committee on Immigration and Naturalization, House of Representatives, Seventieth Congress, First Session, Hearing no. 70.1.6. Washington, DC: Government Printing Office, 1928.

Hearings before the Committee on Immigration and Naturalization, House of Representatives, Sixty-Third Congress, Second Session on HR 6060. Washington, DC: Government Printing Office, 1913.

Relative to the Further Restriction of Immigration: Hearings, 1912, United States, 62nd Congress, Second Session, House Committee on Immigration and Naturalization. Washington, DC: Government Printing Office, 1912.

Reports of the Immigration Commission: Statements and Recommendations Submitted by Societies and Organizations Interested in the Subject of Immigration. Washington, DC: Government Printing Office, 1911.

Restriction of Immigration: Hearings before the Committee on Immigration and Naturalization, House Of Representatives, Sixty-Fourth Congress, First Session on HR 558. Washington, DC: Government Printing Office, 1916.

Periodicals Consulted (1889–1950)

Andover Review
American Journal of Sociology
American Leader
Annals of the American Academy of Political and Social Science
Atlantic Monthly
Century Magazine
Charities and the Commons: A Weekly Journal of Philanthropy and Social Advance
New Republic
New York Times
North American Review
Political Science Quarterly
Scientific American Monthly
Social Service Review
Survey

Published Primary Sources

Abbott, Grace. *The Immigrant and the Community.* New York: Century, 1917.

Buchanan, Patrick. "America in 2050: Another Country." http://buchanan.org/blog/pjb-america-in-2050-another-country-588 (accessed September 20, 2009).

Commons, John R. *Races and Immigrants in America.* 2nd ed. New York: Macmillan, 1920.

Dictionary of American Biography. 1st ed. S.v. "Ward, Robert DeCourcy."

English, Daylanne. *Unnatural Selections: Eugenics in American Modernism and the Harlem Renaissance.* Chapel Hill: University of North Carolina Press, 2004.

Fairchild, Henry Pratt. *Immigration: A World Movement and Its American Significance.* New York: Macmillan, 1913.

Grant, Madison. *The Passing of the Great Race, or the Racial Basis of European History.* 4th ed. 1916. Reprint, New York: Charles Scribner's Sons, 1922.

Hall, Prescott. *Immigration and Its Effects upon the United States.* New York: Henry Holt, 1908.

Jenks, Jeremiah W. and W. Jett Lauck. *The Immigration Problem*. New York: Funk and Wagnalls, 1912.

Murguía, Janet. "The Implications of Immigration Enforcement on America's Children, Presented at: Hearing on ICE Workplace Raids: Their Impact on U.S. Children, Families, and Communities." Publications of the National Council of La Raza, May 20, 2008. http://www.nclr.org/content/publications/detail/52035/ (accessed September 20, 2009).

Official Proceedings of the 25th Annual Convention of the Farmers' National Congress of the United States. Indianapolis: National Farmers' Congress. 1905.

Proceedings of the National Conference for Good City Government. Philadelphia: The League, 1910.

Smith, Richmond Mayo. *Emigration and Immigration: A Study in Social Science.* New York: Charles Scribner's Sons, 1890.

Ripley, William. *The Races of Europe: A Sociological Study.* New York: D. Appleton, 1899.

Ross, E. A. *The Old World in the New: The Significance of Past and Present Immigration to the American People.* New York: Century, 1914.

Twelfth Annual Meeting of the American Sociological Society, Held in Philadelphia, PA, December 27–29, 1917. Chicago: University of Chicago Press, 1918.

Secondary Sources

Adams, Bluford. "World Conquest or a Dying People? Racial Theory, Regional Anxiety, and the Brahmin Anglo-Saxonists." *Journal of the Gilded Age and Progressive Era* 8 (April 2009): 189–216.

Ahmad, Diana L. "Opium Smoking, Anti-Chinese Attitudes, and the American Medical Community." *American Nineteenth Century History* 1 (Summer 2000): 53–68.

Allen, Garland E. "The Eugenics Record Office at Cold Spring Harbor, 1910–1940." *Osiris*, 2nd ser., 2 (1986): 225–64.

———. "The Misuse of Biological Hierarchies: The American Eugenics Movement, 1900–1940." *History and Philosophy of the Life Sciences* 5, no. 2 (1983): 105–28.

Allen, Theodore W. *The Invention of the White Race, Volume One: Racial Oppression and Social Control.* New York: Verso, 1994.

Anderson, Stuart. *Race and Rapprochement: Anglo-Saxonism and Anglo-American Relations, 1895–1904.* Cranbury, NJ: Associated University Press, 1980.

Ayers, Edward L. *The Promise of the New South: Life after Reconstruction.* New York: Oxford University Press, 1992.

Baker, Paula. "The Domestication of Politics: Women and American Political Society, 1780–1920." *American Historical Review* 89 (June 1984): 620–47.

Barkan, Elazar. "Reevaluating Progressive Eugenics: Herbert Spencer Jennings and the 1924 Immigration Legislation." *Journal of the History of Biology* 24, no. 1 (1991): 91–112.

———. *The Retreat of Scientific Racism: Changing Concepts of Race in Britain and the United States between the World Wars.* Cambridge: Cambridge University Press, 1993.

Baron, Ava. "An 'Other' Side of Gender Antagonism at Work: Men, Boys, and the Remasculinization of Printer's Work, 1830–1920." In *Work Engendered: Toward a New History of American Labor*, edited by Ava Baron, 47–69. Ithaca, NY: Cornell University Press, 1991.

Baum, Bruce. *The Rise and Fall of the Caucasian Race: A Political History of Racial Identity*. New York: New York University Press, 2006.

Bayton, Douglas C. "Defectives in the Land: Disability and American Immigration Policy, 1882–1924." *Journal of American Ethnic History* 24 (Spring 2005): 31–44.

Bederman, Gail. *Manliness and Civilization: A Cultural History of Gender and Race in the United States, 1880–1917*. Chicago: University of Chicago Press, 1995.

———. "'Civilization,' the Decline of Middle-Class Manliness, and Ida B. Wells's Anti-Lynching Campaign (1892–94)." *Radical History Review* 52 (Winter 1992): 5–30.

Beeton, Beverly. *Women Vote in the West: The Woman Suffrage Movement, 1869–1896*. New York: Garland, 1986.

Berger, Iris, Elsa Barkley Brown, and Nancy Hewitt. "Symposium—Intersections and Collision Courses: Women, Blacks and Workers Confront Gender, Race and Class." *Feminist Studies* 18 (Summer 1992): 283–326.

Berthoff, Rowland T. "Southern Attitudes toward Immigration, 1865–1914." *Journal of Southern History* 17 (August 1951): 328–60.

Black, Edwin. *War against the Weak: Eugenics and America's Campaign to Create a Master Race*. New York: Thunder's Mouth, 2003.

Blee, Kathleen. *Women of the Klan: Racism and Gender in the 1920's*. Berkeley: University of California Press, 1991.

Bodnar, John. *The Transplanted: A History of Immigrants in Urban America*. Bloomington: Indiana University Press, 1985.

Boris, Eileen. "Reconstructing the 'Family': Women, Progressive Reform, and the Problem of Social Control," in Frankel and Dye, *Gender, Class, Race and Reform*, 81–82.

Boydston, Jeanne. *Home and Work: Housework, Wages, and the Ideology of Labor in the Early Republic*. New York: Oxford University Press, 1990.

Boxerman, Burton A. "Adolph Joachim Sabath in Congress: The Early Years, 1907–1932." *Journal of the Illinois State Historical Society* 66 (Fall 1973): 327–40.

Bredbenner, Candice Lewis. *A Nationality of Her Own: Women, Marriage and the Law of Citizenship*. Berkeley: University of California Press, 1998.

Brodkin, Karen. *How Jews Became White Folks and What That Says about Race in America*. New Brunswick, NJ: Rutgers University Press, 1998.

Brown, Elsa Barkley. "Womanist Consciousness: Maggie Lena Walker and the Independent Order of Saint Luke." *Signs* 14 (March 1989): 610–33.

Brown, Victoria Bissell. "Jane Addams, Progressivism, and Woman Suffrage: An Introduction to 'Why Women Should Vote.'" In *One Woman, One Vote: Rediscovering the Woman Suffrage Movement*, edited by Marjorie Spruill Wheeler, 179–95. Troutdale, OR: New Sage, 1995.

Brown, Wendy. "Tolerance and Equality: 'The Jewish Question' and 'the Woman Question.'" In *Going Public: Feminism and the Shifting Boundaries of the Private Sphere*, edited by Joan Scott and Debra Keates, 15–42. Urbana: University of Illinois Press, 2004.

Buroker, Robert L. "From Voluntary Association to Welfare State: The Illinois Immigrants' Protective League, 1908–1926." *Journal of American History* 58 (December 1971): 643–60.

Carby, Hazel. *Reconstructing Womanhood: The Emergence of the Afro-American Woman Novelist*. Oxford: Oxford University Press, 1987.

Carnes, Mark. *Meanings for Manhood: Constructions of Masculinity in Victorian America*. Chicago: University of Chicago Press, 1990.

Chambers, John Whiteclay, II. *The Tyranny of Change: America in the Progressive Era, 1890–1920*. 2nd ed. New Brunswick, NJ: Rutgers University Press, 2000.

Chauncy, George. *Gay New York: Gender, Urban Culture and the Makings of the Gay Male World, 1890–1940*. New York: Basic Books, 1994.

Cogdell, Christina. *Eugenic Design: Streamlining America in the 1930s*. Philadelphia: University of Pennsylvania Press, 2004.

Cohen, Philip N. "Nationalism and Suffrage: Gender Struggle in Nation-Building America." *Signs* 21 (Spring 1996): 707–27.

Cooper, John Milton, Jr. *The Pivotal Decades: The United States, 1900–1920*. New York: Norton, 1990.

Cornell, Stephen, and Douglas Hartmann. "Conceptual Confusions and Divides: Race, Ethnicity, and the Study of Immigration." In *Not Just Black and White: Historical and Contemporary Perspectives on Immigration, Race, and Ethnicity in the United States*, edited by Nancy Foner and George M. Frederickson, 23–41. New York: Russell Sage Foundation, 2004.

Costin, Lela B. *Two Sisters for Social Justice: A Biography of Grace and Edith Abbott*. Urbana: University of Illinois Press, 1983.

Cott, Nancy F. *The Grounding of Modern Feminism*. New Haven, CT: Yale University Press, 1987.

———. "Marriage and Women's Citizenship in the United States, 1830–1934." *The American Historical Review* 103 (December 1998): 1440–74.

———. *Public Vows: A History of Marriage and the Nation*. Cambridge, MA: Harvard University Press, 2000.

Cunningham, George E. "The Italian, a Hindrance to White Solidarity in Louisiana, 1890–1898." *Journal of Negro History* 50 (January 1965): 22–36.

Daniels, Roger. *Coming to America: A History of Immigration and Ethnicity in American Life*. New York: Harper Perennial, 1990.

———. *Guarding the Golden Door: American Immigration Policy and Immigrants since 1882*. New York: Hill and Wang, 2004.

———. *Not Like Us: Immigrants and Minorities in America, 1890–1924*. The American Ways Series. Chicago: Ivan R. Dee, 1997.

Dale, Robin. *The New Nativism: Proposition 187 and the Debate over Immigration*. Minneapolis: University of Minnesota Press, 2008.

Davis, Allen F. *Spearheads for Reform: The Social Settlements and the Progressive Movement, 1890–1914*. New York: Oxford University Press, 1967.

Dawley, Alan. *Changing the World: American Progressives in War and Revolution*. Princeton, NJ: Princeton University Press, 2003.

———. *Struggles for Justice: Social Responsibility and the Liberal States, 1877–1919*. Cambridge, MA: Belknap, 1991.

Dawson, Graham. *Soldier Heroes: British Adventure, Empires and the Imagining of Masculinities*. London: Routledge, 1994.

D'Emilio, John, and Estelle B. Freedman. *Intimate Matters: A History of Sexuality in America*. New York: Harper and Row, 1988.

Diner, Steven J. *A Very Different Age: Americans of the Progressive Era*. New York: Hill and Wang, 1998.

Divine, Robert A. *American Immigration Policy, 1924–1952*. New Haven, CT: Yale University Press, 1957.

Dubois, Ellen Carol. *Feminism and Suffrage: The Emergence of an Independent Women's Movement in America, 1848–1869*. Ithaca, NY: Cornell University Press, 1978.

————. *Harriot Stanton Blatch and the Winning of Woman Suffrage*. New Haven, CT: Yale University Press, 1997.

Dumenil, Lynn. *The Modern Temper: American Culture and Society in the 1920s*. New York: Hill and Wang, 1995.

Dye, Nancy S. *Equal as Sisters: Feminism, the Labor Movement and the Women's Trade Union League of New York*. Columbia: University of Missouri Press, 1980.

Ewen, Elizabeth. *Immigrant Women in the Land of Dollars: Life and Culture in the Lower East Side, 1890–1925*. New York: Monthly Review, 1985.

Fitzpatrick, Ellen. *Endless Crusade: Women Social Scientists and Progressive Reform*. New York: Oxford University Press, 1990.

Flanagan, Maureen A. *America Reformed: Progressives and Progressivisms, 1890s–1920s*. New York: Oxford University Press, 2007.

————. *Seeing with their Hearts: Chicago Women and the Vision of a Good City*. Princeton, NJ: Princeton University Press, 2002.

Foley, Neil. *The White Scourge: Mexicans, Blacks and Poor Whites in Texas Cotton Culture*. Berkeley: University of California Press, 1997.

Foner, Nancy. *In a New Land: A Comparative View of Immigration*. New York: New York University Press, 2005.

Frankel, Noralee, and Nancy S. Dye, eds. *Gender, Class, Race, and Reform in the Progressive Era*. Lexington, KY: University Press of Kentucky, 1991.

Fraser, Nancy, and Linda Gordon. "A Genealogy of Dependency: Tracing a Keyword of the U.S. Welfare State." *Signs* 19 (December 1994): 323–42.

Freedman, Estelle B. "Separatism as Strategy: Female Institution Building and American Feminism, 1870–1930." *Feminist Studies* 5, no. 3 (1979): 512–29.

Gabaccia, Donna. *From the Other Side: Women, Gender and Immigrant Life in the United States, 1820–1990*. Bloomington: Indiana University Press, 1994.

Gaines, Kevin. *Uplifting the Race: Black Leadership, Politics, and Culture in the Twentieth Century*. Chapel Hill: University of North Carolina Press, 1996.

Gardner, Martha. *The Qualities of a Citizen: Women, Immigration, and Citizenship, 1870–1965*. Princeton, NJ: Princeton University Press, 2005.

Gerstle, Gary. *American Crucible: Race and Nation in the Twentieth Century*. Princeton, NJ: Princeton University Press, 2001.

Gilmore, Glenda Elizabeth. *Gender and Jim Crow: Women and the Politics of White Supremacy in North Carolina, 1896–1920*. Chapel Hill: University of North Carolina Press, 1996.

Ginzberg, Lori. *Women and the Work of Benevolence: Morality, Politics, and Class in the Nineteenth Century United States*. New Haven, CT: Yale University Press, 1990.

Gleason, Philip. "American Identity and Americanization." In *Harvard Encyclopedia of American Ethnic Groups*, 31–57. Cambridge, MA: Belknap, 1980.

————. *Speaking of Diversity: Language and Ethnicity in Twentieth Century America*. Baltimore: Johns Hopkins University Press, 1992.

Glenn, Evelyn Nakano. *Unequal Freedom: How Race and Gender Shaped American Citizenship and Labor*. Cambridge, MA: Harvard University Press, 2002.

Glenn, Susan. *Daughters of the Shtetl: Life and Labor in the Immigrant Generation*. Ithaca, NY: Cornell University Press, 1990.

Goldberg, David. *Discontented America: The United States in the 1920s.* Baltimore: Johns Hopkins University Press, 1999.

Goldstein, Eric L. "'Different Blood Flows in Our Veins': Race and Jewish Self-Definition in Late Nineteenth Century America." *American Jewish History* 85 (March 1997): 29–55.

———. *The Price of Whiteness: Jews, Race and American Identity.* Princeton, NJ: Princeton University Press, 2006.

Gonzalez, Suronda. "Complicating Citizenship: Grace Abbott and the Immigrants' Protective League, 1908–1921." *Michigan Historical Review* 24 (Fall 1998): 56–75.

———. "Immigrants in Our Midst: Grace Abbott, the Immigrants' Protective League of Chicago, and the New American Citizenship, 1908–1924." PhD diss., State University of New York, 2004.

Goodenow, Ronald K., and Arthur White, eds. *Education and the Rise of the New South.* Boston: Hall, 1981.

Gordon, Linda. *Pitied but Not Entitled: Single Mothers and the History of Welfare.* New York: Free Press, 1994.

———. "Putting Children First: Women, Maternalism, and Welfare in the Early Twentieth Century." In *U.S. History as Women's History: New Feminist Essays,* edited by Linda Kerber, Alice Kessler-Harris, and Kathryn Kish Sklar, 63–86. Chapel Hill: University of North Carolina Press, 1995.

Gossett, Thomas F. *Race: The History of an Idea in America.* Dallas: Southern Methodist University Press, 1963.

Gould, Lewis L. *America in the Progressive Era, 1890–1914.* Seminar Series in History. New York: Pearson Education, 2001.

Graham, Sara Hunter. *Woman Suffrage and the New Democracy.* New Haven, CT: Yale University Press, 1996.

Grant, Charles C. "Prophet of American Racism: Madison Grant and the Nordic Myth." *Phylon* 23 (Spring 1962): 173–90.

Greene, Victor R. *The Slavic Community on Strike: Immigrant Labor in Pennsylvania Anthracite.* Notre Dame, IN: University of Notre Dame Press, 1968.

Guglielmo, Thomas. *White on Arrival: Italians, Race, Color and Power in Chicago, 1890–1945.* Oxford: Oxford University Press, 2003.

Guterl, Matthew Pratt. *The Color of Race in America, 1900–1940.* Cambridge, MA: Harvard University Press, 2001.

Hale, Grace Elizabeth. *Making Whiteness: The Culture of Segregation in the South, 1890–1940.* New York: Vintage, 1998.

Hall, Jacquelyn Dowd. *Revolt against Chivalry: Jessie Daniel Ames and the Women's Campaign against Lynching.* New York: Columbia University Press, 1979.

Halle, David. *America's Working Man: Work, Home, and Politics among Blue Collar Property Owners.* Chicago: University of Chicago Press, 1984.

Haller, John S., Jr. *Outcasts from Evolution: Scientific Attitudes of Racial Inferiority, 1859–1900.* Urbana: University of Illinois Press, 1971.

Hawkins, Mike. *Social Darwinism in European and American Thought, 1860–1945: Nature as Model and Nature as Threat.* Cambridge: Cambridge University Press, 1997.

Hawley, Ellis W. *The Great War and the Search for Modern Order: A History of the American People and Their Institutions.* New York: St. Martin's, 1979.

———. *Southern Discomfort: Women's Activism in Tampa, Florida, 1880s–1920s.* Urbana: University of Illinois Press, 2001.

Higginbotham, Evelyn Brooks. "African American Women's History and the Metalanguage of Race." *Signs* 17 (Winter 1992): 251–74.

———. *Righteous Discontent: The Women's Movement in the Black Baptist Church, 1880–1920.* Cambridge, MA: Harvard University Press, 1993.

Higham, John. "Origins of Immigration Restriction, 1882–1897: A Social Analysis." *Mississippi Valley Historical Review* 39 (June 1952): 77–88.

———. *Strangers in the Land: Patterns of American Nativism, 1860–1925.* 2nd ed. 1955. Reprint, New Brunswick, NJ: Rutgers University Press, 1988.

Hirsch, Arnold R. "E Pluribus Duo? Thoughts on 'Whiteness' and Chicago's 'New' Immigration as a Transient Third Tier." *Journal of American Ethnic History* 23 (Summer 2004): 7–44.

Hobson, Barbara, and Ruth Lister. "Citizenship." In *Contested Concepts in Gender and Social Politics,* edited by Barbara Hobson, Jane Lewis, and Birte Siim, 23–48. Cheltenham, UK: Edward Elgar, 2002.

Hodes, Martha. *White Women, Black Men: Illicit Sex in the Nineteenth Century South.* New Haven, CT: Yale University Press, 1999.

Hoganson, Kristin. *Fighting for American Manhood: How Gender Politics Provoked the Spanish-American and Philippine-American Wars.* New Haven, CT: Yale University Press, 1998.

———. "Garrisonian Abolitionists and the Rhetoric of Gender, 1850–1860." *American Quarterly* 45 (December 1993): 558–95.

Horne, Roger. "John R. Commons and the Progressive Context." *Midwest Quarterly* 22 (Spring 1991): 324–37.

Horowitz, Helen L. "Animal and Man in the New York Zoological Park." *New York History* 56, no. 4 (1975): 426–55.

Hutchinson, E. P. *Legislative History of American Immigration Policy, 1798–1965.* Philadelphia: University of Pennsylvania Press, 1981.

Ignatiev, Noel. *How the Irish Became White.* New York: Routledge, 1995.

Irving, Katrina. *Immigrant Mothers: Narratives of Race and Maternity, 1890–1925.* Urbana: University of Illinois Press, 2000.

Isenberg, Nancy. *Sex and Citizenship in Antebellum America.* Chapel Hill: University of North Carolina Press, 1998.

Jacobson, Matthew Frye. *Whiteness of a Different Color: European Immigrants and the Alchemy of Race.* Cambridge, MA: Harvard University Press, 1998.

Johnson, Robert D. "Re-Democratizing the Progressive Era: The Politics of Progressive Era Political Historiography." *Journal of the Gilded Age and Progressive Era* 1 (January 2002): 68–92.

Kazal, Russell A. "Revisiting Assimilation: The Rise, Fall, and Reappraisal of a Concept in American Ethnic History." *American Historical Review* 100 (April 1995): 437–71.

Kennedy, David M. *Over Here: The First World War and American Society.* Twenty-Fifth Anniversary Edition. 1980. Reprint, New York: Oxford University Press, 2004.

Kennedy, Kathleen. *Disloyal Mothers and Scurrilous Citizens: Women and Subversion during World War I.* Bloomington: Indiana University Press, 1999.

Kennedy, Liam. "Alien Nation: White Male Paranoia and Imperial Culture in the United States." *Journal of American Studies* 30 (April 1996): 87–100.

Kerber, Linda. *Women of the Republic: Intellect and Ideology in Revolutionary America.* New York: Norton, 1986.

Kessler-Harris, Alice. *In Pursuit of Equity: Women, Men, and the Quest for Economic Citizenship in Twentieth Century America.* New York: Oxford University Press, 2001.

———. *Out to Work: A History of Wage-Earning Women in the United States.* Oxford: Oxford University Press, 1982.

Kevles, Daniel J. *In the Name of Eugenics: Genetics and the Uses of Human Heredity.* Cambridge, MA: Harvard University Press, 1995.

King, Desmond. *Making Americans: Immigration, Race and the Origins of the Diverse Democracy.* Cambridge, MA: Harvard University Press, 2000.

Kline, Wendy. *Building a Better Race: Gender, Sexuality, and Eugenics from the Turn of the Century to the Baby Boom.* Berkeley: University of California Press, 2001.

Korelitz, Seth. "'A Magnificent Piece of Americanization Work': The Americanization Work of the National Council of Jewish Women." *American Jewish History* 83, no. 2 (1995): 177–204.

Kousser, J. Morgan. *The Shaping of Southern Politics: Suffrage Restriction and the Establishment of the One-Party South, 1880–1910.* New Haven, CT: Yale University Press, 1974.

Koven, Seth, and Sonya Michel, eds. *Mothers of a New World: Maternalist Politics and the Origins of Welfare States.* New York: Routledge, 1993.

Kunzel, Regina. *Fallen Women, Problem Girls: Unmarried Mothers and the Professionalization of Social Work.* New Haven, CT: Yale University Press, 1993.

Kwong, Peter. *Forbidden Workers: Illegal Chinese Immigrants and American Labor.* New York: The New Press, 1997.

Ladd-Taylor, Molly. *Mother-Work: Women, Child Welfare, and the State, 1890–1930.* Urbana: University of Illinois Press, 1994.

Lears, T. Jackson. *Fables of Abundance: A Cultural History of Advertising in America.* New York: Basic Books, 1994.

Lee, Erika. *At America's Gates: The Exclusion Era, 1882–1943.* Chapel Hill: University of North Carolina Press, 2003.

———. "The Chinese Exclusion Example: Race, Immigration, and American Gatekeeping, 1882–1924." *Journal of American Ethnic History* 21 (Spring 2002): 36–62.

Leonard, Henry. "The Immigrants' Protective League of Chicago." *Journal of the Illinois State Historical Society* 66, no. 3 (1973): 271–84.

Leong, Karen J. "'A Distant and Antagonistic Race': Constructions of Chinese Manhood in the Exclusionist Debates, 1869–1878." In *Across the Great Divide: Cultures of Manhood in the American West,* edited by Matthew Basso, Laura McCall, and Dee Garceau, 131–48. New York: Routledge, 2000.

Lissak, Rivka Shpak. *Pluralism and Progressives: Hull House and the New Immigrants, 1890–1919.* Chicago: University of Chicago Press, 1989.

———. "The National Liberal Immigration League and Immigration Restriction, 1906–1917." *The American Jewish Archives* 47, no. 2 (1994): 197–246.

Lopez, Ian F. Haney. *White by Law: The Legal Construction of Race.* New York: New York University Press, 1996.

Ludmerer, Kenneth M. "Genetics, Eugenics and the Immigration Restriction Act of 1924." *Bulletin of the History of Medicine* 46, no. 1 (1972): 59–81.

Luibhéid, Eithne. *Entry Denied: Controlling Sexuality at the Border.* Minneapolis: University of Minnesota Press, 2002.

MacLean, Nancy. *Behind the Mask of Chivalry: The Making of the Second Ku Klux Klan.* New York: Oxford University Press, 1994.

Marilley, Suzanne M. *Woman Suffrage and the Origins of Liberal Feminism in the United States, 1820–1920.* Cambridge, MA: Harvard University Press, 1996.

McCormick, Richard. *The Party Period and Public Policy: American Politics from the Age of Jackson to the Progressive Era.* New York: Norton, 1970.

McGerr, Michael. *A Fierce Discontent: The Rise and Fall of the Progressive Movement in America.* New York: Free Press, 2003.

McLaren, Angus. *The Trials of Masculinity: Policing Sexual Boundaries, 1870–1930.* Chicago: University of Chicago Press, 1997.

McMillen, Neil R. *Dark Journey: Black Mississippians in the Age of Jim Crow.* Urbana: University of Illinois Press, 1990.

Meyerowitz, Joanne. *Women Adrift: Independent Wage Earners in Chicago, 1880–1930.* Chicago: University of Chicago Press, 1988.

Mink, Gwendolyn. *The Wages of Motherhood: Inequality in the Female State, 1917–1942.* Ithaca, NY: Cornell University Press, 1995.

Montgomery, David. "Workers' Control of Machine Production in the Nineteenth Century." *Labor History* 17 (Fall 1976): 485–509.

Muncy, Robyn. *Creating a Female Dominion in American Reform, 1890–1935.* New York: Oxford University Press, 1991.

Newman, Louise Michele. *White Women's Rights: The Racial Origins of Feminism in the United States.* New York: Oxford University Press, 1999.

Ngai, Mae M. *Impossible Subjects: Illegal Aliens and the Making of Modern America.* Princeton, NJ: Princeton University Press, 2004.

Nicolosi, Ann Marie. "'We Do Not Want Our Girls to Marry Foreigners': Gender, Race and American Citizenship." *NWSA Journal* 13 (Fall 2003): 1–21.

Nugent, Walter. *Crossings: The Great Transatlantic Migrations, 1870–1914.* Bloomington: Indiana University Press, 1992.

Painter, Nell Irvin. *Standing at Armageddon: The United States, 1877–1919.* New York: Norton, 1987.

Parmet, Robert C. *Labor and Immigration in Industrial America.* Boston: Twayne, 1981.

Pascoe, Peggy. "Miscegenation Law, Court Cases, and Ideologies of 'Race' in Twentieth-Century America." *Journal of American History* 83 (June 1996): 44–69.

Pavalko, Ronald M. "Racism and the New Immigration: A Reinterpretation of the Assimilation of White Ethnics in American Society." *Sociology and Social Research* 65, no. 1 (1980): 56–77.

Paul, Diane. *Controlling Human Heredity: 1865–Present.* Atlantic Highlands, NJ: Humanities Press, 1995.

Peffer, George Anthony. *If They Don't Bring Their Women Here: Chinese Female Immigration before Exclusion.* Urbana: University of Illinois Press, 1999.

Peiss, Kathy Lee. *Cheap Amusements: Working Women and Leisure in Turn-of-the-Century New York.* Philadelphia: Temple University Press, 1986.

Perry, Elizabeth Israels. "Men Are from the Gilded Age and Women Are from the Progressive Era." *Journal of the Gilded Age and Progressive Era* 1 (October 2002): 25–48.

Petit, Jeanne. "Breeders, Workers and Mothers: Gender and the Congressional Literacy Test Debates, 1896–97." *Journal of the Gilded Age and Progressive Era* 3 (January 2004): 35–58.

Pickus, Noah. *True Faith and Allegiance: Immigration and American Civic Nationalism.* Princeton, NJ: Princeton University Press, 2005.

Pierson, Ruth Roach, and Nupur Chaudhuri, eds. *Nation, Empire, Colony: Historicizing Gender and Race.* Bloomington: Indiana University Press, 1998.

Portnoy, Alisse. *Their Right to Speak: Women's Activism in the Indian and Slave Debates.* Cambridge, MA: Harvard University Press, 2005.

Reid, Donald. *Paris Sewers and Sewermen: Realities and Representations.* Cambridge, MA: Harvard University Press, 1991.

Reuben, Julie A. "Beyond Politics: Community Civics and the Re-Definition of Citizenship in the Progressive Era." *History of Education Quarterly* 37 (Winter 1997): 399–420.

Roediger, David R. *The Wages of Whiteness: Race and the Making of the American Working Class.* New York: Verso, 1991.

———. *Working toward Whiteness: How America's Immigrants Became White.* New York: Basic Books, 2005.

Rogow, Faith. *Gone to Another Meeting: The National Council of Jewish Women, 1893–1993.* Tuscaloosa: University of Alabama Press, 1993.

Ross, Dorothy. *The Origins of American Social Science.* Cambridge: Cambridge University Press, 1991.

Rotundo, E. Anthony. *American Manhood: Transformations in Masculinity from the Revolution to the Modern Era.* New York: Basic Books, 1993.

———. "Learning about Manhood: Gender Ideals and the Middle-Class Family in Nineteenth Century America." In *Manliness and Morality: Middle-Class Masculinity in Britain and America, 1800–1940,* edited by J. A. Mangan and James Walvin, 35–51. New York: St. Martin's, 1987.

Russett, Cynthia Eagle. *Sexual Science: The Victorian Construction of Womanhood.* Cambridge, MA: Harvard University Press, 1989.

Rutherford, Jonathan. *Forever England: Reflections on Race, Masculinity and Empire.* London: Lawrence and Wishart, 1997.

Ryan, Mary P. *Cradle of the Middle Class: The Family in Oneida County, New York, 1790–1865.* Cambridge: Cambridge University Press, 1981.

Sanchez, George. *Becoming Mexican American: Ethnicity, Culture and Identity in Chicano Los Angeles, 1900–1945.* New York: Oxford University Press, 1993.

Sapiro, Virginia. "Women, Citizenship and Nationality: Immigration and Naturalization Policies in the United States." *Politics and Society* 13, no. 1 (1984): 1–26.

Shah, Nayan. *Contagious Divides: Epidemics and Race in San Francisco's Chinatown.* Berkeley: University of California Press, 2001.

Sarvasy, Wendy. "Beyond the Difference versus Equality Policy Debate: Postsuffrage Feminism, Citizenship, and the Quest for a Feminist Welfare State." *Signs* 17 (Winter 1992): 329–62.

Salyer, Lucy E. *Laws Harsh as Tigers: Chinese Immigrants and the Shaping of Modern Immigration Law.* Chapel Hill: University of North Carolina Press, 1995.

Saxton, Alexander. *The Rise and Fall of the White Republic: Class Politics and Mass Culture in Nineteenth Century America.* New York: Verso, 1990.

Schaffer, Ronald. *America in the Great War: The Rise of the War Welfare State*. New York: Oxford University Press, 1991.

Seltzer, Mark. *Bodies and Machines*. London: Routledge, 1992.

Shanks, Cheryl. *Immigration and the Politics of American Sovereignty, 1890–1990*. Ann Arbor: University of Michigan Press, 2001.

Siim, Birte. *Gender and Citizenship: Politics and Agency in France, Britain and Denmark*. Cambridge: Cambridge University Press, 2000.

Sklar, Kathryn Kish. *Florence Kelley and the Nation's Work*. New Haven, CT: Yale University Press, 1995.

———. "'Some of Us Who Deal with the Social Fabric': Jane Addams Blends Peace with Social Justice, 1907–1919." *Journal of the Gilded Age and Progressive Era* 2 (January 2003): 80–96.

———. "Two Political Cultures in the Progressive Era: The National Consumer's League and the American Association of Labor Legislation." In *U.S. History as Women's History: New Feminist Essays*, edited by Linda Kerber, Alice Kessler-Harris, and Kathryn Kish Sklar, 36–62. Chapel Hill: University of North Carolina Press, 1995.

Skocpol, Theda. *Protecting Soldiers and Mothers: The Political Origins of Social Policy in the United States*. Cambridge, MA: Belknap, 1992.

Slotkin, Richard. *Gunfighter Nation: The Myth of the Frontier in Twentieth Century America*. New York: Atheneum, 1992.

Smith, Rogers M. "The 'American Creed' and American Identity: The Limits of Liberal Citizenship in the United States." *Western Political Quarterly* 41 (June 1988): 228–40.

———. *Civic Ideals: Conflicting Visions of Citizenship in United States History*. New Haven, CT: Yale University Press, 1997.

Solomon, Barbara Miller. *Ancestors and Immigrants: A Changing New England Tradition*. Cambridge, MA: Harvard University Press, 1956.

Spiro, Jonathan Peter. *Defending the Master Race: Conservation, Eugenics and the Legacy of Madison Grant*. Burlington: University of Vermont Press, 2009.

Steinson, Barbara. *American Women's Activism in World War I*. New York: Garland, 1982.

Stepan, Nancy Leys. *The Hour of Eugenics: Race, Gender and Nation in Latin America*. Ithaca, NY: Cornell University Press, 1991.

Stern, Alexandra Mina. *Eugenic Nation: Faults and Frontiers of Better Breeding in Modern America*. Berkeley: University of California Press, 2005.

———. *The Hour of Eugenics: Race, Gender and Nation in Latin America*. Ithaca, NY: Cornell University Press, 1991.

Stocking, George W., Jr. "Lamarckianism in American Social Science: 1890–1915." *Journal of the History of Ideas* 23 (April–June 1962): 239–56.

———. *Race, Culture and Evolution: Essays in the History of Anthropology*. New York: Free Press, 1968.

Strange, Carolyn. *Toronto's Girl Problem: The Perils and Pleasures of the City, 1880–1930*. Toronto: University of Toronto Press, 1995.

Stromquist, Shelton. *Re-inventing "The People": The Progressive Movement, the Class Problem and the Origins of Modern Liberalism*. Urbana: University of Illinois Press, 2006.

Takaki, Ronald. *Strangers from a Different Shore: A History of Asian Americans*. Boston: Little, Brown, 1989.

Testi, Arnoldo. "Gender and Reform Politics: Theodore Roosevelt and the Culture of Masculinity." *Journal of American History* 81 (March 1995): 1509–33.

Townsend, Kim. *Manhood at Harvard: William James and Others*. New York: Norton, 1996.

Vought, Hans P. *The Bully Pulpit and the Melting Pot: American Presidents and the Immigrant, 1897–1933*. Macon, GA: Mercer University Press, 2004.

———. "Division and Reunion: Woodrow Wilson, Immigration, and the Myth of American Unity." *Journal of American Ethnic History* 13, no. 3 (Spring 1994): 24–50.

Wagoner, Jennings L., Jr. "Charles W. Eliot, Immigrants, and the Decline of American Idealism." *Biography* 8, no. 1 (1984): 25–36.

Ware, Vron. *Out of Whiteness: Color, Politics and Culture*. Chicago: University of Chicago Press, 2002.

Weinberg, Julius. "E. A. Ross: The Progressive as Nativist." *Wisconsin Magazine of History* 50, no. 3 (Spring 1967): 242–53.

Welch, Richard E., Jr. "The Federal Elections Bill of 1890: Postscripts and Prelude." *Journal of American History* 52 (December 1965): 511–26.

White, Deborah Grey. *Aren't I a Woman: Female Slaves in the Plantation South*. New York: Norton, 1985.

Willrich, Michael. "The Two Percent Solution: Eugenic Jurisprudence and the Socialization of American Law, 1900–1930." *Law and Labor History Review* 16 (Spring 1998): 63–111.

Winter, Thomas. *Making Men, Making Class: The YMCA and Workingmen, 1877–1920*. Chicago: University of Chicago Press, 2002.

Zaeske, Susan. *Signatures of Citizenship: Petitioning, Antislavery, and Women's Political Identity*. Chapel Hill: University of North Carolina Press, 2003.

Zeidel, Robert F. *Immigrants, Progressives and Exclusion Politics*. DeKalb: Northern Illinois University Press, 2004.

———. "Peopling the Empire: The Great Northern Railroad and the Recruitment of Immigrant Settlers to North Dakota." *North Dakota History* 60 (Spring 1993): 14–23.

Zeiger, Susan. "She Didn't Raise Her Boy to Be a Slacker: Motherhood, Conscription, and the Culture of the First World War." *Feminist Studies* 22 (Spring 1996): 6–39.

Zieger, Robert H. *America's Great War: World War I and the American Experience*. Lanham, MD: Rowman and Littlefield, 2000.

Index